Collection Management for School Library Media Centers

Collection Management for School Library Media Centers

Brenda H. White, Ph.D.
Editor

The Haworth Press
New York • London

Collection Management for School Library Media Centers has also been published as *Collection Management,* Volume 7, Numbers 3/4, Fall 1985/Winter 1985-86.

The Haworth Press, Inc., 28 East 22 Street, New York, NY 10010-6194
EUROSPAN/Haworth, 3 Henrietta Street, London WC2E 8LU England

Library of Congress Cataloging in Publication Data
Main entry under title:

Collection management for school library media centers.

 Includes bibliographies and index.
 1. School libraries—Collection development. 2. Instructional materials centers—Collection development. 3. Audio-visual library service. 4. Media programs (Education) I. White, Brenda H.
 Z675.S3C66 1986   025.2'1878   85-21945
 ISBN 0-86656-433-0
 ISBN 0-86656-416-0 (pbk.)

Collection Management for School Library Media Centers

Collection Management
Volume 7, Numbers 3/4

CONTENTS

Collection Management for School Library Media Centers

Introduction

Brenda H. White

This book is intended for all those persons interested in school library media centers. The wide range of articles provides theoretical as well as practical views of collection management in school settings. The authors include professors of library science, school library media specialists, and experts from state departments and businesses.

The assumptions upon which this book rests are that school library media centers exist to facilitate student learning and that their collections are necessary to learning. Therefore, collections are developed to provide the resources to allow learning to occur. Practicing school library media specialists, librarians and students of librarianship and of that special branch of librarianship known as school library mediaship will all find much to interest them here.

The book is divided into five sections. Part One; The Schools and Collection Development, is made up of eleven articles that center on general issues affecting collection development in schools. The section opens with a major bibliographic essay and continues with an overview article. Subsequent articles focus on particular topics such as collection mapping, budget, administration policy and the effects of business and industry and state agencies upon local library media centers.

Part Two; Networking and Collection Development, explores the possibilities and problems of sophisticated resource sharing using telecommunications technology. The role of the school is explored in networks that encourage certain collection sites to become comprehensive.

Part Three; School and Public Cooperation, includes four articles that explore various aspects of cooperation among school and public libraries. While the same clients may be served in both sorts of library, use of the libraries varies because the clients expectations and the libraries' missions are different. The ways in which the differences have an impact on cooperative efforts is the subject of these essays.

Part Four; Collections Management in Particular Areas and Formats, begins with an article on using reviews to select books in mathematics. The section also includes an article on building collections in religion as a subject of study. Articles follow on collecting in the formats of video, films, computer software, government documents and periodicals.

The final section, Part Five; Intellectual Freedom and Collection Management, reminds one of the effect of social issues on collections. Awareness of the sometimes subtle pressures of self-censorship as one selects materials to represent the range of opinion on a topic is the theme of this section.

As a whole these essays provide a wide-ranging view of the problems and possibilities for collection development and management within the school library media center. They remind the reader that more than ever the school and the library media center are part of the wider world. Collections for schools reflect that awareness.

SECTION I
THE SCHOOLS AND
COLLECTION DEVELOPMENT

Essays in this section cover the general issues and trends in collection development. This section begins with DeLoach and DeLong's bibliography that neatly sets the stage for the rest of this collection of essays. Topics in this section include techniques of collection development (Loertscher, Laughlin, Grebey, Smith, Saley and Yesner) and the effects of specific activities on collection development (Perica, Williams, and Spriestersbach).

Collection Development in School Library/Media Centers: A Selected and Partially Annotated Bibliography

Marva L. DeLoach
Dianne S. DeLong

This bibliography includes literature published during the last five years in the areas of general collection development sources, censorship, networking/cooperation, nonprint materials, microcomputer/information technology, disabled/handicapped learners and ethnocultural minorities. All items were reviewed by the authors and all entries are annotated.

INTRODUCTION

Collection development has taken on a new urgency in recent years. Demands for a wide variety of new topics; requests from previously underserved populations; the influx of newer technologies; expanding curricula; changing roles of school library media centers; increased episodes of censorship; and shrinking finances are only a few of the factors which have had a resounding impact upon collection development processes in the school library media center. These elements, coupled with the evolution of the school library's collection from a bookcentered collection to a media collection,

Marva L. DeLoach is Associate Professor and Head, Cataloging and Records Maintenance Division, Illinois State University, Normal, IL 61761 and Dianne S. DeLong is Assistant Professor and Laboratory Schools Cataloger, Illinois State University, Normal, IL 61761.
The authors wish to thank Fred M. Peterson, University Librarian, Bryant H. Jackson, Associate University Librarian, Helga Whitcomb, ILL Assistant, and Chrystie Marksteiner, Student Assistant for their assistance in bringing this article to fruition.

have changed the complexion of collection development. Therefore, media specialists have been forced to become more conscientious and sophisticated in their collection development efforts.

The professional literature contains a wealth of material that is designed to assist the media specialist in collection building. Unfortunately, many media specialists are unable to stay abreast of the literature because of many other demands upon their time. This bibliography is intended to alert those interested in collection development in school library media centers to collection development literature which has been published during the last five years.

Compilation of the bibliography began with a review of some definitions of collection development. The *ALA Glossary* (American Library Association, 1983) defines collection development as

> A term which encompasses a number of activities related to the development of the library collection, including the determination and coordination of selection policy, collection use studies, collection evaluation, planning for resource sharing, collection maintenance, and weeding.

Selection, on the other hand, is defined by the *ALA Glossary* and G. Edward Evans (Libraries Unlimited, 1979) respectively as the process of deciding which "specific documents should be added to a library collection,"

> and which materials to acquire for a library collection. It may involve deciding between items that provide information about the same subject; . . . or deciding whether an item could stand up to the use it could receive. In essence, it is a matter of systematically determining quality and value.

Still other definitions lists such elements as identifying strengths and weaknesses of the materials collection in terms of patron needs and community resources and attempting to correct weaknesses; ongoing evaluation, and effective, timely selection of media collections by bibliographic specialists.

The selection/evaluation component of collection development is highlighted in the bibliography. Other components of collection development received less in depth treatment: collection use studies, detailed collection evaluation, collection maintenance and weeding/deselection. Resource sharing is marginally addressed.

The bibliography begins with sources detailing the many roles of school library media centers/media specialists and discussing the administration of modern media centers. This is followed by sections on general collection development sources and collection development for media centers. Other topics are censorship, networking/cooperation, nonprint materials, microcomputer/information technology, disabled/handicapped learners and ethnocultural minorities. Topics such as sexism and ageism and subject disciplines are not singled out because they are deemed too specialized for this more general bibliography. Emphasis upon microcomputer technology, with the greater emphasis upon software, prevails because of the rapid expansion of microtechnology software and the major role that microtechnology plays in all aspects of information professions. Other information technology and nonprint media are treated to a lesser degree. A selected list of review periodicals for microcomputer software and non-print media is included but not annotated.

To be included in the bibliography, an item had to be personally reviewed by the authors. Many items were deselected after review because they were considered inappropriate. Some items which the authors wanted to include were not available for review and therefore were omitted. Most of the entries were published between 1979 and July 1984. A few are included because they are classics; others because they were the most recent or most pertinent information available on a topic or because of their indirect or potential impact on the collection development process. Another limitation on inclusion was North American, mostly U.S., publications.

Attempts were made to avoid unecessary duplication of items which are cited in bibliographies, mediagraphies and filmographies which are part of this article. Although attempts were made to minimize biases, final inclusion or exclusion of an entry reflects the personal biases of the authors.

The reader is reminded also to consult institutional sources which specialize in specific topics and/or formats. Several agencies provide evaluation and/or selection aids which the authors think are especially useful. These include the National Information Center for Educational Media which publishes about a dozen NICEM Indexes; EPIE (Educational Products Information Exchange) Institute and Nolan Information Management Services which publish software sources; and the Council on Interracial Books for Children which seeks to promote equity in children's literature as well as to promote the concept of multiracial and multicultural society. Other agencies provide similar services.

Finally, this bibliography is intended to be used as a tool—a beginning point, and does not purport to usurp or to substitute for the ultimate decision on an item's usefulness. Such a decision can only be borne by individual users.

MEDIA CENTERS

Cleaver, Betty P., and Taylor, William D. *Involving the School Library Media Specialist in Curriculum Development.* Chicago: American Association of School Librarians, American Library Association, 1983.

The authors advocate involvement of the media specialist with the school's instruction program at its inception rather than after the planning is completed. The focus of the book is on working with faculty to provide a full array of media for the implementation of the curriculum. The authors present the TIE (Teaching, Involving, Evaluating) model for practical, systematic cooperation, and conclude the book by presenting a method for analyzing the decision-making process and "simulated" situations in which readers can evaluate their role as decision makers.

Davies, Ruth Ann. *The School Library Media Program: Instructional Force for Excellence.* 3rd ed. New York: R. R. Bowker, 1979.

Reflects the changes and critical challenges that will face those in school media centers in the 1980's. The School Media Center is an appropriate learning resource for those preparing to be school media specialists. It also provides much valuable resource material for practicing librarians trying to define their role in the context of the "emerging social, economic, and political trends" of the 1980's. A major emphasis is that of the curriculum support role which the school librarian plays.

Freeman, Patricia. *Pathfinder; an Operational Guide for the School Librarian.* New York: Harper, 1975.

Designed for the novice, this work offers practical planning information on administering the media center and its collections as well as suggests methods of service to school clientele. Extensive bibliographies are valuable additions to this work.

Galvin, Thomas J., Kimmel, Margaret Mary, and White, Brenda H., eds. *Excellence in School Media Programs.* Chicago: American Library Association, 1980.
A collection of pieces by 20 authors, this Festschrift celebrates the dynamism and professional commitment of Elizabeth T. (Betty) Fast. Discusses various aspects of school media programs including a communication audit, inconsistency in selection standards, the right and needs of children and parents, difficulties in professional training and field work, media production by children, evaluation techniques, district services, professionalism, federal legislation, networking, and continuing education.

Gillespie, John Thomas, and Spirt, Diana Louise. *Administering the School Library Media Center.* New York: R. R. Bowker, 1983.
The book opens with the development of school libraries into media centers, then moves to practical chapters on administrative responsibilities (functions, program development, budget, staff, facilities, selection, acquisition, managerial concerns). Also includes chapters on "Computers and the School Library Media Center", "Networks and Networking", "Beyond the Single School Library Media Center" and a section on book fairs.

Hale, Robert G. and others. *A Guide to School Library Media Programs.* Connecticut State Department of Education, 1982. (ERIC ED 230 201)
Presents guidelines for establishing, modifying and building library media programs that effectively meet the needs of students and faculty. Discusses the curriculum, learning resources, program management and the impact of technology on programs.

LiBretto, Ellen V., ed. *New Directions for Young Adult Services.* New York: R. R. Bowker, 1983.
Intended for library professionals concerned with public library programs for teenagers, this work offers 17 previously unpublished essays on materials, services, and management concerns unique to the young adult area. This book brings together practitioner-oriented information on young adult services. It discusses nonprint media, microcomputers, services, participation, merchandising, literary analysis, censorship issues, booktalking, resource sharing, coordination with other community services, library education, professional organizations, and state policies and standards. The American Library Association Young Adult Services Division publications on youth participation in decision making and competencies for young adult librarians are included as appendices. An index provides quick reference to topics, book titles, authors, and organizations.

Martin, Betty. *A Survival Handbook for the School Library Media Specialist.* Hamden, CT: Library Professional Publications, 1983.
Provides coping strategies for dealing with the stress associated with the expanding role of the media specialist, especially relationships with various publics. Includes extensive bibliographies on the role of the media specialist and materials for special groups.

Prostano, Emanuel T., and Prostano, Joyce S. *The School Library Media Center.* 3rd ed. Littleton, CO: Libraries Unlimited, 1982.

Focuses on the purpose, structure, and function of the school library media center. It presents the library media center as a unified system of elements existing within and for the educational program of the school. Emphasis is placed on the application of basic management functions— planning, organizing, staffing, directing, and controlling—to the library media program in the individual school.

Taggart, Dorothy T. *Management and Administration of the School Library Media Program.* Hamden, CT: Library Professional Publications, 1980.
Designed for the inexperienced practitioner, this work provides innovative ideas on program planning which are also practical.

Thomason, Nevada Wallis, ed. *The Library Media Specialist in Curriculum Development.* Metuchen, N.J.: Scarecrow Press, 1981.
The editor limits the scope of the book to the school library media specialist's role in curriculum development. Articles are by media specialists and library educators and were published in the past two decades. The subjects range from the media specialist as an educational change agent to curriculum involvement through professional relationships. The book provides a concise introduction to some of the crucial questions which library media specialists confront in the area of curriculum. It is especially useful for practitioners who are looking for succinct articles about curriculum involvement. A bibliography of over 150 books, articles, and theses provides further reading.

Turner, Philip M. *Handbook for School Media Personnel.* 2nd ed. Littleton, CO: Libraries Unlimited, 1980.
Designed specifically for the person charged with administering the school audiovisual center, this popular handbook is a compendium of practical information for handling everyday organization and operation. The topics covered include faculty communication; equipment selection, maintenance, and distribution; local production of audiovisual instructional materials by both the media staff and students; utilization of student helpers; software selection, arrangement, and distribution; and inservice training for the teaching faculty in equipment operation and software production. The bibliography of further resources for media personnel is grouped to correspond to chapter subjects. Sample forms and checklists are provided.

COLLECTION DEVELOPMENT—GENERAL

Perkins, David L., ed. *Guidelines for Collection Development.* Chicago: American Library Association, 1979.
This handy volume offers a framework for the consideration of collection management in all types of libraries. The guidelines are grouped into four major divisions: (1) Formulation of Collection Development Policies; (2) Evaluation of the Effectiveness of Library Collections; (3) Review of Library Collections; and (4) Allocation of Library Materials Budgets. There is a bibliography for each major topic.

Bonk, Wallace John, and Magrill, Rose Mary. *Building Library Collections*. 5th ed. Metuchen, NJ: Scarecrow Press, 1979.

One of the standard textbooks in this vitally important area. It is a classic. Includes chapters on community studies, resource sharing, cooperative acquisition programs, and library networks, as well as restructured chapters on collection maintenance, weeding, and preservation. Most chapters contain helpful references to utilized material and listings of reference books with brief annotations.

Broadus, Robert N. *Selecting Materials for Libraries*. 2nd ed. New York: H. W. Wilson, 1981.

Broadus' work focuses on the selection function. It is primarily concerned with selection as it relates to small and medium-sized libraries. The largest part of the work discusses selection by subject field. The author provides an overview of each discipline, discusses the characteristics of its literature, and suggests aids for selection.

Evans, G. Edward. *Developing Library Collections*. Littleton, CO: Libraries Unlimited, 1979.

Helpful for its traditional introduction to the background and processes of collection development in all types of libraries. Indentifies six basic elements—community survey, collection development/selection policies; selection of books and audiovisuals, acquistions, weeding, and evaluating the collection—and the interrelated nature of these components. Introduces concepts of collection development and discusses sources of materials; gives practical guidance in community survey techniques, collection development policies, selection of materials, weeding, and collection evaluation; and discusses the influences on collection development of copyright, cooperative system, and censorship.

Gardner, Richard K. *Library Collections: Their Origin, Selection, and Development*. New York: McGraw-Hill, 1981.

Presents a lengthy discussion of the publishing industry and book trade, e.g., how library materials are produced and marketed; describes how one finds out about library materials through trade bibliographies, reviewing media, and retrospective tools; and discusses the theory and principles of selection, selection procedures, weeding and storage, collection evaluation and standards, resource sharing, and censorship. Short lists of suggested readings follow each section. Three appendices reprint documents on collection development policies, standards for library collections, and censorship.

Godden, Irene P., Fachan, Karen W., and Smith, Patricia A., with assistance of Sandra Brug, comps. *Collection Development and Acquistions, 1970–80; An Annotated, Critical Bibliography*. Metuchen, NJ: Scarecrow Press, 1982.

Intended to bring together the "best" or most "useful" articles reflecting trends in acquisitions and collection development during the seventies, as well as current and best texts and monographs.

Katz, William A. *Collection Development: The Selection of Materials for Libraries*. New York: Holt, Rinehart, and Winston, 1980.

Text focusing on the selection aspects of collection development. Covers all types of libraries; print and non-print materials; and censorship and selection. Bibliographic citations integrated in text. Good bibliographical guide to the literature of collection development.

Stueart, Robert D., and Miller, George B. Jr., eds. *Collection Development in Libraries: A Treatise.* Greenwich, CT: JAI Press, 1980.
The purpose of this work is "to present theories, techniques and state-of-the-art analysis which have wide application to academic, research, public, school and special libraries".

Wofford, Azile. *Book Selection for School Libraries.* New York: H. W. Wilson, 1962.
A classic in book selection. Discusses specific selection problems including series, classics and censorship and special groups. Good overview of selection principles.

COLLECTION DEVELOPMENT—SCHOOL MEDIA CENTERS

Altan, Susan. "Collection Development in Practice in an Independent School." *Catholic Library World* 54 (October 1982): 110–112.
Discusses collection development practices employed at two media centers of the Columbus School for Girls, an independent day school. Includes general criteria for selection as well as specific criteria for the school. Lists sources of reviews and materials.

Carter, Betty and Harris, Karen. "The Children and the Critics: How Do Their Book Selections Compare?" *School Library Media Quarterly* 10 (Fall 1981): 54–58.
Compares children's choices with librarians' choices, showing a small percentage of matches. Discusses the librarian's obligation to provide some popular materials and some from the reviewers' choice lists.

Gallagher, Sister Mary. "Trends and Issues in Literature for Young Adults." *Catholic Library World* 54 (October 1982): 116–118.
Discusses problems of selecting fiction for young adults and sources of reviews. Provides a sample list of books for young adults on problems they may experience.

Hearne, Betsy Gould. *Choosing Books for Children: a Commonsense Guide.* New York: Delacorte Press, 1981
Good starting point for anyone interested in exploring books for children. Includes chapters on "Trying to Be Human"; "The Picture Book for Children—Dead or Alive?"; "The Goose Is Loose—Sex, Violence, Obscenity, Tragedy, Scariness, Life and Other Controversies"; and "Treasure Hunt—How to Track Down Good Books" with suggested reading levels for materials.

Lamb, Dee Anne. "Television and the New Media Age" *Current Studies in Librarianship* 3 (Spring/Fall 1979): 12–21.

Discusses the effects of television viewing on pre-school children and how librarians can select materials with these effects in mind.

Livingston, Myra Cohn. ". . . Climb into the Bell Tower." *Library Media Quarterly* 11 (Winter 1983): 134–139.

Philosophical discussion of reasons school librarians should select good literature and help children discover it.

Miller, Marilyn L. "Collection Development in School Library Media Centers: National Recommendations and Reality." *Collection Building* 1 (1978): 25–48.

Discusses the history of standards and their changes, and changing patterns of selection. Lists three bibliographies of research on school libraries to 1975.

Pillon, Nancy Bach. *Reaching Young People Through Media.* Littleton, CO: Libraries Unlimited, 1983.

This book is a collection of 15 original articles on the role of the young adult librarian in our high-technology age, written by prominent young adult specialists. This collection is designed as a handbook for practicing librarians in public libraries or secondary schools.

Reeser, Cheryl. "Silk Purse or Sow's Ear: Essential Criteria in Evaluating Children's Literature." *Idaho Librarian* 34 (October 1982): 157–158.

Lists evaluation criteria and stresses working directly with children in helping them select their reading.

Rovenger, Judith. "Matter of Bias" *School Library Journal* 29 (May 1983): 34–35.

Calls for selectors of children's books to be aware of their own biases and to distance themselves from them when selecting.

Silver, Linda R. "Judging Books is Our Business." *School Library Journal* 25 (January 1979): 35.

Argues that librarians should use a higher set of standards for book selection rather than buy poor materials just because they are popular.

Taylor, Mary M., ed. *School Library and Media Center Acquisitions Policies and Procedures.* Phoenix, AZ: Oryx Press, 1981.

Based on 233 selection policies and 157 questionnaires received by the author, this report of policies and procedures provides much useful information for schools and school systems which need to develop and adopt policies for the first time and for others which have policies in need of revision or expansion.

Thomas, Lucille C. "Building School Library Media Collections." *Bookmark* 41 (Fall 1982): 16–19.

Defines collection development and collection development policies; discusses writing of a collection development policy and provides forms; and discusses methods of collection evaluation.

Thomason, Nevada W. "Evaluating a School Media Center Book Collection." *Catholic Library World* 53 (Spring 1981): 87–88.
Suggests ways to evaluate the book collection on a one-time and continuing basis.

Thompson, Phillip R. "On Bad Books." *Wilson Library Bulletin* 58 (January 1984): 354–355.
Argues that librarians should take the responsibility of selecting good literature and not popular bad literature.

Van Orden, Phyllis J. *The Collection Program in Elementary and Middle Schools: Concepts, Practices, and Information Sources.* Littleton, CO: Libraries Unlimited, 1982.
This work focuses on the internal and external relationships impacting the media program and their implications for the collection program in the elementary and middle schools.

Van Orden, Phyllis, and Phillips, Edith B., eds. *Background Readings in Building Library Collections.* 2nd ed. Scarecrow Press, 1979.
Collection of articles taken mostly from the major periodical literature from 1969 to 1978. Covers general topics of creating, maintaining and evaluating collections. Recommended reading at the end of sections covers subjects not included in the collection.

CENSORSHIP

American Library Association, Office for Intellectual Freedom. *Censorship Litigation and the Schools: Proceedings of a Colloquium Held January 1981.* Chicago: American Library Association, 1983.
The conference produced a wealth of valuable material that can assist a beleaguered school library in resisting attacks by a censorship-minded public. The book provides practical strategies that schools can utilize in their fight against censors.

American Library Association, Office for Intellectual Freedom. *Intellectual Freedom Manual,* 2nd ed. Chicago: American Library Association, 1983.
Designed to be consulted both before and during confrontations with censors, this updated edition provides sections on the Library Bill of Rights, the freedom to read, intellectual freedom and the law, and what to do before the censor comes. There also is a valuable chapter on the ways and means of state coalitions and local lobbying for intellectual freedom. An annotated reading list is included.

Asheim, Lester E. "Selection and Censorship: a Reappraisal." *Wilson Library Bulletin* 58 (November 1983): 180–184.
Argues that it is the "defense of ideas" that is important, not a particular title or point of view, in the fight against censorship.

Bosmajian, Haig, comp. *Censorship, Libraries, and the Law.* New York: Neal-Schuman, 1983.

Bosmajian has compiled a group of spirited essays which helps explain the legal verbiage handed down in the now-famous Island Trees case, which attempted to delineate the powers of a school board in removing controversial books from a library's shelves. Presents a good analysis of the Court's positions in the case in easily understandable language for laypeople.

Busha, Charles H., ed. *Censorship in the Eighties.* Philadelphia, PA: School of Library and Information Science, Drexel University, 1982.

This special issue of the *Drexel Library Quarterly* defends intellectual freedom and discusses recent censorship issues. A bibliography of items published between 1970 and 1981 is included.

Folke, Carolyn. "Selective Bibliography on School Materials Selection and Censorship." *Wisconsin Library Bulletin* 77 (Spring 1981): 37–41.

A selective, annotated bibliography updating a 1975 edition from the State Superintendent of Public Instruction in Wisconsin. Includes titles from 1953–1981.

Hole, Carol. "Who me, censor?" *Top of the News* 40 (Winter 1984): 147–153.

A lively philosophical discussion of the problems of censorship versus selection.

Hunter, Darlene. "Accessibility to Media in the School Library." *Catholic Library World* 53 (February 1982): 288–289.

Argues that students should have the same guarantees to freedom as adults in having access to media. A checklist for survival against censorship is included, as well as guidelines for writing a materials selection policy.

Immroth, Barbara F. "Limiting What Students Read: Books and Learning Materials in Our Public Schools, How They Are Selected and How They Are Removed." *Texas Library Journal* 57 (Winter 1981): 113.

Reports on a survey conducted under the auspices of the American Library Association, American Association of PubLishers and the Association for Supervisors of Curriculum Development. Stresses the need for a material selection policy.

Livingood, Mary Jean. "The Selection Policy as the School Library's Defense Against the Censor." *Texas Library Journal* 56 (Spring 1980): 57–59.

Discusses reasons for having a selection policy and an advisory committee.

Manual on Intellectual Freedom. University, AL: Alabama Library Association 1979. (ERIC ED 180 470)

Prepared as a handbook for school librarians. Includes texts of Library Bill of Rights, School Library Bill of Rights and the ALA Freedom to Read Statement.

Miller, Joan M. "Why Are You Putting That On Yourself?" *Ohio Media Spectrum* 34 (Summer 1982): 14–15.

Discusses briefly the librarian's responsibility to select responsibly for the age group served and with the principles of the Library Bill of Rights in mind.

Mosley, Madison. "The School Library in Court." *School Library Journal* 28 (October 1981): 96–99.

A summary of some US court cases involving materials in school library media centers which have set precedents. These cases offer 3 guidelines for media specialists to use in coping with selection of materials which might cause censorship problems.

Oboler, Eli M. "The Controversy Surrounding Values Education." *School Library Journal* 27 (October 1980): 115–117.

Discusses implications for librarians in selection and censorship of materials for values clarification education.

Oboler, Eli M. *Defending Intellectual Freedom: The Library and the Censor.* Westport, CT: Greenwood Press, 1980.

Oboler has dealt forthrightly and incisively with such topics as: "The Free Mind: Intellectual Freedom's Perils and Prospects," "The Politics and Censorship," "The Young Adult and Intellectual Freedom," "The Etiology of Censorship," "Public Relations and Fighting Censorship," and "The Censorship Battle in a Conservative State." There are also editorials and letters on intellectual freedom, reviews of recent literature on intellectual freedom, notes and maxims, and an Intellectual Freedom Creed.

Raywid, Mary Anne. "Censorship: New Wrinkles in an Old Problem." *High School Journal* 62 (May 1979): 332–338.

A philosphical discussion of censorship as a broad complex issue, and as applied to selecting books for a school library versus a public library.

Robotham, John, and Shields, Gerald. *Freedom of Access to Library Materials.* New York: Neal-Schuman, 1982.

Useful both as a library school text and as a handbook for the practicing librarian, this is a well-organized, readable review of the present state of the ongoing struggle between freedom and censorship in U.S. libraries. The book offers sensible advice on handling complaints. Examples of complaint forms are provided, but there are offered cautions against viewing them as a panacea.

Woods, L.B. and Salvatore, Lucy. "Self-censorship in Collection Development by High School Library Media Specialists." *School Media Quarterly* 9 (Winter 1981): 102–108.

Discusses a study by questionnaire of whether high school library/media specialists practice self censorship, and whether titles absent from a collection would be ordered if the librarian was aware of their absence or whether titles on the list would be restricted. Lists controversial titles used as basis for the study.

NETWORKING/COOPERATION

Aaron, Shirley L. *A Study of Combined School-Public Libraries.* Chicago: American Association of School Librarians, American Library Association, 1980.

Presents five elements responsible for the renewed interest in the combined school-public library in recent years—need for better utilization for tax monies; broader acceptance of the community school concept and expansion of its media center services to the whole community; increasing perception of the roles of public and school libraries as parallel; and growing demand for access to the nonprint resources of information available in school media centers. Appendices A-F may be considered as step-by-step directions for those wishing to consider the feasibility of combining a school/public library.

Dyer, Ester R. *Cooperation in Library Service to Children.* Metuchen, NJ: Scarecrow Press, 1978.

Dyer's unbiased report summarizes the issue in a carefully organized, readable and usable fashion. Two successful experiments are mentioned only briefly. Dyer concludes that so long as administrators and coordinators continue their rhetoric, school and library cooperation will remain a figment of an undefined future. This book is revealing reading and a necessary introduction to the inherent problems of the issue. Includes a bibliography on cooperation.

Markuson, Barbara Evans, and Woolls, Blanche, eds. *Networks for Networkers: Critical Issues in Cooperative Library Development.* New York: Neal-Schuman, 1980.

With an impressive array of practical and very useful information on library networks, Barbara Evans Markuson and Blanche Woolls have provided the library and information science community basic information on networks as a mechanism for connecting libraries to foster and expedite information sharing.

Rogers, Joann V. "Networking and School Media Centers" In *Advances in Librarianship,* Michael H. Harris, New York: Academic Press, 1981, pp. 77-107.

A state-of-the-art review in school networking. Discusses barriers to cooperation and suggests some solutions. Extensive references included.

The Role of the School Library Media Program in Networking. Washington: Task Force on the Role of the School Library Media Program in the National Program, National Commission on Libraries and Information Science; distr., Washington: GPO, 1978.

Attempts to define the potential role of the school library/media specialists and school media program in a national resource sharing network. Covers rationale for the inclusion of schools, potential contributions of school libraries, benefits, problems, and recommendations. Concentrates on immediate (within two years), intermediate (three to five years), and long-range recommendations.

Woolard, Wilma Lee Broughton. *Combined School/Public Libraries: A Survey with Conclusions and Recommendations.* Metuchen, NJ: Scarecrow Press, 1980.

The survey was designed to identify advantages and benefits of combining school and public libraries; problems, weaknesses and limitations; how matters of governance are determined; and what pre-existing conditions within schools and communities appear to be conducive to effecting combined facilities.

REFERENCE WORKS/SELECTION AIDS

American Library Association. Ad Hoc Committee for the Fourth Edition of References Sources for Small and Medium-sized Libraries. *Reference Sources for Small and Medium-sized Libraries.* 4th ed. Chicago: American Library Association, 1984.

Reviews reference sources in all subjects for children and young adult audiences.

American Library Association. Association for Library Service to Children. *Let's Read Together: Books for Family Enjoyment.* 4th ed. Chicago: American Library Association, 1981.

Cites many titles relevant to the interest of young people today. Age and grade interest levels range from preschool to ages 13 and up. All titles selected were in print as of early 1980, including timeless favorites as well as selections published during the past decade. A convenient table of contents quickly leads the user to a variety of topics, such as divorce, death, disabilities, human sexuality, mystery and suspense stories, picture story books, etc.

American Library Association. Association for Library Services to Children, and Young Adult Services Division. *Selecting Materials for Children and Young Adults: A Bibliography of Bibliographies and Review Sources.* Chicago: American Library Association, 1980.

Bracken, Jeanne, and Wigutoff, Sharon. *Books for Today's Young Readers: An Annotated Bibliography of Recommended Fiction for Ages 10–14.* Old Westbury, NY: Feminist Press, 1981.

Examines fiction published from 1977 to 1980 and presents choices for books which combine a good, readable story with sensitivity to stereotyping in regard to gender, race, ethnicity, age, class, sexual preference, and physical and mental capabilities. Seven themes found in adolescent literature are presented in bibliographic essays, and each essay is followed by an annotated bibliography of recommended titles.

Children's Catalog, 1981. 14th ed., with supplements. New York: H.W. Wilson, 1981.

Christensen, Jane, and others. comps. *Your Reading: A Booklist for Junior High and Middle School Students.* New ed. Urbana, IL: National Council of Teachers of English, 1983.

Cianciolo, Patricia Jean. *Picture Books for Children.* 2nd ed., rev. and enlarged. Chicago: American Library Association, 1981.

The Elementary School Library Collection: A Guide to Books and Other Media, Phases 1-2-3, 14th ed. Newark, NJ: Bro-Dart Foundation, 1984. Provides a list of books, periodicals, and audiovisual materials for preschool through sixth grade. According to the introduction, *ESLC* includes high-quality materials designed to be housed in building-level library media centers.

Elleman, Barbar. *Popular Reading for Children: A Collection of the Booklist Columns.* Chicago: American Library Association, 1981.

Emmens, Carol A., ed. *Children's Media Market Place.* 2nd ed. New York: Neal-Schuman, 1982
The major part of the directory is divided into areas of interest, such as publishers of children's materials, audiovisual producers, periodicals for children and professionals, review journals, and reviewers of children's media. Wholesalers, juvenile bookstores and clubs, children's radio and television program sources, public library coordinators of children's and young adult services a calendar of events and conferences awards honoring excellence in children's media, and bibliography of selection tools are listed.

Field, Carolyn W., ed. *Special Collections in Children's Literature.* Chicago: American Library Association, 1982.

Gillespie, John T., and Gilbert, Christine B., eds. *Best Books for Children: Preschool through the Middle Grades.,* 2nd ed. New York: R. R. Bowker, 1981.
One of the foremost tools for aiding librarians and teachers in collection building and readers' guidance arranged in 35 subject areas which are subdivided. Fiction is also subdivided by type of story. Books for preschool through sixth grade, with some coverage for grades 7 through 9. Sources named are: *Children's Catalog, Elementary School Library Collection, Children's Books* (Library of Congress), *Notable Children's Books* (Association for Library Service to Children), *Children's Books* (New York Public Library), "Outstanding Science Trade Books for Children" (Science and Children), "Notable Children's Trade Books in the Field of Social Studies" (Social Education), *Booklist, Bulletin of the Center for Children's Books, Horn Book* and *School Library Journal.*

Greene, Ellin, and Schoenfield, Madalynne, comps. and eds. *A Multi-Media Approach to Children's Literature: A Selective List of Films, Filmstrips, and Recordings Based on Children's Books.* 2nd ed. Chicago: American Library Association, 1977.
Desiring to help teachers and librarians locate nonprint forms of a story suited for preschoolers to sixth graders, the authors' objective is to lead children ultimately to enjoyment of imaginative literature. Preceding the list are six pages of resources to assist programming. These include related readings, selection aids, program aids, and sources of realia.

Haviland, Virginia. *The Best of Children's Books,* 1964–1978. Washington: Library of Congress; distr., Washington: CPO, 1980.

Lynn, Ruth, comp. *Fantasy for Children: An Annotated Checklist and Reference Guide.* New York: R. R. Bowker, 1983.

Meacham, Mary. *Information Sources in Children's Literature: A Practical Reference Guide for Children's Librarians, Elementary School Teachers, and Students of Children's Literature.* Westport, CT: Greenwood Press, 1978.

Guide to sources on children's trade books (K–6), selection aids and review media, children's book authors, illustrators, and awards. Lengthy evaluative descriptions for some 200 items.

National Association of Independent Schools, Ad Hoc Committee, comp. *Books for Secondary School Libraries.* 6th ed. New York: R. R. Bowker, 1981.

"A comprehensive bibliographic guide and selection aid for librarians, teachers, administrators and others involved in developing book collections to meet the needs of college-bound students". Fiction is omitted. A seven-page section at the beginning of the book is devoted to professional tools, and a separate section lists more than 500 reference works.

Peterson, Carolyn Sue, and Fenton, Ann D. *Reference Books for Children.* Metuchen, NJ: Scarecrow Press, 1981.

Polette, Nancy. *Nancy Polette's E is for Everybody: A Manual for Bringing Fine Picture Books into the Hands and Hearts of Children.* 2nd ed. Metuchen, NJ: Scarecrow Press, 1982.

This resource guide to picture books is designed to assist teachers, librarians, and parents in presenting and using books with students in grades K–8.

Richardson, Selma K. *Magazines for Young Adults: Selections for School and Public Libraries.* Chicago: American Library Association, 1984

Roginski, Jim, comp. *Newberry and Caldecott Medalists and Honor Book Winners: Bibliographies and Resource Material Through 1977,* Littleton, CO: Libraries Unlimited, 1983.

Small, Robert C. Jr., and others. *Books for You: A Booklist for Senior High Students.* New ed. Urbana, IL: National Council of Teachers of English, 1982.

White, Mary Lou, ed. *Adventuring with Books: A Booklist for Pre-K—Grade 6.* New ed. Urbana, IL: National Council of Teachers of English, 1981.

Wittig, Alice J. *U.S. Government Publications for the School Media Center.* Littleton, CO: Libraries Unlimited, 1979.

Gives a brief introduction to the history of government printing, the Superintendent of Documents Classification System, and the depository library system. Also includes a list of suggested basic reference tools—including indexes and selection aids—and a bibliography of helpful professional books on government documents. Complete instructions on how to order government publications are included also.

Wynar, Christine Gehrt. *Guide to Reference Books for School Media Centers.* 2nd ed. Littleton, CO: Libraries Unlimited, 1981.

Each of the entries provides full bibliographic data, including LC card number. Prices quoted are those shown in *Books in Print* 1980–81 or in publishers' announcements. The code letter "E" flags entries that are suitable for elementary school students or for professional use in the elementary school. Annotations describe the content and level of presentation, and indicate strengths or weaknesses of the titles. Citations to reviews in major review sources are appended.

The guide is also a source for locating infrequently used books which can be requested through interlibrary loan. Thus, it is both a selection and reference tool to be consulted frequently by school media specialists, teachers, principals, and public librarians.

NONPRINT

Berry, James and Thomas, James L., eds. *Current Trends in Media for Children.* Minneapolis, MN: Dennison, 1982.

Designed to assist librarians to quickly identify important and necessary items for building an up-to-date collection, especially in light of shrinking budgets. Includes annotated bibliographies on many problems facing young people.

Brown, Lucy Gregor. *Core Media for Elementary Schools.* 2d ed. New York: R. R. Bowker, 1979.

Designed to provide a qualitative selection guide to nonprint media titles. The majority of the titles are for sound or captioned filmstrips, kits, recordings, and some 16mm films. Study prints, art prints, 8mm loops, slides and transparencies are listed also. Covers a wide variety of subject and ability levels for grades K-6. Arranged by DDC numbers cataloging data; and *Sears* subject headings, with cross references. Brief annotations and citations to reviewing sources are included. A directory of producers/distributors is appended.

Brown, Lucy Gregor. *Core Media Collection for Secondary Schools.* 2nd ed. New York: R. R. Bowker, 1979.

The core media collection gathered for this guide encompasses some 16mm films, 35mm filmstrips, and other assorted nonprint formats recommended by a wide range of review journals and media specialists as suitable for instructional use in grades 7–12. Features arrangement by *Sears* subject headings, with cross references; DDC numbers and cataloging data; contents and brief annotations; and citations to recommending sources. A directory of producers/distributors is a helpful appendix.

Cabeceiras, James. *Multimedia Library; Materials Selection and Use.* New York: Academic Press, 1978.

Handbook for the selection of various types of communication media. Discusses trends, the need for a system of media selection, the use of selection aids, and the role of a learning center. Covers selection of special kinds of materials such as films and realia. Geared toward school libraries.

Craig, James. "Evaluating Materials: A System for Selection of Non-print Materials." *Media Spectrum* 9 (1982): 5–6.
   Describes a program for encouraging teachers to request and preview non-book materials. Includes form samples.

Daniel, Evelyn H. *Media in the Library: A Selected, Annotated Bibliography.* Syracuse, N.Y.: ERIC Clearinghouse on Information Resources, 1978. ERIC ED 168–590.
   About one-fourth of the materials are marked with an asterisk (*) as "particularly important." This smaller selection will be a service to the practicing media specialists, library school students, and educational technologists to whom this well-organized guide to nonprint is addressed. These titles are arranged in chapters comprising general works, selection of materials and equipment, managing the media center, operation and production, media in context, media and teaching, and research and special issues.

Duane, James E. *Media About Media: An Annotated Listing of Media Software.* Englewood Cliffs, NJ: Educational Technology Publications, 1981.
   Bibliography of nonprint media software produced within the last decade. Entries are listed alphabetically by title under each subject and lists type of media, year of release or revision, producer/distributor with address, purchase/rental cost, grade/audience level and content description.

Ellison, John W. "Non-print Selection: A Combination of Methods." *Catholic Library World* 54 (October 1982): 119–21.
   Provides a basic introduction and general guidelines for selection of non-print material.

Jonassen, David H. *Nonbook Media: A Self-paced Instructional Handbook for Teachers and Library Media Personnel.* Hamden, CT: Library Professional Publication, 1982.
   A combination reference guide and how-to handbook. Summarizes the fundamentals of educational technology theory and provides instruction in audiovisual media production and equipment operation. Chapters on the systems approach, behavioral objectives, communication models, graphics, transparencies, slides, filmstrips, audio media, film, video, programmed and computer-based instruction, games and simulations, and media selection. Discussion of topics is brief. Cites relevant sections in educational technology texts and includes a fairly current bibliography of books, articles, and nonprint resources. Self-evaluative tests enable specialists to diagnose their need to consult the collateral readings.

Sive, Mary Robinson. *Media Selection Handbook.* Littleton, CO: Libraries Unlimited, 1983.

Provides a summary of useful bibliographic tools for non-print materials, as well as a series of case studies demonstrating sensible procedures for identification and verification of appropriate media.

Sive, Mary Robinson. *Selecting Instructional Media: A Guide to Audiovisual and Other Instructional Media Lists.* 3rd ed. Littleton, CO: Libraries Unlimited, 1983.

Designed to assist media specialists, teachers and other educators in areas such as the selection and pruchase of instructional media, curriculum development, and school media center operation. Includes both coprehensive lists as well as lists by subjects and by media format.

Woodbury, Marda. *Selecting Materials for Instruction.* Littleton, CO: Libraries Unlimited, 1979-1980.

Three volume set: subtitled (1) *Issues and Policies,* (2) *Media and the Curriculum,* and (3) *Subject Areas and Implementation.* Each volume can be used separately or combined with the other two volumes. Issues and Policies is a handbook for establishing an effective and efficient selection process; Media and the Curriculum approaches the acquistions and evaluation of materials in various print and nonprint media; and Subject Areas and Implementation aids the selector in choosing materials for specific areas of study.

Talmage, Harriet. "Selecting Non-Print Materials to Best Fit the Curriculum: A Teaching/learning Center Partnership. *Ohio Media Spectrum* 32 (1980): 4–7.

Suggests language and criteria to be used by teachers and media specialists in selection of non-book materials. Includes sample form.

MICROCOMPUTER/INFORMATION TECHNOLOGY

Adler, Anne and others, comps. *Automation in Libraries: A LITA Bibliography, 1979–1982.* Ann Arbor, MI: Pierian Press, 1983.

Extensive bibliography on library automation. This is the sixth bibliography since 1967 by LITA and "it is possible that this will be the last" because the subject is expanding so rapidly. It covers many subjects including microcomputer software and school libraries. Annotations would have added to the value of this resource.

American Association of School Librarians Committee for Standardization of Access to Library Media Resources. "Microcomputer Software and Hardware: An Annotated Source List. How to Obtain, How to Evaluate, How to Catalog, How to Standardize." *School Library Media Quarterly* 12 (winter 1984): 107–119.

Includes a list of microcomputer software producers and distributors, sources of evaluations, listing of software available, sources of cataloging examples, and a software evaluation form.

Anderson, Eric. "Software Selection Considerations." *Access: Microcomputers in Libraries,* 2 (July 1982): 10–11, 17, 23.
Details criteria for school librarians to use in selecting educational software. Emphasis is on use with the Apple II, but criteria is general enough for use with other systems.

Barrette, Pierre P. "Microcomputers in the School Media Program." *Catholic Library World* 53 (October 1981): 125–132.
Discusses the impact of microcomputers on school media centers and specialists, including problems of aquiring computers and software as well as problems associated with professional development for the media specialist.

Barrette, Pierre P. "Selecting Digital Electronic Knowledge: A Process Model." *School Library Media Quarterly* 10 (Summer 1982): 320–326.
Cites need for policies and collection development plan for digital electronic materials. Lists types of application programs and presents a detailed model for evaluation of a software package.

Bewsey, Julia J. *Microcomputers and Libraries: An Annotated Bibliography.* New York: Vantage Information Consultants, due 1984.
Intended to identify "all pertinent books, bibliographies, and periodical or serial articles within the last few years for those wishing to acquaint themselves with this topic." Annotations are concise and are categorized into 10 sections including books, bibliographies, general articles, hardware, software, school libraries and items unavailable for annotation.

Bland, Barbara B. "Evaluation: The Key to Selecting Quality Microcomputer Courseware for School Media Collections." *North Carolina Libraries* 40 (Fall-Winter 1982): 191–197.
Describes services of the Materials Review and Evaluation Center, Division of Educational Media, North Carolina Department of Public Instruction, Raleigh. Services include its Advisory Lists of Computer Courseware.

Block, David and Kalyoncu, Aydan. "Selection of Word Processing Software for Library Use." *Information Technology and Libraries* 2 (September 1983): 252–260.
Discusses uses for microcomputer word processing software in libraries and evaluates four word processing packages.

Chambers, Val, and Haycock, Ken B. "Microcomputers: A Guide to Periodicals for Teachers and Librarians. *Emergency Librarian* 10 (January/February 1983): 18–22.
An annotated bibliography of selected periodicals on microcomputer applications in education and libaries.

"Computers in the Schools" *Educational Technology* 21 (October 1981).
Issue on computer technology and its potential impact on learning.

Costa, Betty, and Costa, Marie. *A Micro Handbook for Small Libraries and Media Centers.* Littleton, CO: Libraries Unlimited, 1983.
General introduction to the use of microtechnology in libraries for the

novice. Appendices include a glossary, lists of resources and a section on computer care and maintenance. Shows how microcomputers can be used as a management tool. Describes three basic generic software packages: word processing, data-base management, and spread-sheet programs with practical tips for selection. Provides a system for researching hardware and software and presents checklists of criteria and things to consider.

Daniel, Evelyn H. *Media and Microcomputers in the Library: A Selected Annotated Resource Guide.* Phoenix, AZ: Oryx Press, 1984.
   Includes sources "for current, accurate, practical information on computers and nonprint media (audio, film, photographic, toys, video) and their use in libraries." Covers material published since 1978 and indicates the most useful informative material with an asterisk. Very comprehensive.

Dewey, Patrick R., and Garber, Marvin. "Organizing and Storing Diskettes." *School Library Journal* 30 (April 1984): 32.
   Brief discussion of storage problems and a Chicago Public Library branch's solution.

Dowling, Karen H., ed. "Technology in the School Media Center." *School Library Quarterly* 10 (Summer 1982).
   Issue devoted to various technologies in the school media center.

Falk, Howard. "Computer Software and Equipment Considerations." *School Library Journal* 28 (November 1981): 29–32.
   Introduction to terminology and computer capabilities.

Gallagher, Francine L. "What Educators Want in Microcomputer Software." *Catholic Library World* 55 (February 1984): 290–293.
   Discusses criteria for evaluating software for instructional purposes.

Glotfelty, Ruth. "Stalking Microcomputer Software." *School Library Journal* 28 (March): 91–94.
   Discusses the establishment of a computer program in a high school. Lists, with evaluations, educational software programs for use with Apple Computers. Lists dealers and distributors who did and did not supply programs for prepurchase evaluation.

Gordon, Anitra, and Zinn, Karl. "Microcomputer Software Considerations." *School Library Journal* 28 (August 1982): 25–27.
   Discusses factors in the selection of microcomputer software. Lists sources of information and factors to consider when starting a program of microcomputer use.

Griffis, Joan E. "The Challenge of Computer Software Evaluation." *Catholic Library World* 55 (April 1984): 403–404.
   Discusses problems of software reviews and evaluation. Suggests steps librarians can take to encourage producers of software to permit prepurchase evaluation of software.

Kilpatrick, Thomas R. "Annotated Bibliography: Microcomputers in Libraries." *ACCESS: Microcomputers in Libraries,* 3 (Spring 1983): 12, 33–52.

An extensive annotated bibliography representing the literature of the microcomputer in the library setting up to Autumn 1982. Includes articles about micros and software in all types of libraries.

Lathrop, Ann. "Microcomputer Courseware: Selection and Evaluation." *Top of the News* 39 (Spring 1983): 265–274.

Discusses how to evaluate courseware that is obtained on an approval basis. Includes bibliography of evaluation instruments, guidelines and criteria, and sources of courseware reviews, as well as an evaluation form.

Lathrop, Ann, and Goodson, Bobby. *Courseware in the Classroom.* Reading, MA: Addison-Wesley, 1983.

Contains practical information on courseware selection, its organization and its integration into the classroom. Discusses uses of the computer as a teaching tool, various types of available courseware and course evaluation. Suggests ways of setting up computer work stations.

Loertscher, David V. "Analyzing Microcomputer Software." *School Library Journal* 29 (November 1982): 28–32.

Suggests ways to use ideas from commercial software to produce local software for specific purposes. Lists and discusses the usefulness of several commercial packages.

Marcum, Deanna H., and Boss, Richard W. "Information Technology." *Wilson Library Bulletin* 56 (January 1982): 364–365.

Brief basic introduction to terms and considerations in the purchase of microcomputers.

Mason, Robert M. "Micro Market Place: Have the Principles for Selecting a Micro Changed?" *Library Journal* 109 (January 1984): 60–61.

Asserts that fundamental principles for selecting microcomputers remain the same, although there is more information available for those making the selection.

Mason, Robert M. "Searching for Software: Finding and Buying the Right Stuff." *Library Journal* 108 (April 15, 1983): 801–802.

Discusses methods and sources for identifying software and information about software.

Matthews, Joseph R. *Choosing an Automated Library System: A Planning Guide.* Chicago: American Library Association, 1980.

The work is essentially a how-to-do-it guide, presenting useful information and suggestions from "how to begin" through needs analysis, considering alternatives, selection, contracting, installations, and implementation. Appendices present more detailed information about particular areas in the library that might be considered for automation.

Miller, Inabeth. "Microcomputers and the Media Specialist: an Annotated Bibliography." Syracuse, N.Y.: ERIC Clearinghouse on Information Resources, 1981. (ERIC ED 222 182).

Selected bibliography of articles appearing from 1978–1981 covering microcomputers and other nonprint media.

Miller, Inabeth. *Microcomputers in School Library Media Centers.* New York: Neal-Schuman, 1984.

Designed to assist the school librarian who is considering adopting microtechnology. Inadequate financial support forces school librarians to seek alternative funding. Chapter on software covers selection, resources, vendors, etc. Current applications also discussed.

Miller, Inabeth. "Microcomputers in Media Centers: Selecting Software." *Collection Building* 5 (Summer 1983): 3–17.

Discusses publishers of software for schools. Gives sources of reviews and discusses previewing and evaluating software.

Naumer, Janet Noll. "Microcomputer Software Packages: Choose with Caution." *School Library Journal* 29 (March 1983): 116–119.

Bibliography of specific application programs for library tasks and instructional uses. Several have brief evaluations. Includes a list of distributors and producers with addresses.

Newmark-Kruger, Barbara. "All the Things You Need to Know About Microcomputers and Were Afraid to Ask: A Bibliography. *Top of the News* 39 (Summer 1983): 341–346.

A selected list of materials covering the use of microcomputers in home, school and small business. Materials with brief annotations are listed for various age levels.

Nicklin, R.C., and Tashner, John. "Micros in the Library Media Center?" *School Media Quarterly* 9 (Spring 1981): 168–172, 177–181.

Discusses factors to consider in buying hardware and software, including costs, uses and management.

Nolan, Jeanne M., ed. *Micro Software Evaluation.* Torrance, CA: Nolan Information Management Services, 1984.

Contains critical evaluations of library and information management microcomputer software, indicating strengths and weaknesses, ease of use, etc. Evaluations are by professionals who are actually using the programs.

Nolan, Jeanne M., ed. *Micro Software Report: Volume II.* Library Ed. 2nd ed. Torrance, CA: Nolan Information Management Services, 1983.

Includes library applications software which appeared in the literature from July 1982–July 1983. Updates volume I which lists materials appearing between July 1981 and July 1982. Intended to serve as a comprehensive tool for library and information management microcomputer software. Lists sources of reviews.

Rosaschi, Jim. "Avoid Worthless Micro-related Purchases." *ACCESS: Microcomputers in Libraries* 2 (January 1982): 6, 26–27.

Suggests areas of consideration that will assist the novice in avoiding/minimizing unwise purchases. Includes a recommended list of sources for software and hardware, reviews, and evaluations.

Rorvig, Mark E. *Microcomputers and Libraries: A Guide to Technology, Products and Applications.* White Plains, NY: Knowledge Industry, 1981.

Good introduction to the use of microcomputers in libraries with explanations of hardware and software applications in libraries.

Sherouse, Vicki M. "Purchasing a Microcomputer for the School Media Center." *Ohio Media Spectrum,* 34 (1982): 7–9.

Describes 4 categories of uses for microcomputers in schools, including computer literacy, programming skills, computer assisted instruction and administration. Describes brands of hardware for each application.

Tashner, John, ed. *Improving Instruction with Microcomputers: Readings and Resources for Elementary and Secondary Schools.* Phoenix, AZ: Oryx Press, 1984.

Gives an overview of the use of microcomputers in schools. Discusses computer literacy, hardware, software, intergrating computers into the school curricula and training educators to use computers. Includes a glossary, lists of resources and annotated bibliographies.

Tenopir, Carol. "In-house Databases I: Software Sources." *Library Journal* 108 (April, 1983): 639–641.

Lists and discusses directories of software specifically for libraries.

Tenopir, Carol. "In-House Databases II: Evaluating and Choosing Software.." *Library Journal* 108 (May 1, 1983): 885–888.

Discusses how to assess what is needed, evaluating vendors, and evaluating software. Lists some software packages for creating in-house databases.

Thomas, James L., ed. *Microcomputers in the Schools.* Phoenix, AZ: Oryx Press, 1981.

This collection of articles discuss the selection and use of microcomputers in schools. Includes articles on selection, software development, curriculum applications and equipment. Appendices and bibliographies provide further information and resources including a glossary and articles on funding sources for microcomputers and student use of computers.

Thomason, Nevada. "Microcomputers and Automation in the School Library Media Center." *School Library Media Quarterly* 10 (Summer 1982): 312–319.

Basic description of microcomputers and their uses in school libraries. Lists some sources of review and purchasing information and includes a bibliography.

Toler, Donna J. "So You Want to Buy a Microcomputer!" *Florida Media Quarterly* 6 (Spring 1981): 11–12.

Briefly defines basic microcomputer terms and selection criteria.

Troutner, Joanne. *The Media Specialist, the Microcomputer, and the Curriculum.* Littleton, CO: Libraries Unlimited, 1983.

Designed as a guide for integrating the microcomputer into the school and the media program. Provides an overview of the media specialist's roles in the integration process. Selection and evaluation of computer software and hardware and establishment of a computer lab are discussed. Concludes with concerns such as cataloging software and the future role of the microcomputer and the role that media specialists will play.

Troutner, Joanne J. "Microcomputer Books for Core Collections." *School Library Journal* 30 (September 1983): 41–44.
Annotated list of books recommended to be the most useful as a core collection on microcomputers.

Truett, Carol. "The Search for Quality Micro Programs: Software and Review Sources." *School Library Journal* 30 (January 1984): 35–37.
This annotated list includes directories, review journals and other sources of information about software.

Twaddle, Dan R. "Microcomputers in Public Libraries and School Media Centers: A Selected Survey of Periodical Literature." *Kentucky Libraries* 47 (Spring 1983): 18–25.
Annotated list of articles on microcomputers for school and public libraries. Items selected for first time readers on the subject.

Wichert, M. Lou. "Computer Software Evaluation Challenge for Media Specialists." *Media Spectrum* 9 (1982): 8–9.
Step by step instructions for evaluating software in hand.

Woolls, Blanche. "Selecting Microcomputer Software for the Library." *Top of the News* 39 (Summer 1983): 321–326.
Discusses criteria developed from a review of more than 20 recent articles.

Woolls, Blanche E. and Loertscher, David V. "Some Surefire Microcomputer Programs." *School Library Journal* 28 (August 1982): 22–24.
Annotated list of software intended for use with students and "recommended for first purchases." Programs cover various subjects and grade levels for high school and elementary pupils.

SELECTED PERIODICALS

ACCESS: Microcomputers in Libraries. Oakridge, OR: DAC Publications.

Booklist. Chicago: American Library Association.

CMC (Computers in the Media Center) *News.* Cannon Falls, MN: Jim Deacon.

Classroom Computer News. Watertown, MA: Intentional Educations.

The Computing Teacher. Eugene, OR: University of Oregon.

Digest of Software Reviews: Education. Fresno, CA: School and Home Courseware.

Educational Computer Magazine. Cupertino, CA: Edcomp.

Electronic Education. Tallahassee, FL: Electronic Communications.

Electronic Learning. New York: Scholastic.

Media and Methods. Philadelphia, PA: North American Publishing Company.

Micro-Courseware PRO/FILES and Evaluations. New York: EPIE Institute, Columbia University.

School Courseware Journal. Fresno, CA: School and Home Courseware.

School Library Journal. New York: R. R. Bowker.

School Media Quarterly. Chicago: American Library Association.

Sightlines. New York: Educational Film Library Association.

Small Computers in Libraries. Tucson, AZ: Graduate Library School, University of Arizona.

Software Review. Westport, CT: Meckler Publishing.

T.H.E. Journal. Action, MA: Information Synergy. (Free to qualifying Educators)

DISABLED/SPECIAL LEARNERS

Baker, D. Philip, and Bender, David R. *Library Media Programs and the Special Learner.* Hamden, CT: Shoe String Press, 1981.

A monograph on factors, backgrounds, and requirements for superior media programs for special learners, with presentations on 27 "exemplary programs": 14 for special learners, 8 for mentally and physically limited or disabled, and 5 for gifted and talented.

Baskins, Barbara H., and Harris, Karen H. *The Mainstreamed Library: Issues, Ideas, Innovations.* Chicago: American Library Association, 1982.

Forty-seven articles, primarily reprints, are arranged under six headings—physical environment, materials selection, technology, software, program, and outreach—in this reader designed for use by librarians in all types of settings as a guide "to develop a full range of services for patrons with exceptional needs.

Browns, Freda, and Arnell, Diane. *A Guide to the Selection and Use of Reading Instructional Materials.* Washington: Alexander Graham Bell Association for the Deaf, 1981.

Focusing on the deaf child, this source book is designed to assist those responsible for teaching deaf children to become proficient readers. Discusses the basal reading programs and other resources.

Davis, Emmett A., and Davis, Catherine M. *Mainstreaming Library Service for Disabled People.* Metuchen, NJ: Scarecrow Press, 1980.

Focuses on providing library services through regular community information centers (school and public libraries). Discusses overcoming issues such as "handicapism" through effective staff training, and integrated system design, improved selection and service, and non-stereotyped processing and display. Valuable suggestions on staff training and developing a "mainstreamed" philosophy of library service are included.

Dequin, Henry C. *Librarians Serving Disabled Children and Young People.* Littleton, CO: Libraries Unlimited, 1983.

This book is intended to help those librarians who serve disabled children and young people from kindergarten through high school and emphasizes the services that librarians can provide. The book covers assesing the need for library services; attitudes; serving individual abilities, needs, and interests; general and special library services; library programs; locating, evaluating, and selecting materials; and equipment and devices. Appendices contain criteria for the selection and evaluation of instructional materials and other media.

Dresang, Elisa T. "Materials and Services for Children and Young Adults with Disabilities." *Information: Reports and Bibliographies II* 3 (1982): 73–79.

Discusses "principles of materials selection and premises of service" to handicapped children. Includes a bibliography of materials and sources.

Elswit, Sharon. "Special Books for Special People." *School Library Journal* 28 (December 1981): 28–29.

An annotated bibliography of "first class books" about the disabled for children, labeled for grades K–9.

Hirsberg, Robin. "Developmentally Disabled in Literature for Young People." *Catholic Library World* 53 (April 1982): 391–394.

Discusses books published from 1967–1977, fiction and non-fiction, from picture books to young adult books. Intended to introduce librarians to the needs of the developmentally disabled.

Kraus, W. Keith. "Adolescent Novels About Physical Handicaps: The Beginning of Long Term Therapy." *Catholic Library World* 53 (September 1981): 78–80.

Discusses evolution of the young adult novel and mentions a few recent titles dealing with the handicapped.

Lucas, Linda, and Karrenbrock, Marilyn H. *The Disabled Child in the Library: Moving into the Mainstream.* Littleton, CO: Libraries Unlimited, 1983.

This book is designed to assist school and public librarians in successfully designing and implementing services in mainstream libraries. Includes basic information about currently available resources and offers practical approaches for beginning library service to disabled children. Needs assessment, materials and equipment, services, legislation, environmental design, and planning are discussed. A bibliography and list of standard criteria for the selection and evaluation of instructional materials are offered in the appendix.

Macon, Myra, ed. *School Library Media Services to the Handicapped.* Westport, CT: Greenwood Press, 1982.

Provides a philosophical framework for school media specialists with little or no background on the subject. Discusses selecting media for the mainstreamed library. Extensive appendices include a directory of selection sources and an annotated bibliography about disabled individuals.

Metcalf, Mary Jane. "Helping Hearing Impaired Students." *School Library Journal,* 25 (January 1979): 27–29.

Describes visual aids that can be used to help hearing impaired children participate in library story hours as well as programs for library instruction and encouraging reading. Factors to be considered in selecting appropriate library materials for this group are discussed, and book selection aids and information sources are indicated.

Moon, Ilse B. "Free and Inexpensive Materials on Aids and Devices for the Physically Handicapped." *Collection Building* 4 (1982): 57–63.

Annotated bibliography of sources of free and inexpensive materials.

Offerman, Sister Mary Columba. "The Handicapped Person: A Bibliography." *Catholic Library World* 55 (February 1984): 287–289.

Annotated bibliography of books for children and young adults about handicapped people.

Petrie, Joyce. *Mainstreaming in the Media Center.* Phoenix, AZ: Oryx Press, 1982.

This book provides a background for understanding mainstreaming and defines the philosophy of the media center. Suggestions are provided for media center planning. Sources of further information that will facilitate efforts to mainstream in the media center are cited throughout the book and an extensive bibliography appears at the end of the work.

Needham, William L., and Jahoda, Gerald. *Improving Library Service to Physically Disabled Persons: A Self-Evaluation Checklist.* Littleton, CO: Libraries Unlimited, 1983.

This work is designed as a checklist and reference source for self-evaluation of services and facilities for librarians and library administrators. Provides suggestions for evaluating general library services to disabled persons for school libraries/media centers and other types of libraries. Contains lists of resources including organizations, sources for print and nonprint materials (braille, recordings, etc.) and professional readings.

Thomas, Carol H., and Thomas, James L., eds. *Meeting the Needs of the Handicapped: A Resource for Teachers and Librarians.* Phoenix, AZ: Oryx Press, 1980.

Articles published between 1973 and 1979 are reproduced in this work, especially those whose ideas for one or more groups of handicapped students are replicable. There are sections on general concepts related to PL94-142 and PL95-602; students who are mentally retarded, learning disabled, hard of hearing, visually handicapped, and orthopedically impaired; and on vocational preparation, as well as appendices on materials selection, producers of materials, and organizations and publications related to the handicapped.

Velleman, Ruth A. *Serving Physically Disabled People: An Information Handbook for All Libraries.* New York: R. R. Bowker, 1979.
Discusses school libraries in the context of the development of special education and library services to students with special needs. Public libraries are discussed in a broader context of service to the handicapped. A suggested core special education collection is included.

Wilms, Denise. "Children's Books on Disabilities." *Booklist* 78 (November 1, 1981): 395–397.
An annotated bibliography divided into fiction and non-fiction categories. Titles are labeled by grades and ages.

Wright, Keith C., and Davie, Judith F. *Library and Information Services for Handicapped Individuals.* 2nd ed. Littleton, CO: Libraries Unlimited, 1983.
Addresses the library's critical role in informing handicapped persons and their advocate. Designed to encourage information professionals to develop an increasing knowledge and understanding of handicapped individuals; to outline programs and services that can be modified to meet needs in different settings; and to integrate different service groups into library programming and information services.
Resources, services and programs for public librarians and media specialists are included as practical suggestions for implementation in existing environments.

ETHNOCULTURAL MINORITIES

Austin, Mary C., and Jenkins, Esther C. *Promoting World Understanding Through Literature, K–8.* Littleton, CO: Libraries Unlimited, 1983.
Designed primarily for classroom teachers, but valuable source for media specialists. Blacks and Black-American; Native North Americans; and Mexicans and Mexican-Americans are the focus of this work. Asians and Asian-Americans will be included in subsequent volumes.
Presents rationale for bringing multiethnic literature into the mainstream of the curriculum. Practical aids for implementing a program are included in sections on planning a multiethnic program, selecting media for children, and evaluating a multiethnic literature program. Includes both annotated and unannotated resource lists.

Bareno, Laura A., and others. *A Guide for Developing Ethnic Library Services.* Hayward, CA: California Ethnic Services Task Force, 1979.
Offers practical advice on most aspects of collection development including community analysis and selection, evaluation, funding and administration of ethnic library services.

Biro, Ruth Ghering. "Multicultural Resources for Libraries." *Catholic Library World* 51 (March 1980): 331–335.
Discusses sources of multicultural information. Bibliography "identi-

fies selected titles and information sources pertinent to various ethnic and multicultural areas."

Buttlar, Lois and Wynar, Lubomyr R. *Building Ethnic Collections: An Annotated Guide for School Media Centers and Public Libraries.* Littleton, CO: Libraries Unlimited, 1977.
Provides resources on more than thirty ethnic groups including the four major ethnic minorities. Other ethnic groups include Jewish, Polish, Irish, Italian and Appalachian Americans. This guide is intended "to fill an existing gap in literature related to ethnicity."

Chambers, Joanna Fountain. *Hey Miss! You Got a Book for Me?: A Model Multicultural Resource Collection: Annotated Bibliography.* 2nd ed., Austin, TX: Austin Bilingual Language Editions, 1981.
Valuable and useful annotated bibliography of library materials for children and young adults. Most items are in English, with Spanish and bilingual formats well represented, along with a few titles in English and another language such as Chinese, French, Greek, Filipino, or Vietnamese.

Duran, Daniel Flores. *Latino Materials: A Multimedia Guide for Children and Young Adults.* New York: Neal-Schuman, 1979
Intended to facilitate the evaluation, selection and purchase of Latino materials, this work concentrated on works of special interest to Chicanos/Mexican Americans and Puerto Ricans.

Dyer, Esther R. *Cultural Pluralism & Children's Media.* Chicago: American Association of School Librarians, American Lirary Association, 1978.
This is the first in a series on issues of concern to media specialists and addresses the value of culturally pluralistic materials and service for library/media programs. Discusses the potential role of the media center in smoothing the transition from a melting pot to a multicultural philosopy.
The principles discussed may well form the basis for serious study and thought as the needs of students and the design of a total library/media collection are examined.

Freudenthal, Juan R. "Latin American/Spanish-speaking Cultures: Steps in Collection Building." *Catholic Library World* 55 (November 1983): 174–178.
An annotated bibliography of bibliographies and selection tools for materials by and about Spanish speaking cultures.

Josey, E.J., and DeLoach, Marva L., eds. *Ethnic Collections in Libraries.* New York: Neal-Schuman, 1983.
Various authors stress the importance of a well-balanced ethnic collection in the context of library services to ethnic communities. Wendell Wray presents a major article on "Criteria for the Evaluation of Ethnic Materials" that provides very helpful guidelines for librarians and ethnic specialists engaged in building ethnic collections. Adele Dendy's chapter on nonprint resources is especially important to the media specialist.

While not specifically addressed to school media personnel, the section
on major ethnic collections is helpful for anyone concerned with building
ethnic collections.

MacCann, Donnarae, and Woodward, Gloria, eds. *Cultural Conformity in
Books for Children; Further Readings in Racism.* Metuchen, NJ: Scarecrow Press, 1977.
 Suggests that librarians must play a key role in advancing multicultural
 education. Provides chapters on selection of multicultural materials as
 well as measures for combatting racial sterotypes in children's literature.
 Also includes a list for further reading.

McCormick, Regina. "Ethnic Studies Materials for School Libraries: How
to Choose and Use Them." *Catholic Library World* 51 (March 1980):
339–41.
 "Contains suggestions designed to help school librarians and media
 specialists identify, analyze, select, and use ethnic studies materials for
 their media centers."

Schon, Isabel, comp. *Books in Spanish for Children and Young Adults: An
Annotated Guide/Libros Infantiles y Juveniles en Español: Una Guia
Anotada.* Metuchen, NJ: Scarecrow, 1978.
 Works in Spanish by Hispanic authors of Latin American Countries
 and Spain are highlighted.

Schon, Isabel. "Recent Detrimental and Distinguished Books about Hispanic People and Cultures." *Top of the News* 38 (Fall 1981): 79–85.
 A bibliographic essay discussing in detail 15 titles published since 1979.
 Nine are considered to perpetuate old stereotypes while six offer "authentic and sensitive portrayals" of the Hispanic people.

Shaw, Spencer G. "Legacies for Youth: Ethnic and Cultural Diversity in
Books." *School Library Journal* 30 (December 1983): 17–21.
 Discusses past images of racial and ethnic minorities in children's literature. Proposes the librarians provide materials which will instill pride
 in cultural heritage and understanding of others.

Tatum, Charles M. *A Selected and Annotated Bibliography of Chicano
Studies.* 2nd ed. Lincoln, NE: Society of Spanish and Spanish-American
Studies, 1979.
 Aimed at secondary schools and colleges, this work is designed to
 assist uninitiated persons who desire to establish or expand programs on
 Chicanos. Addresses all aspects of Chicano heritage and includes both
 print and nonprint materials.

Wynar, Lubomyr R. and Buttlar, Lois. *Ethnic Films and Filmstrip Guide
for Libraries and Media Centers: A Selective Filmography.* Littleton, CO:
Libraries Unlimited, 1980.
 Annotates aboout 1400 films and filmstrips on 46 American ethnic
 groups.

Mills, Joyce. *The Black World in Literature for Children; A Bibliography of
Print and Non-print Materials.* Atlanta; School of Library Service, Atlanta University, 1975–

The purpose of this bibliographical series "is to make historical notation of, as well as to give today's public information about the availability of, juvenile materials by and about black people in the United States and Africa." Age or grade levels are indicated for items. Critical evaluations, with recommendations, are indicated for most works.

Nichols, Margaret Irby and others. "Minority Reference Sources: An Annotated Bibliography" *Texas Library Journal* 58 (Summer 1982): 37–41.

Identifies reference sources for a general library with several sources aimed at children and young adults. Limited to Black Americans, Mexican Americans and Native Americans.

Nichols, Margaret S., and O'Neill, Peggy. *Multicultural Resources for Children: A Bibliography of Materials for Preschool Through Elementary School in the Areas of Black, Spanish-speaking, Asian American, Native American, and Pacific Island Cultures.* Stanford, CA: Multicultural Resources, 1977.

Includes materials, (with suggested grade levels) on major ethnocultural minorities that were assembled for a demonstration collection. Appendices address evaluation of ethnic materials and distributors and publishers of ethnic materials for children.

Ounanian, Lee Allison. "Taking Aim at Cultural Sterotypes." *Top of the News* 40 (Fall 1983): 77–80.

Bibliography of titles for young adults which are designed to help clear up stereotypes about other cultures.

Report of the Task Force on Library and Information Services to Cultural Minorities. Washington: National Commission on Libraries and Information Science; distr., Washington: GPO, 1983.

The report is a useful source of information on minorities and provides helpful data for librarians and information services professionals.

The major divisions of the report focus on library and information needs, library personnel, services and programs, materials and resources, and financing library programs for cultural minorities.

Rollins, Charlemae Hill, ed. *We Build Together; A Reader's Guide to Negro Life and Literature for Elementary and High School Use.* 3rd ed. Champaign, IL: National Council of Teachers of English, 1967.

A classic in ethnic resources.

Ruth, Grace W. "Selecting Children's Books to Meet Multicultural Needs." *Catholic Library World* 55 (November 1983): 169–173.

Suggests a philosophy for providing multicultural materials and lists sources of information for collection building.

The Curriculum
and Materials Selection:
Requisite for Collection Development

Lotsee P. Smith

Principles of selection are reviewed in the light of curricular changes, the effect of national attention to education and changes in media used. The need to stay abreast of changing trends is highlighted.

Reading, Writing and Arithmetic—the basic curriculum taught in our first public schools. How far we've expanded those 3 R's in the past century and a half. Now "reading" includes such components as vocabulary, comprehension, and word attack skills. In fact, we often don't even call it reading anymore; we call it language arts. And "arithmetic" is now "mathematics." Writing got integrated into language arts somewhere along the way. Art, music, social studies, and physical education became standard courses in the curriculum as years went by, but it was the decades of the 1960's and 1970's that really witnessed a proliferation of elective curriculum topics. Courses in career exploration, interpersonal and group communication, psychology, theatre arts, building trades, metal working, and sociology are only a few examples of the wealth of subjects available to students. Critics protested that electives were being accepted for graduation credits at the expense of the basics and pressured educators to "go back to the basics." National sentiment has recently seemed to lend support to that argument and we presently see many states undergoing substantial educational reforms.

Attempts at formulating a coherent national policy on edu-

Dr. Smith is Associate Professor at the Texas Woman's University School of Library Science, Denton, TX.

cation go back at least to the early part of this century (1918) when a Commission on the Reorganization of Secondary Education issued the seven cardinal principles as major goals for secondary education.[1] The seven major headings were: Health, Command of Fundamental Processes, Worthy Home Membership, Vocation, Citizenship, Worthy Use of Leisure Time, and Ethical Character. These statements were followed periodically by others made by various commissions, committees, organizations, and White House Conferences.

The development of library collections has been closely related to curricular trends and in the period of roughly one hundred and fifty years of public school development in the United States school libraries have had their own evolution. They have gone from being an assortment of adult level books collected in whatever space was available with no professional library personnel to being an integral part of the school program with highly trained professionals managing collections of diverse subjects and formats in specially designed facilities usually called Media Centers.

Collections slowly became tied more specifically to the curriculum, and guidelines or principles of selection emerged. Idealistic and often eloquent, they became part of a collection development policy which guided school librarians toward better and more relevant collections. They ranged from the traditional, "Materials acquired should meet high standards of quality in content, expression and format"[2] to the logical, "Every library collection should be built up according to a definite plan or a broad general foundation."[3] Some authorities like Helen Haines cautioned selectors that choices would be difficult.

> A principle often affirmed, but to be applied with caution, is: Give preference to an inferior book that will be read over a superior book that will not be read. This involves opposed "values" and deserves most consideration in selection of fiction. With a wide and discriminating knowledge of books, it is almost always possible to choose a book that on its own plane possesses both value and interest.[4]

Time and circumstances have not eroded the idealism in Helen Haines' principle. In fact, some contemporary texts on collection development still pay homage to this noble vestige of professional librarianship. Today, principles of selection are not given the separate distinction they once were. This is not from lack of deference to standard library practice, but rather from the recognition that every library/media center is different and the professional who develops the collection therein must be cognizant of the needs of the school it serves. Also, many of the statements now contained in the basic documents included in selection policies (The Library Bill of Rights, The Freedom to Read) are in essence statements of principles. The task of the professional who develops the school collection is to relate material content and format to the educational goals of the institution, the instructional objectives of the curriculum, and needs of the learner consistent with selection principles set forth in the selection policy.

The purpose of the collection is usually threefold: (1) to support and enrich the curriculum, (2) to provide material for recreational reading, viewing and listening, and (3) to provide professional aids for teachers. Many media specialists would carry these further and add that they must be integrated into the instructional program. To do this implies intimate knowledge of the curriculum.

A number of factors affect the curriculum and some of the major ones are discussed here. The media specialist will need to keep informed in these areas in order to stay abreast of trends that affect the collection.

Political influences come in two modes, those which have direct authority such as legislative mandates and those which have no authority, but which have influence, such as national studies or reports. Curricular changes and the resultant adjustment in media center collections are often the result of decisions made by political figures who pass laws, allocate funds, and even specify procedures. They, in turn, are responding to pressures from organizations, interest groups, or events. One author noted that "Curriculum in American schools has often been developed from the top down . . . during the 1890's the school books reflected specifically the recommendations of the report (of the Committee of Ten, 1893) and public school systems were profoundly influenced in organizing their 'courses of study' by its recommendations."[5]

Indirect political factors, while not carrying direct authority, can, however, have great influence and effect. For example, the recent report issued on the quality of education in America by the President's National Commission on Excellence in Education hit hard at the current status of the curriculum in U.S. schools in its report, *A Nation at Risk: The Imperative for Educational Reform.* Stating, "Our society and its educational institutions seem to have lost sight of the basic purpose of schooling and of the high expectations and disciplined effort needed to attain them,"[6] it described the secondary-school curricula of being "homogenized, diluted and diffused."[7]

Curricular recommendations for high schools made by the Commission included a core for a modern curriculum of Five New Basics:

  a. Four years of English;
  b. Three years of mathematics;
  c. Three years of science;
  d. Three years of social studies; and
  e. One-half year of computer science.[8]

For grades 1–8 the Commission recommended a curriculum designed to provide a sound base in the areas of "English language development and writing, computational and problem-solving skills, science, social studies, foreign language, and the arts."[9]

Although the purpose of the report was to help define the problems afflicting American education, its issuance and strong language caused an uproar in both the library and public school communities. Librarians reacted swiftly by issuing two reports of their own. *Alliance for Excellence* was the response eminating from five seminars held around the country and sponsored by the U.S. Department of Education's Center for Libraries and Education Improvement. Citing deficiencies in the holdings of school library media centers due to adverse forces (budget cuts and inflation), the report states they cannot "provide a wide variety of up-to-date, relevant learning materials fully complementary to and supportive of the current emphasis on the New Basics."[10]

The American Library Association outlined its reaction in the task force's statement entitled *Realities: Educational Reform in a Learning Society.* Among its actions called for is,

"Public officials should: provide funds for sufficient library books, audiovisual materials, magazines, computer software, and other materials to support teaching and learning and to permit participation by school libraries in library networks for sharing of resources."[11] Members of the National Commission on Libraries and Information Science studied the report and adopted a statement reading in part, "School libraries should hold the materials to complement and supplement texts used in various academic studies. They should introduce students to the use of their own and other libraries as places holding the record of our culture and resources for continuing reference and learning."[12]

Reactions by public officials were equally swift across the country, for within a year forty states had increased their academic requirements in high schools. Thirty more changed their curriculum standards and/or adopted new procedures for choosing textbooks in addition to other educational reforms and major legislative changes.

Economic factors have greatly affected collection development in the past few years. Media specialists have seen the cessation of federal funds to which they could lay sole claim. Now they must compete with other components within the school system under the Education Consolidation and Improvement Act, Chapter II funds. In some areas of the country taxpayers have revolted and local funds have been reduced. The cost of materials has escalated so much that less and less can be bought. This economic pressure has forced media specialists to rethink and use their best discretion in applying selection principles and criteria to the purchase of new material.

Commercial factors, those created by the publishing and producing industry, have also increased the need to make changes in the application of standard selection guidelines. One of the most significant is that of books quickly going out of print, often within a few months. This is forcing librarians to make decisions without the benefit of standard reviewing tools. Another is the number of new companies, periodicals, and vendors particularly in computer software. Do standard selection principles still apply? A persistant problem, too, is the lack of good material in certain areas, e.g., books by and about minorities. There appears to be a distinct lack of effort on the part of publishers recently in seeking out and encouraging minority authors. While we have long had principles, "see to it that no race, nationality . . . is overlooked,"[13] and criteria specifically for selection of ethnic material, there is a definite shortage of good material in this area.

Social changes have had a profound effect on the curriculum and library materials. Events and circumstances have led the schools to extend the limits of intellectual freedom. Whereas material was once selected to "shield the child from complex and difficult personal and social problems,"[14] now almost any issue can be realistically presented. Community standards have changed and educational priorities have fluxuated with citizens' attitudes. In the past decade or so this has swung in some communities from "social adjustment" as a top priority to a "back to basics" movement. Pluralism is not only tolerated but encouraged. Purposes of collections have expanded from just support and enrichment of the curriculum to materials that include personal development needs. This requires selection of materials that "give them intellectual stimulation, emotional backup, psychological information and philosophical realization."[15]

And, last, are technological factors. This topic is discussed at length elsewhere in this issue, but no one has escaped the implications that the influx of hardware, software, new formats of storing, retrieving and making available materials. Adapting to these changes and the willingness to share resources and/or to participate in cooperative selection or retrieve information electronically provide new frontiers in collection development.

In view of these factors, what are the implications for material selection? In some ways it almost creates a contradiction because on one hand educational reforms have specified a much more rigorous adherence to learning tasks, to classroom time periods and specified competencies diverting attention away from individualized learning but at the same time a trend toward individuality of each media center in meeting the needs of each school continues. In curriculum-related activities there is more rigidity. In the media center uniqueness of local situations and less recognition of the need to compare one's center to "standards" set out by the profession is accepted practice.

How the educational reforms currently underway are going to affect the collection development policies of school librarians no one can say with certainty, but it is clear that the curriculum will remain the primary requisite for materials selection in the schools.

REFERENCE NOTES

1. Ruth Ann Davies, *The School Library Media Program* (New York: R. R. Bowker, Co., 1979), pp. 16–17.
2. John Wallace Bonk and Rose Mary Magrill, *Building Library Collections*, 5th ed. (Metuchen, N.J.: The Scarecrow Press, Inc., 1979), p. 7.
3. Ibid., p. 5.
4. Helen E. Haines, *Living with Books*, 2nd ed. (New York: Columbia University Press, 1965), p. 42.
5. Richard L. Morrill, "The School Libraries and Progressive Educators: Two Points of View," *School Media Quarterly* 9 (Chicago, Ill: American Association of School Librarians, Spring, 1981): 146.
6. National Commission on Excellence in Education, *A Nation at Risk: The Imperative for Educational Reform* (Washington, D.C.: U.S. Department of Education, 1983), pp. 5–6.
7. Ibid., p. 18.
8. Ibid., p. 24.
9. Ibid., p. 26–27.
10. Libraries and a Learning Society, *Alliance for Excellence* (Washington, D.C.: U.S. Department of Education, 1984), p. 14.
11. Task Force on Excellence in Education, *Realities: Educational Reform in a Learning Society* (Chicago, Ill.: American Library Association, 1984), p. 61.
12. National Commission on Libraries and Information Science, "News Release," (Washington, D.C.: NCLIS, January 18, 1983), p. 2.
13. National Commission on Libraries and Information Science, *Library and Information Service Needs of the Nation: Proceedings of a Conference on the Needs of Occupational, Ethnic and Other Groups in the United States* (Washington, D.C.: NCLIS, 1974), p. 5.
14. Bonk and Magrill, *Building Library Collections*, p. 44.
15. NCLIS, *Library and Information Needs of the Nation*, p. 159.

The Elephant Technique of Collection Development

David V. Loertscher

Described here is a technique of collection development called collection mapping in which three collection segments are charted: the base collection, general emphasis areas and specific emphasis areas. Information is given on how to make a collection map and on how to use it for evaluating and improving the collection.

There is a tidbit of sage advice that goes something like this: "If you want to eat an elephant, cut it up into little pieces." Snakes have never learned that tidbit and sometimes that ignorance is fatal. If you have studied snake teeth recently, you know that they curve inwardly toward the belly. Such a structure is wonderful for many purposes, but once food starts down the snake throat, the curve of the teeth prevents the snake from regurgitating its prey. So it's all or nothing. The snake either eats the whole animal in one bite or dies.

It is said that confession is good for the soul. In this article, I would like to review my past collection development methods (which I shall dub the snake method), and suggest an alternative elephant method.

A number of years ago, I was an elementary school library media specialist in Elko, Nevada. The collection at that school contained 10,000 books, 2,000 filmstrips and a variety of other media. Later, I served as a high school library media specialist in Idaho Falls, Idaho and again had a large multimedia collection. The high school was on modular scheduling at the time and a number of curricular areas did not have a

Dr. Loertscher is Associate Professor of Library Science at the University of Arkansas.

text book. Teachers and students relied on the library media collection for all teaching and learning materials.

As I look back at the methods I used to build those two collections, I get an uneasy feeling that even though I tried my best, I used the snake method of collection development and should have used the elephant approach. How did I choose materials? Where did I get my ideas? Why didn't I change my methods sooner when I had nagging feelings of distress? Since hindsight is always better than foresight, I shall outline my mistakes and hope that some reader will not make the same ones I did.

The snake method of collection development is a spin-off of the public library approach to collection development. That approach is great for public libraries but doesn't work in schools because of a fundamental difference in purpose. I may not have applied what I learned in library school very well, but here are the patterns I used:

1. I surveyed my community (the school and a brief overview of the curriculum). Mistake: While I had a general idea of what was taught, I did not make a thorough study of the various units that would be taught in the courses. Only after several years at the school did I start to recognize, "Oh, yes, there's the insect collecting unit again."
2. I had all the standard basic book collection lists and used them to build the collection so that some sort of balance was achieved. Mistake: While the standard lists are helpful, they are not created with a specific school or curricular need in mind. I was building a public library collection in a school and that is not what was needed.
3. I faithfully read selection periodicals each month, checking the most positively reviewed materials for purchase. I did try to keep in mind what I already had and what we needed. Mistake: I was selecting the cream of the crop across all areas of publishing—building balance as often as I selected for a curricular objective.
4. When I was given money and a deadline for purchase, I invited teachers and students to submit ideas for materials. Mistake: Teachers and students may know what they needed this week and last week but are often not helpful beyond that.

5. I kept a consideration file. At purchasing time, I prioritized the cards in the file and spent until the money was gone. Mistake: Many of the cards in the file became useless because I couldn't remember why I had been interested in that item in the first place. My priority sort was very subjective and often too hurried.

There were a host of other problems besides those listed. For example, I'd purchase a critically acclaimed title and then find that it would not serve the needs of the students for their assignments. The problem wasn't the book's quality; it just wasn't the right book for a particular need. There seemed to be many shelf sitters which were highly esteemed by some reviewer but of little value to an Indian student living on a reservation in Nevada.

Looking back, I realize that I wasted money. Even though I had 10,000 volumes on the shelves, the collection did not respond to user's needs often enough. I found a number of teachers who would rather have had $100 a year to buy the things they wanted for their room rather than give the $100 to the library media center. There was the auto shop teacher who wanted all the car repair manuals in his auto shop. There was the home economics teacher who wanted the large charts, posters and filmstrips in her kitchen permanently. These teachers did not think of the library media center as a place to obtain their instructional materials. We were supposedly geared up for the academic departments.

Several years ago, I began working on the problem of collection development as a part of creating evaluation methods for school library media centers. That effort has resulted in a collection mapping technique with an accompanying computer program which will be published shortly by Neal Schuman.[1] The technique will be described here but not in complete detail.

THE ELEPHANT METHOD

The library media specialist who wishes to build a collection systematically should remember the sage advice to cut up an elephant into small pieces before eating. Why not divide the collection into a number of small manageable segments which match the various parts of the curriculum? Each of these pieces could then be built, weeded, or maintained as curriculum needs dictated. Each segment would have a corresponding piece of the total budget pie depending on the priorities assigned to the goal of expansion, replacement only, or de-emphasis.

Such an idea is not new. Academic libraries often have collection targets. These are areas of specialty where the goal is to collect everything in a topical area. These specialties often revolve around certain strong professors or departments of the university. They often support doctoral programs and research centers and are deemed a major reason to study at that university. Likewise, special libraries try to build in-depth collections in very narrow subject fields and only in areas which support the work of their specialized clientele.

For the school library media center, it would seem theoretically defensible to divide collection development into three main areas:

1. The building of a balanced or basic collection to serve a wide variety of interests and needs.
2. The creation of broad emphasis areas which would contain materials in a particular curricular area such as U.S. History over and above what a balanced collection might contain.
3. The collection of materials for in-depth coverage of specific curricular units such as the Civil War.

Each of these main areas could be subdivided as many times as necessary to match the needs of a particular school. How would the system work?

Step #1: Create a collection map which will put in graphic form the various segments of the collection.

A collection map is a visual supplement to the card catalog which graphically displays the breadth and depth of a library media collection. Such a map would be displayed on a large poster in the library media center for all to view. It would serve as a key to the collection showing strengths, collection targets and collection size in a single chart. Each school's collection map might be completely different than the collection map of a neighboring school. In fact, several schools could coordinate their selection policies to create complementary collections which would be shared regularly.

Four sample collection maps follow. The reader should note the three main segments of the map—the base collection, the general emphasis areas and the specific emphasis areas. The emphasis areas can be multimedia or a single medium. Each is charted on a relative scale to show excellence in terms of size. The map has the underlying assumption that bigger is better. If the library media specialist regularly weeds the collection and keeps each segment "in tune" with the curriculum, the map is indicative of both quality and quantity.

Creating a collection map takes about three to five hours depending on the types of records kept and the experience which the person has with the collection. The technique is basically this:

a. Count the total number of items both print and audiovisual in each of the Dewey Decimal areas (Reference, 000, 100, 200 . . .)

b. Decide what general emphasis areas support whole courses such as U.S. History, Chemistry, General math, etc. Count the number of items for each topic (count the number in Reference, 000, 100, 200 . . .)

c. Decide what specific emphasis areas support specific units of instruction such as Civil War, insects, dinosaurs, etc. Count the number of items for each topic (count the number in Reference, 000, 100, 200 . . .)

d. Divide the total size of each emphasis collection by the number of students in the school and chart the resulting items/student figure on the collection map.

e. Add up the total of all emphasis items in each Dewey Area (Reference, 000, 100, 200 . . .) and subtract each total from the total number of items in each category as counted in (a) above. These remaining items represent the true basic collection size. Total all the basic items and divide the result by the number of students in the school and then chart this items/student figure on the collection map.

SAMPLE COLLECTION MAPS

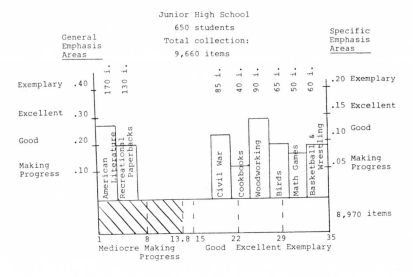

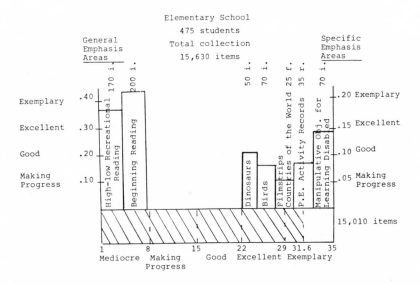

If the library media specialist has estimated rather than counted exact numbers of items, the map is a quick way to visualize the whole in smaller pieces.

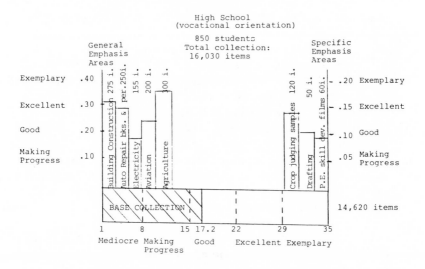

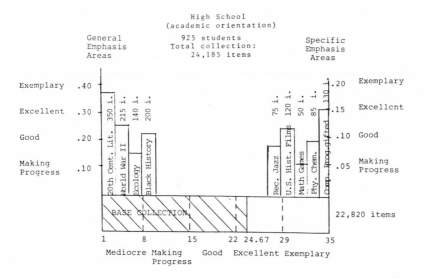

Step #2: Use the collection map as a planning tool, a bragging tool, and a begging tool.

The collection map which may have several or numerous segments could be used for:

a. Showing faculty and students the strengths of a collection.
b. Evaluating whether the strengths of a collection match the curriculum of a school.
c. Suggesting the most logical areas of the curriculum that can be served the most effectively.
d. Suggesting purchasing targets.
e. Suggesting areas of the collection that might be irrelevant.
f. Demonstrating areas of need and areas of excellence.

Step #3: Evaluate how well each of the segments is reacting to the demands made upon it.

The best evaluative tool of a collection is how it responds to usage demands. Every time a major demand is placed upon one of the emphasis areas of the collection or upon the base, the library media specialist and the teacher should evaluate how well the collection responded. With input from the students, these two people can quickly rate the collection on the following points:

a. Diversity of formats available (both books and AV).
b. Recency of the collection (Were the materials up-to-date?).
c. Relevance of the collection to unit needs.
d. Duplication (Was there enough materials for the number of students taught?).
e. Reading/viewing/listening level (Was it ok for all students?).

The answers to those questions and the resulting systematic follow-up in an acquisition program, weeding activity, or replacement task provide the key to an improved collection development program.

Step #4: Use the evaluation sheets from step #3 to build a sound acquisition program.

Short and long range collection goals are easy to build when the collection is segmented. Some essential questions could be asked which would lead to goal statements. Do the emphasis areas fit the curriculum of this school? If not, would it be better to give or trade these emphasis collections to another school which would have more use for them? What emphasis areas should be built in the next five years? Which emphasis areas should be improved? What curricular trends will affect the emphasis areas of the collection as they now exist?

New emphasis area targets could be handled like community fund drives with a thermometer chart put on the collection map indicating funding needs and progress toward funding goals.

Consideration files can be divided into sections matching the sections of the collection map. Percentages of the budget can be assigned to purchase materials in each of the target areas. Ordering periods might be adjusted to allow for purchase of materials in time for teaching units. Bibliographies and selection tools would be used to find materials for specific needs rather than for general broad interests. Smaller consideration files by topic area would be managed more effectively.

Step #5: Build a budgeting system which matches the segments of the collection map.

There are a number of types of budget systems which can easily be adapted to the collection target system advocated here. Breaking a lump sum of money into segments which supports certain collection targets is much easier to understand by administrators and certainly easier to defend. Budget cuts or improvements can be decided jointly by administrators and library media specialists with full knowledge of exactly what parts of the collection will be affected.

ELEPHANT STEW

This article has described a manual system of keeping track of segments of the library media collection and conscientiously building, maintaining, or weeding each of the segments. Those readers who have computerized their card catalog realize that much of this segmentation can be done within current computer systems as a by-product of the program.

Perhaps the elephant stew of the future would be to track each unit for a teacher which would not only be a total bibliography of materials for that unit, but would present analyses of types of materials available, duplicates, new items, replacement items, age, and progress on goals for that segment of the collection.

REFERENCE

1. Loertscher, David V., Woolls, Blanche, and Stroud, Janet G. *Evaluating School Library Media Programs.* Neal Schuman, 1985. The computer collection mapping program can be obtained from: David V. Loertscher, P.O. Box 1801, Fayetteville, AR 72702 for $10.

Collection Development in Elementary School Library Media Centers

Mildred Knight Laughlin

In order to face wisely depleting budgets, increased demand, and accountability requirements, elementary school library media specialists must evaluate critically their approach to collection development. This article examines selection as an evaluation continuum beginning with an expressed need and ending with eventual discard of those materials added to the collection.

School library media specialists have historically been concerned with selection of appropriate materials to satisfy the requests of their users. However, the practice of selection has been in many instances limited in scope, fraught with errors in identifying critical needs, and limited in the involvement of users in the total process.

In an effort to rectify haphazard selection practices, it would be wise for all school library media specialists to discard the term selection in favor of the more inclusive term "evaluation." As evaluation is defined as examining and assessing the worth, quality and value of specific materials in meeting user needs, one sees the task as much more than selection. Evaluation involves a continuum, a process covering every aspect of use from determining need to assessing appropriateness of specific materials, through considering alternatives to accomplishing use objectives more efficiently or at lower cost, to actual use of acquired materials, the initial determination of effectiveness, the constant monitoring of value, and final withdrawal.

Dr. Laughlin is a professor at the School of Library Science, the University of Oklahoma, Norman, Oklahoma.

Dorothy Broderick in *Library Work With Children* points out that many library media specialists spend more time on the selection of materials than any other professional activity, yet with fewer results to show for their work except crowded shelves. Library media specialists read thousands of reviews, examine and read hundreds of books, preview many audio-visual materials, and the end result is a haphazard combination of works that we term the library collection. Worse yet some principals force library media specialists to ignore reputable jobbers as a source for materials and instead allow remainder salesmen to sell a supply of trade books at bargain prices. Even if the salesman sets up displays of books from which students and teachers may choose, the process is merely selecting the best of the worst and has no relationship to collection need or literary value.

Even when library media specialists select books of literary quality to purchase from reputable jobbers, this does not insure an adequate collection. Too often the selector assumes the necessity of ordering all current award winning books even if collection priority would not evidence the need for those particular titles. Often starred reviews have more weight upon materials chosen than the relationship of content to library needs.

Most library media specialists recognize the importance of an appropriate selection policy, but seldom is concern expressed for an overall collection policy. This document is also needed to provide focus for collection development in relation to the goals of the parent institution. It should identify areas in which general materials are needed, which in-depth collections of materials are appropriate, and when all quality materials on the subject are demanded. A well developed collection policy could result in increased cooperation between school and public libraries or among schools in a district. Often it is not feasible or cost effective for each library to build an extensive collection in a given area that is heavily used only a small portion of the year. An agreement by which each library will develop an in-depth collection for one of a number of areas and share upon request is many times a more logical arrangement to satisfy total user needs.

The development of a collection policy does not mean that the belief in the value of the traditional selection policy is discarded. Instead, it merely expands the concept of clarifying the philosophy and objectives of materials selection which is the major reason for needing a stated selection policy. It was encouraging to read recently a selection policy in use which stated "criteria for materials selection includes literary and artistic worth, suitability of content and vocabulary to the age of the readers, and the contribution of the material to the balance of the total collection."

Obviously, a selection policy should also establish responsibility for selection, give criteria for general and specific subjects, identify procedures for selection and gift acceptance, and outline the process for handling questioned materials. It is *very* important that the policy developed be a positive document. Because many selection policies were created as a protective device in case a book was challenged, that portion of the document is often longer and more specific than the philosophy, criteria, and procedures for selection. A selection policy should be examined yearly to see if it remains appropriate. If revisions are needed, the amended policy should be examined and approved by the Board of Education. This examination for relevancy also has merit because Board members change and all should be cognizant of the document that has at one time received Board approval.

In the total evaluation process for acquisition and use of materials, the needs, interests, and abilities of the patrons *must* be considered. Many times school library media specialists will say "Most of the materials in the collection are too difficult for our students." This sad fact may have resulted from a past practice of building a basic collection for new schools by ordering those titles listed in the H.W. Wilson's *Children's, Junior High* and *Senior High Catalogs*. This was an easy approach that attempted to insure quality but did not necessarily meet specific community needs. On the other hand, it is easy to fulfill the needs of vocal patrons to such an extent that an in-depth Shakespearean England section can be built for sixth grade social studies because of one teacher's unique interest. At some point, this specialized collection may remain on the shelves when the teacher leaves or retires. Library media specialists must assume the final responsibility of choosing materials with serious thought for total needs.

However, the library media specialist must encourage wide

participation in the choosing of materials for purchase. Although the AASL guidelines *Media Programs District And School* asserted in 1975 that "Selection of materials is a cooperative process involving the media staff, curriculum consultants, teachers, students, and community representatives," it is safe to say that in few instances do students and community representatives play an active role in determining needs. Reader polls, informal discussions with the Parent Teachers Organization library committee, and active encouragement of student/teacher contributions to a Suggestions For Purchase box placed on the circulation desk are a few of many ways to enlist wide participation in collection development.

Wise suggestions demand that library media specialists assist teachers, students and parents in awareness of appropriate criteria for materials selection in all formats. James Cabeceiras in *The Multimedia Library* has recorded criteria for evaluation of major categories of media. After these general suggestions are adapted to meet the unique, specific needs of each school, appropriate means should be adopted to insure that all patrons are aware of these criteria. In addition to aiding wise materials evaluation, cognizance of the unique values of each medium will assist students and teachers in choosing the appropriate medium for a specific information need.

It is imperative that library media specialists read widely, regularly, and critically in order to spend limited funds with wisdom. Establishing a sensible, specific plan for reading is important. An elementary school media specialist easily can determine to read at least an average of one children's book per day. Three hundred sixty-five does not adequately cover the year's output of publications, but it enhances ability to read critically, and by following a determined reading plan, plus reading reviews in credible sources, wise evaluation is possible. In addition, only through wide reading can library media specialists guide patrons to those materials that will meet best their information and interest needs.

Reviewing tools should never be considered the answer to *all* evaluation problems. There are too few reviews of new materials for specialized needs, few reviews of materials *not* recommended for purchase, and too great a time lag between publication/production and review, but current and retrospective reviewing tools must be examined regularly. That, plus patron involvement in reading and preview, will enhance wise choices of materials to satisfy collection needs. A comparison of related titles to see which is more appropriate is essential. Obviously, everything can not be purchased, and library media specialists must keep a running file of order cards—a "want list" based on reading and preview, patron suggestions, and needs revealed when there was no available source to answer a specific question. Library media specialists never know when a parent teacher organization or library donor may make funds available, and often there is little time for wise choice based on need if want files are not available. The end of a fiscal year sometimes results in unspent funds, and if the school administrator is made aware that the library always contains an available list of needed materials, he/she may turn to the library media specialist instead of the band or athletic department to "use up" funds.

The evaluation continuum must specifically address the *use* of materials purchased. Media specialists should plan specific ways to let the patrons know about new materials received before they are placed on the regular shelves. In addition, it is imperative that a form be developed to notify with ease the teacher, parent or student about the arrival of the specific title he or she suggested. At that point, it is easy to ask that person for a reaction to the material after reading, listening, or viewing it. This initial reaction of users is important, as it either reinforces or leaves open to question the appropriateness of the new material for the collection. This initial reaction, in addition to aiding the library media specialist in reading/listening/viewing guidance alerts her/him to any need for further monitoring.

Probably the most neglected area of the evaluation continuum is "discard." Principals and library administrators often treasure numbers of quantitative reports of holdings, teachers hesitate to allow discard of materials they *might want* to use someday, and library media specialists are too pressed with immediate tasks to assume the time-consuming details of discard. This process is easy to postpone, yet often patrons can't find new materials they would profit from using because those sources are hidden among the countless unattractive, less useful titles housed on the same shelf.

John Gillespie and Diana Spirt suggest in *Administering the School Library Media Center* that four to five percent of the established school library collection should be discarded each year. This "ball-park" figure should evidence to most library media specialists their neglect of this important aspect of the evaluation continuum. Yet most would agree that when the subject matter of the material is out of date, mediocre or inaccurate, is unsuitable for a particular grade level, is damaged beyond repair, or is unused, it should be evaluated for discard.

Choosing materials to satisfy user needs and keeping the collection relevant is one of the most important professional tasks for which the library media specialist is responsible. However, if the selection concept is extended to one of evaluation in which overall collection needs are examined, user cooperation is enlisted, initial and constant monitoring of use is deemed important, and appropriate discard practices are adopted, the collection development process will be enhanced and the user will profit.

REFERENCES

American Association of School Librarians, ALA and Association for Educational Communications and Technology. *Media Programs District and School.* Chicago: ALA, 1975, 62

Broderick, Dorothy M. Library Work With Children. New York: H.W. Wilson, 1977, 3–7.

Cabeceiras, James. *The Multimedia Library.* 2nd ed. New York: Academic Press, 1982.

Gillespie, John T. and Diana L. Spirt. *Administering the School Library Media Center.* New York: R.R. Bowker, 1983, 309.

Woodbury, Marda. *Selecting Materials For Instruction.* Littleton: Libraries Unlimited, 1980.

The Effects of Small Budgets on the Principles of Development of Collections for Small School Library Media Centers

Al Saley

Practical suggestions for extending the small budget's buying power are given, following a discussion of the need for comparative statistics.

Small library media centers with small budgets can maximize their expenditures to further develop the collection without violating sound principles of collection development. In purchasing print and nonprint resources there exists the opportunity to take advantage of promotions, special sales and higher than average discounts in an attempt to acquire additional materials. The acquisition of paperback books, government documents, periodicals, remainder books, free and inexpensive materials as well as a major public relations campaign to receive gifts can all aid to a larger degree in obtaining a greater number of materials than would be possible if one were to adhere solely to the practice of employing the traditional current review-purchase approach. Today more than ever before, warehouse sales of university presses as well as commercial publishers can increase the number of titles purchased for that same dollar. With a strengthened school library media center collection small school library media centers will then be better able to contribute as well as to reap

Al Saley is a school library media specialist at the Mountain Lakes High School, Mountain Lakes, New Jersey.

the benefits of networking. A vital first step is to know one's own collection.

STATISTICS

School library media specialists are at a distinct disadvantage in their effort toward collection management without reliable statistics on school library media center expenditures and acquisitions.

During the sixties and seventies, an attempt was made to compile school library media center statistics but unfortunately in most states this hasn't continued. The New Jersey Department of Education, Public and School Library Services Bureau, issued *Statistics: New Jersey Media Programs 1968–69, 1969–70.* The statistics in the report were extracted from applications for Federal funds under Title II of the Elementary and Secondary Act, Public Law, 87-10.

These statistics were used by doctoral students, the school media association and the department of education in an attempt to further the development of school library media centers of the state. The statistics were also used to encourage the local district to support school library media program development using the *Standards*[1] as a guide. It is difficult to make a case for increased support for school library media centers without a comparison of statistics on the local level.

Marilyn Miller reported the results of a questionnaire survey relating to expenditures for school library media centers for the 1982–83 school year. Miller with Barbara Moran[2] concluded that:

> School library media specialists have obviously made progress over the last 20 years in their efforts to provide a library resource center in every school. There are, however, disquieting signs in this data. We are obviously a long way from seeing adequately stocked and adequately maintained multimedia collections in all schools, since more than one quarter of the respondents fear they will have lower budgets in 1983–84. At the reported level of present funding, collection erosion is a serious threat; the lack of available money for AV resources

comes at a time when we purport to know a great deal about the value of multimedia resources and their use in the teaching-learning process.

Miller and Moran[3] also point out the difficulty in assessing the development of school library media center service because of the irregularity and lack of availability of dependable statistics.

The ABILITY to assess the development of school library service in the United States has been a persistent problem which is hampered by the irregularity of the availability of dependable statistics. For instance, during the last 20 years, only three national surveys of public school library media centers (LMCs) have been published. In 1963, a landmark survey, *Public School Library Statistics 1962–63,* was published by the U.S. Office of Education. Fourteen years later, the department published Statistics of *Public School Library Media Centers, 1974 (LIBGIS I).* This was followed by *Statistics of Public School Libraries/Media Centers 1978 (LIBGIS II),* published in 1981. The time lag between these reports, the failure of any other government department or professional organization to systematically gather statistics on LMCs, and the decision of the current federal administration to diminish the government's role in providing statistical data have prevented school librarians from monitoring levels of expenditures for resources and programs in LMCs.

It must be conceded that it is nearly impossible to account for all funding for LMCs. From building to building, district to district, county to county, and state to state, there is no uniformity to the way in which funds are obtained for and how they are allocated to LMCs.

Milbrey L. Jones[4] reporting on the 1979 National Center For Education Statistics, provides the average number of books and audiovisual titles held by the private school media center as:

The average number of books and audiovisual titles held by private school library media centers—about 4,198 and

531 per school, respectively—indicates very small collections. . . . An average of 340 books per school and about 57 audiovisual titles per school were added in 1978–79, showing very marginal additions to collections. Whether looking at book collections or audiovisual collections or number of periodical subscriptions held at the end of the 1978–79 school year, the collections of many private school library media centers are far below the standards recommended by the American Association of School Librarians (AASL) and the Association for Educational Communications and Technology (AECT).

Jones[5] further reports on expenditures for school library media center materials as being:

The mean per pupil expenditure for library books and for all other types of library media resources will not add many items to a library media center's collections. For example, an annual expenditure of $5.56 per pupil for library books in a school of 1,000 students would add fewer than 300 books to a library media center collection.

An example of the importance of statistics and how an analysis can be made from them is evident in *Analyses of New Jersey Public Library Statistics for 1982.*[6] This analysis was prepared under the direction of the Office of Library Planning and Development from the annual reports submitted by public libraries of New Jersey. The information allows a comparison among groups of libraries as follows:

Study of the averages gives a good general picture of each population group and each expenditure level. The average of each data element not only describes the group as a whole but also can provide interesting comparisons with other groups. For example, a county library may wish to compare its member libraries and itself with other county library systems.

Comparisons among different population groups or expenditure categories can suggest general trends. For example, local tax support per capita increases from $1.43 in the $0–9,999 expenditure category, to $3.37 in

the $10,000–$24,999 group, then $6.09, $8.79, dips to
$7.46 in the $75,000–99,000 group, then increases to
$10.80, $12.10, $13.03, dips again to $12.35, then increases from $13.07 to $13.48 in the $750,000–999,999
group, then drops to $13.22 in the over-$1,000,000 category. The average library's local tax support per capita in
New Jersey is $9.81.

A telephone inquiry was made by the author to sixteen
school library media centers in an attempt to determine a
correlation between the monies allocated for materials and
the number of titles added to the collection for the school
year 1983–84. While the sample is small, some interesting
observations can be made. Of the sixteen schools contacted,
twelve were high schools with various groupings of grades:
eight through twelve to ten through twelve; one middle school
and three elementary schools. The following averages were
obtained: the staffing pattern consisted of one professional
usually with at least one support staff for each 500 students,
the collection size averaged 20,000 volumes, the periodical
budget averaged $2,235, the print budget averaged $10,000,
the non-print budget averaged $5,142, the number of titles
added to the print collection averaged 891, and the number of
items added to the non-print collection averaged 70.

This survey of a very small sample reveals higher than national averages for school library media centers and yet shows
how far behind the recommended *Standards*[7] we are. Frances
Henne, Professor Emeritus, Columbia University, advocated
a need for a high school collection of 50,000 in the early
1960's. The 1975 *Standards*[8] indicates a 60,000 collection. It
appears as if we are only one third of the way toward that
collection size.

How then can we obtain the necessary resources with the
small allocations available to us? It is imperative to maximize
each expenditure we make. We can solicit support from
within and outside the community, we can take advantage of
free and inexpensive materials, we can consider paperback
editions, we can take advantage of remainder books and we
can make the effort to secure as many items as possible with
the small budgets with which we work.

PERIODICALS

The purchase of periodicals through a subscription agency has many advantages. Dorothy M. Broderick[9] points out that:

> By using a subscription agency, you prepare one list of periodicals to be ordered which can probably go for the cost of one ounce postage (at worst, two). One bill is received from the subscription agency which requires less human help to process. And there you are, for a smidgen of what it costs to do it yourself, you have obtained high quality service and saved several hours of time as well as saved hard cash.

Subscription agencies also offer a discount. While the average discount on the total amount may be 5 to 6%, it can often reach has high as 9 to 10%. The discount rate depends on a number of factors such as: the number of titles; number of subscriptions to a particular title; specific titles; and the number of years subscribing to a given periodical.

An additional service provided by a subscription agency that is worth time and money is the inquiries necessary concerning missing issues. Some agencies retain back issues of some periodicals just for that purpose.

Subscription agencies are able to provide personal attention. Many agencies have local offices providing a customer service representative for each account. In addition, the agencies often exhibit at library conferences where personal contact can be made.

One problem in the use of subscription agencies for the school library media specialist evolves when the decision on the selection of an agency is made in isolation, such as decisions based solely on the amount of discount offered in the bid process. This change to another subscription agency requires another round in developing rapport, which had been established with the former agency.

The cost of a periodical subscription can be reduced when a subscription can be made for a period of time beyond one year. For example, the current subscription price to *Natural History* is $18.00. A two year subscription is $28.00 and a three year subscription is $36.00. The savings for a three year subscription is obvious.

Many school districts are reluctant to allow this kind of extended purchasing. A case can be made to show the resultant savings.

It is helpful to prepare a visual presentation of the current periodical procedure with a comparison of what can be gained through an extended subscription plan. There is no magic formula in developing such a plan but generally a beginning procedure would be to allocate a portion of the current periodical budget for this purpose. The presentation may often result in an increased periodical budget for the given year if an overall savings can be realized over a three to five year plan, taking into consideration inflation.

It is well to point out that communication between the administration, central administrative office and the school library media specialist is imperative in order to make purchasing more fruitful. Monies other than those allocated on the line item may be available for the school library media center to aid in the periodical development plan. Another important factor to consider is the monies realized from the subscription agency discount. It can often become a part of the general fund rather than a way to increase the periodical collection. The argument that "you receive what you ordered" doesn't add up since in most cases what you ordered is only a fraction of what is really needed because of the original periodical budget allocation.

One approach to this dilemma is to submit a list of periodicals exceeding the allocation and to be prepared to have the list returned after the bid process. The discount factor can then be used to subscribe to additional titles.

MICROFORMS

The use of microforms in even the smallest school library media center has been well documented in the literature. The convenience, savings in shelf space, permanence and ease in use are decided advantages.

The two major suppliers of microforms, University Microforms International and Bell & Howell have been offering bonus packages for quite a few years. These bonuses include equipment and additional titles.

The current bonus offering from Bell & Howell is five backfile years of periodicals for the price of four which represents a 20% savings. University Microforms International is currently offering free microform equipment when a minimum of 20 new or additional serials are purchased.

Periodicals on microform can be an ongoing item on a "wish list." Whenever funds become available they are easily purchased and are a vital component of the school library media center collection.

PAPERBACK BOOKS

There is no longer any argument about the place of the paperback in the school library media center collection. Over the years many individuals have advocated the acquisition of paperbacks as a means of revitalizing and extending the collection. The appeal of paperbacks and their timelines is without question and now numerous examples can be found on how paperbacks can stretch the budget.

Librarians resisted jumping on the bandwagon of providing paperbacks some years ago because of the difficulties encountered in purchasing and processing. Other factors including a short shelf life contributed to the resistance to acquiring them. Studies now show the cost effectiveness of paperbacks based on the initial purchase price and on their circulation life.

The early beginnings of the thirty-five cent paperback with pages that yellowed and spines that deteriorated still continues, but we now have a wide choice of quality paperbacks to select from, often with a shelf life comparable to the hardbound counterpart.

The Bowker Annual, 1983 relates that the 1981 decline of 10.5% in adult trade paperbacks might be attributed to a whopping 24.5% price increase. The increase reflects the complexity, quality and richness of content and illustration as well as inflation.

A random sample of paper back titles in the Mountain Lakes, New Jersey high school library media center shows price increases in the cost of paperbacks from the 1960 Signet

Classic of *Animal Farm* at fifty cents to a 1983 copy of Bantam's *The Heart of a Woman* at $3.50.

Connie C. Epstein in the February and November, 1983 issues of *School Library Journal* offers bibliographies of paperbacks to expand the high school collection with titles having teenage appeal. Prices in these bibliographies average $10.00.

Daniel Melcher[10] writing in *Melcher on Acquisitions* in a chapter on "How to Buy Paperbacks" recommends that mass market titles best be purchased from a wholesaler service, as for a newsstand, as follows:

> Far and away the easiest way to buy the lower priced paperback would be to buy exactly as your local newsstand does. Let his wholesale service to you from the same truck, on the same schedule. That truck would bring you, with full return privileges, a full assortment of each month's new mass market titles, some 300–400 of them, sweetened up with staples like Spock and the Pocket Dictionary. And it will take away what hasn't "sold". Such a local news wholesaler would operate on about a 40% margin and let you have 20%.

This procedure would be like having your own materials selection center. It might just be possible on a situation where a book store or book sales were a part of the school activities.

Kliatt Paperback Book Guide offers a subscription service to some 1200 book reviews each of paperback originals, reprints and new editions. The reviews include both curriculum and leisure reading materials. The use of this service can be for both current and retrospective acquisitions.

Oftentimes a book title is available in both hardcover and paperback as it is issued. The decision on which edition to purchase would be based on need, its use and ultimately the budget.

Hardbound editions of almost any paperback are being offered by a number of firms. Again, decisions concerning the perception of circulation, and the concern for shelf life can determine the need for the additional cost involved in the hardbound paperback edition.

There are many paperback booklists available in almost all subject areas. The Connie Epstein lists referred to earlier are prime examples. Badham S. Wynar's *Reference Books in Paperback: An Annotated Guide* provides an opportunity for small school library media centers to purchase expensive reference materials in paperback at a much reduced cost. Our experience with the annual almanacs in both formats bears this out.

The 1969 *Standards*[11] discussed the widespread use of paperbacks as well as their use as textbooks. It was common at that time to abandon the standard hardbound text for a number of paperback titles. The care and handling of paperbacks in many cases was difficult. Losses were greater for the paperback than for the standard textbook. Unfortunately, in the small school situation, it was not the library media center who administered the paperback textbook program or the standard textbook program either. There are many advantages for this approach but without adequate staff or facilities it is not a feasible undertaking.

Interestingly, paperbacks are not treated separately in the 1975 *Standards*.[12] The use of paperbacks is an accepted fact.

GOVERNMENT DOCUMENTS

The cost of government publications has increased greatly in recent years. The once inexpensive documents now approach prices in the commercial book world. However, these publications are an important part of the school library media center collection and when available, the paperbound editions are affordable.

Acquiring government documents is simplified through the use of a deposit account obtained through the United States Government Printing Office, Superintendent of Documents, Washington, D.C. 20402. A school library media center may choose to encumber a sum of money to be placed into the account from which the subscriber can make purchases. Deposit account statements are then issued on a monthly basis resulting in a savings in both time and effort.

The once regularly issued and popular *Selected U.S. Government Publications* has now become irregular. A recent

U.S. Government Books: Publications for Sale by the United States Government Printing Office, lists some one thousand popular publications. The catalog is arranged by subject and is easy to use. Those with deposit accounts can call in orders which is an added convenience.

The *Monthly Catalog of U.S. Government Publications* lists all publications of the Government issued during each month. The annual subscription rate of $125.00 makes it too expensive for the small school library media center. However, access to the *Monthly Catalog* can be made at one of the Federal Depository Libraries.

A recent issue of *The Federal Depository Library Program*[13] was made available to all public libraries. It included items of information relating to the program.

> These libraries participate in the Depository Library Program established by Congress to allow the public free access to Government publications. Each year Depository Libraries select titles from more than 25,000 new publications issued by our Government. Fifty regional Depository Libraries receive every unclassified Government publication of interest to the public and have undertaken the responsibility of retaining this material permanently, on paper or microfiche. Inter-library loan and reference services are also provided.
>
> The Depositor Library Program originated in the early 1800's when a joint resolution of Congress directed that additional copies of the House and Senate Journals and other documents be printed and distributed to institutions outside the Federal establishment. Over the years the Depository Library System has expanded and today there are more than 1,370 participating libraries.

The informational depository library program offers book marks, poster sets, brochures and listing of the depository libraries. New Jersey, for example, has forty-three such collections.

Students need to be made aware of the availability of these materials and be able to make use of them to a far greater degree than is now occurring.

The *Consumer Information Catalog* which is available in

bulk (twenty-five copies or more) cannot be obtained from an individual mailing list. There is a maximum of 20 free pamphlets from a particular quarterly catalog. The catalog is available from the Consumer Information Center, Department H, Pueblo, Colorado 81009.

Periodicals such as *Booklist* supply a sampling of recent government publications for sale by the Superintendent of Documents. Other periodicals also provide similar information. *Changing Times* and *Good Housekeeping* are prime examples.

Some government publications can be obtained free from members of Congress. *The Yearbook of Agriculture* and the *Congressional Record* are common examples. Both publications are important to the high school library media center collection.

FREE AND INEXPENSIVE

There is a wealth of free and inexpensive materials available for use in school library media center collections. Unlike being able to use a periodical subscription agency or a book wholesaler, the free and inexpensive books, periodicals, brochures and vertical file materials must be requested on an individual basis.

Acquiring the available materials can be a time consuming process. Devising a plan or procedure that can be retrieved on a moment's notice will ease the acquisition of these materials.

Parent and student volunteers can be recruited to aid in the mechanics of writing for the materials. Staff members will often volunteer their time or can be encouraged to do so if they are participating in the selection process. Making use of the post card, unless school letterhead stationary is stipulated, simplifies the ordering process and reduces the overall cost. Post cards can be run through copy or mimeo machines with the few standard lines of a general request allowing space to write in or type the specific item sought. The return address is most often easily stamped on the card.

There are many sources of information for free and inexpensive materials. *Books In Print*[14] lists twenty-six titles of which nine are from the Educators Progress Service, Inc. The long standing *Free and Inexpensive Learning Materials*[15] issued from George Peabody College For Teachers, Trevarrow's *Book of Free Books* from Domus Press, *Freebies Magazine* of Santa Monica, California and *The Freebies Book–Thousands of Things You Can Get Free (or Almost Free From Associations)* published by the American Society of Association Executives are all excellent sources.

There are many periodicals available at no cost and can contribute to extending the collection. Some examples include: *The Journal, School Product News, The Rotarian, Video Pro, Leatherneck, Matrix, Yale Scientific, School Guide* and *Aerospace.*

The American Library Association's (ALA) publication *Information For Everyday Survival: What You Need and Where to Get It*[16] contains a list of materials for information on everyday problems. The introduction suggests that:

> Librarians can use the list as a reference aid and as a buying guide for pamphlet collections, deposit collections and collections for adults with low reading skills. Teachers can use the lists as a source of supplementary materials. Counselors and others engaged in problem solving can use the list to find information to meet the special needs of their clients.

As these materials are received, they can be allowed to accumulate in arranged categories for routing, for the vertical file, for processing or for display.

REMAINDER BOOKS

While there remains a paucity of literature on remainder books, judgements can still be made concerning their value based on what is available. Tony Leisner's[17] summary points out the problems involved with remainders as well as the cost.

> Save up to 80% off list! You've all seen the ads and flyers and catalogs with claims of incredible discounts for books. Some of you have ordered from these catalogs with great success, but more often you don't, because it looks either too good to be true or the requirements of ordering are too complex for your library. Others, who

have made the attempt to order, have been disappointed by order fulfillment or the lack of card kits and now hestitate to purchase from the catalogs. Another source of irritation is that vital information, such as copyright date, binding and indexing data, is often missing. Aside from all this, the more basic question remains un-answered. You are still asking, "Why are these books priced so low? There are no exact statistics available, but my own research indicates that libraries spend over 8 million dollars a year buying remaindered books. It is a sizable industry and an important part of the acquisition process. If the book you need is no longer listed as "in print" or your jobber can't supply it, then maybe one of us has it.

Remainder books are big business. Access to remainders can occur in a number of ways from remainder catalogs to automobile trunk vendors.

Some catalogs are intentionally or unintentionally deceiving in their presentation and annotations. There often is the omission of important information such as edition, copyright and reprint editions while on the other hand some car trunk vendors using book jackets for their display are often astute enough to include dates, index, reprint edition, reviews and the like on the inside of the jacket.

As an aid in the selection of remainders it is helpful to maintain a desiderata file based on reviews. The file can contain these titles which do not require an immediate purchase but would add depth to the collection. It is also for those titles which one would judge might be remaindered.

J. Wandres[18] supplies an example of remainder bargains and how two librarians use remainders:

> Bargains can include $79.95 art books on sale for $19.95, lavishly illustrated imported reference works for a fraction of their list price; fiction gothics, romances, mysteries and westerns for $1.29 to $1.69—often less than their prices in paperback.
>
> How does the small librarian who does her or his own acquisitions, and the big city system with a central acquisitions office approach the buying of remainders?

The search begins with a note on library letterhead to the several remainder book companies listed in Literary Market Place (or in this article) asking for their lists.

Although they will send a catalog, some remainder wholesalers may advise, pointedly, that they do not service library accounts. This is because they are not set up to handle an order for one or two copies of a book—it isn't profitable for them to do so.

How can a librarian best use a remainder dealer? Richard Reed, acquisitions librarian for the 20-branch Miami-Dade library in Florida, says "We use them to pick up titles that we didn't get the first time around." Reed also says he uses remainder houses for multiple copies of books in high demand as well as for replacements.

Richard Provinsal, assistant superintendent of technical processes for the 50-branch Queens Borough system in New York, says, "What my people go for are the imports from England. They're more readily available through remainder houses here than by ordering direct from the original publisher." Provinsal also says that by ordering through remainder wholesalers he gets the books for less, and quicker.

The librarian for the fine arts department of a small midwestern college says he depends on two remainder houses that specialize in art books for his acquisitions. "It's the only way I can survive on the budget I'm given."

Thomas Weyr[19] points out the commercial aspects of remainder books:

Today the business is no longer only remaindered books. Remainder houses call themselves promotional publishers and deal as much in reprints and original book packaging as they do with publishers' overstock. The business has acquired some of the frantic aspects associated with the Seventh Avenue "rag trade" and the stock market pit. It is a fast-paced, risky, high-volume, low-overhead and tight-margin kind of operation where everybody seems to do three or four jobs at once.

In the trade, "bargain books," as they like to be

known, are a big-ticket, year-round business pushed by major chains like Waldenbooks and B. Dalton and large discounters like Crown Books and Barnes & Noble Stores that once spurned displaying or selling remainders, or did so reluctantly once or twice a year, now consider bargain books an integral part of the sales mix.

Adhering to the principles of book selection outlined by Mary Duncan Carter in *Building Library Collections*[20] we can enhance and extend school library media center collections without violating sound selection procedures through careful remainder book purchasing.

GIFTS

Extending the collection through gifts can be an important means of acquiring library materials. While one cannot depend on a systematic approach to this type of collection development, the effort involved can be worthwhile.

A 1964 publication on library administration, edited by Roberta Bowler, provides the following advise to public libraries which can serve the school library media center[21]:

> The admonition always to look a gift horse in the mouth must have been written with librarians in mind. Probably few institutions are the target of so much attempted bibliophilanthropy as are public libraries. Every librarian knows that come spring there will be telephone calls about what was found in the attic. And cartons of books are packed that might contain anything from a physics text of 1896 to a rare pamphlet on local history.
> One of the best methods for dealing with this chronic gift problem is a clear statement the book selection policy to the effect that gifts will be subjected to the same searching scrutiny as are new books, with reference to their value for the library and the community. All gifts should be accepted only with the provision that if the library has no use for them they may be disposed of without any red tape as the library decides best.

It is a good idea never to turn down any gift offer without inquiring into its nature. Again and again treasures have been found in piles of junk and every librarian owes it to his institution and his community to have a careful check made of any list or lot of books offered.

Further advise offered by Bowler[22] includes:

An alert librarian can extend his book budget considerably through the expenditious acquiring of gifts. These come in various forms. Money itself is always welcome, particularly if no strings are attached. Money is given on occasion to build up a specific collection or specific subject, for establishing a new service, as a subscription to a magazine or a service, as a memorial to or appreciation of an individual, for specific items too expensive for the library's budget, or it may simply be given or willed for use at the library's discretion.

Foundations; government units; charitable, educational, religious, and scientific institutions or organizations; foreign governments; publishers, business firms; authors—these are among those who will on occasion make their publications available free to a library. Libraries also exchange their publications and sometimes their unneeded or discarded duplicates with one another. The U.S. Book Exchange was established for this purpose. There are also individuals who make donations, varying from great collections of rare books to attic junk; from buttons to stuffed bison.

There are pitfalls as well as gains among gifts. Some must be avoided because they come tied by expensive strings: a library cannot dissipate its service, its time, or its space to establish and maintain patches of special collections or material requiring special handling; it will get caught in embarrassing and long drawn out wrangles or explanations if it accepts materials without the clear understanding that it is free to add or not add them to its collections; it can find itself buried with unusable books, flora and fauna, and objects d'art if a firm stand is not taken against accepting or in regard to disposal.

At the beginning of each school year, requests to students and parents can result in obtaining back issues of periodicals, books and phonograph recordings. Regular publicity made in and outside the school can bring good results. Parent volunteers whether in the school library media center or elsewhere in the school serve as an excellent contact.

Once the pattern of gift giving is established, you may very well find that you are inundated with materials. Periodicals can then be shared with the various departments of the school. A good way of instilling in students the care and concern for school library media centers resources is to provide a spot for cutting up articles or pictures from the duplicates you acquire. It is also a good strategy to share these materials with the local public library or schools in and outside the school district.

Teacher and parent loans of books, especially some best selling titles can also bring a new vitality to the collection. Providing a shelf or two with these "on-loan to the library media center" generates considerable interest and results in few overall losses.

Working cooperatively with whatever group in your community who may be sponsoring a book sale is also profitable. Often the media specialist can be the first purchaser at the sale. If it is a parent-teacher undertaking, they may put aside titles they feel would be of value such as books of drama and poetry.

Cooperation and good rapport with the local public library is always essential. Their book sale, their gifts, their duplicate new book titles can often be directed to you. The public library has an already established pattern in most communities of welcoming and receiving many gifts of materials. This same pattern can be established for the school library media center. A sharing of these materials between the public and school library media center can become an important element of cooperation between the two institutions.

Public libraries have long used a paperback exchange shelf, corner or even a cardboard box. "Take one, Leave one" is often the motto. Students and staff respond well to this approach and often whole collections of science fiction, mysteries, fantasy and more have appeared in the exchange area.

NETWORKING

The 1970's ushered in the concept of networking in a formal way. Today many states have enacted legislation allowing multitype networks to occur and school library media centers share a role in this structure. David Bender[23] reports a long standing tradition of cooperation between schools and public libraries.

> Cooperative activities are not new to school library media personnel. Jointly developed and cooperatively sponsored activities are in operation throughout the country. However, most of these activities have occurred via informal arrangements, thus making their continuation somewhat less than certain. For a change in personnel could bring an end to such cooperative endeavors. Also, such arrangements usually exist at the local levels, without any sharing on a regional or statewide basis. Examples of these activities include:

1. informal meetings between public and school librarians to address mutual concerns
2. exchanging lists of collection holdings
3. jointly planned summer library programs
4. joint compilation of community resources
5. joint planning of community programs
6. joint material evaluation, selection, acquisition, and processing programs
7. placement of public library book catalogs in school libraries
8. joint development of storytelling groups to improve techniques and skills
9. reciprocal borrowing and lending of materials
10. class-orientation visits to the public library
11. book talks by public librarians given in the school
12. providing the public library with curriculum guides and units of instruction
13. inservice programs designed around topics of mutual interest and concern
14. production facilities for materials
15. preparation of union lists or catalogs

16. access to specialized and computerized data bases
17. joint film cooperatives.

Bender[24] cautions that networks are not designed to reduce the budget, but rather to enhance the existing school library media program:

> Cooperative activities emanating from any system or network should not be designed to supplant the existing library media program. The services provided should increase the offerings of a single library, therefore supplementing existing operations.

The American Library Association of School Librarians (AASL) issued an important document in 1978 on *The Role of the School Media Program in Networks and Interlibrary Cooperation*. The report was developed from an AASL Committee on networking. Franckowiak[25] and others have emphasized the contributions that school library media centers can make in their participation in networks:

> In addition to benefiting from participation in networks, schools have a substantial contribution to make to these efforts. School media programs have had a long history of concern for the application of newer materials of instruction and their attendant technologies to the teaching and learning processes. The kindergarten through twelfth grades in public and private schools in the country have taken the leadership in embracing and attempting to realize the potential of audiovisual technology and its contribution, in combination with a variety of traditional formats, to the process of education.
>
> School media personnel have considerable skills in the evaluation, selection, organization, and utilization of the full range of print and nonprint materials. School media programs have traditionally been concerned with handling a variety of information packages, because this was the way information came to them, in a form most readily applicable to curriculum and personal needs. Schools have taken the lead in viewing instructional objectives

and the need for information as a primary concern. School media programs have applied scientific processes to the selection of the appropriate medium to meet the instructional objectives of the full range of print and non-print resources, as well as community resources and information, is vital to the education process. Schools have significant collections of print and nonprint materials and the equipment necessary for listening and viewing as well as producing a variety of media.

School library media centers should be and can become equal partners in the evolving cooperative efforts now occurring. The cost of such participation is being explored in many areas from state aid, federal monies and local contractual arrangements. The anticipation of access to materials on a moments notice is gratifying indeed and the opportunity for this access will generate greater support for the school library media program.

SUMMARY

A special theme issue of the January/February, 1983 *The Book Report* provides numerous suggestions on "Surviving the Budget Squeeze". The article *51 Ways to Save and Earn Money for the Library Budget* submitted by library media specialists are grouped into categories: Sales and Donations, Cooperation, Do It Yourself, Recycling, Book Clubs, For the Asking, Paperbacks, Procedure, Free Information and an invitation to become a book reviewer for the *Journal* and keep the book reviewed which can then be added to the school library media center collection.

The energy shortage in the late 1970's brought out the creative and clever efforts of Americans to cope with that situation. As school library media specialists, we can and do cope with small budgets in small school settings. As our world expands through information science and our full potential is realized, we will be able to gain additional financial support to strengthen our collections and participate in sharing resources from other collections.

REFERENCES

1. American Association of School Librarians and Association for Educational Communications and Technology, *Media Programs: District and School* (Chicago and Washington, D.C.: American Library Association and Association for Educational Communications and Technology, 1975).

2. Marilyn Miller and Barbara B. Moran, "Expenditures For Resources In School Library Media Centers FY '82-'83", *School Library Journal*, 30, No. 2 (October 1983):113-14.

3. Miller and Moran, "Expenditures For Resources", p.105.

4. Milbrey L. Jones "NCES Survey of Private School Library Media Centers, 1979", *"The Bowker Annual of Library and Book Trade Information"* (New York: R. R. Bowker Company, 1983) p.354.

5. Jones, "NCES Survey", p.353.

6. Office of Library Planning and Development, *Analyses of New Jersey Public Library Statistics for 1982* (N.J. State Department of Education, Division of the State Library, January, 1983):5.

7. *Standards*, p.70.

8. *Standards*, p.70.

9. Dorothy M. Broderick, "Subscription Agencies: Money Savers", *Voice of Youth Advocates*, 4, No. 6 (February 1982):22.

10. Daniel Melcher, *Melcher On Acquisitions* (Chicago: American Library Association, 1971) p.75.

11. American Library Association and the National Education Association, *Standards For School Media Programs* (Chicago and Washington, D.C., 1969).

12. *Standards*, 1975, p.70.

13. *Depository Libraries: Your Source For Government Information* (Brochure S/N 021-000-38000-8, U.S. Government Printing Office, STOP: MK, Washington, D.C. 20401).

14. *Subject Guide To Books in Print, 1983-1984* (New York, R. R. Bowker Company, 1983) p.2195.

15. Norman R. Moore, ed., *Free and Inexpensive Learning Materials* (George Peabody College for Teachers, Incentive Publications, 1983).

16. Priscilla Gotsick et al. comp., *Information For Everyday Survival: What You Need and Where To Get It* (Chicago, American Library Association, 1977).

17. Leisner, Tony. "Speciality Jobbers Are Special". *EMANATIONS*, 3, No. 2 (Winter, 1980):11

18. Wandres, J. "Remainder Books: An Offer You Can No Longer Afford To Refuse" *Collection Management* (LJ Special Report #11):2-3.

19. Thomas Weyr, "The Bargain Hunters", *Publishers Weekly*, 225 No. 14 (April 6, 1984):32.

20. Mary Duncan Carter, Wallace John Bonk and Rose Mary Magrill, *Building Library Collections* (Metuchen, NJ, Scarecrow Press, 1974).

21. Roberta Bowler, ed., *Local Library Administration* (Chicago, International City Manager's Association, 1964):193-94.

22. Bowler, "Local Library Administration", p.205.

23. David R. Bender, "Networking and School Library Media Programs", *School Library Journal* 26, No. 3 (November, 1979):31.

24. Bender, "Networking", p.32.

25. Bernard Franckowiak, "Networks, Data Bases and Media Programs: An Overview", *School Library Quarterly* 6, No. 1 (Fall 1977):15.

Core Collections in Small Media Centers

Betty Grebey

This paper will address the various connotations of core collections, the problems of building and maintaining a core collection in a small school media center, the impact of publishing on collection building, and the advantages and disadvantages of certain selection tools.

A core collection often has the connotation of a base collection or an opening-day collection. This definition embraces a quantitative requirement. Recommended numerical guidelines per type of media exist in various state and national standards. The theory of such a collection is that this group of materials will meet the minimal basic needs of the student and faculty.

A second connotation concerns the adequacy and depth of the subject content of the library's collection. A balanced collection is a concept found frequently in the literature when the overall subject content of a collection is discussed. Historically, a balanced collection refers to a given percentage of titles in each Dewey class. Today's philosophy as stated in *Media Programs: District and School* stresses the need for the media specialist to make decisions concerning the number of materials in any given subject area needed to support the individual media program and to fulfill its users' needs.[1] This means the collection may not be "balanced" in the traditional sense.

There is yet a third meaning of this term which involves a library's efforts to acquire all recommended materials on a given subject. This practice of buying everything is not usually followed in school media centers because of cost restrictions and lack of need for all these materials.

Mrs. Grebey is the district coordinator of libraries in the Downingtown Area School District.

Basic book selection criteria, selection policies, and collection evaluation techniques have all been discussed thoroughly and often in library literature, textbooks, and library school curricula. Because of such treatment, these topics, though relevant to the overall concept of collection management, will not be examined in detail in this paper. However, some essential factors affecting collection-building in schools need to be reiterated.

One of these factors is that, ideally, the school media collection will meet the goals of local, state, and national educational agencies. These goals must include support for the ever-changing informational, recreational, and instructional needs of the students and faculty.

Knowledge of the local community is another factor. The community should be examined in terms of its political, social, geographical, economic and cultural characteristics.[2]

By the same rationale, the individual school community must also be studied. One of the factors in this aspect is a thorough knowledge of the curriculum. A collection cannot and will not meet the needs of the students or faculty if the librarian does not know the courses of study. A familiarity with faculty needs logically follows the curricular study. To become thoroughly familiar with the curriculum and faculty methodology, the librarian should be able to answer the following questions about each course of study:

1. Which teachers use the media collection?
2. How do they use the library?
3. What type of assignments are made using the collection?
4. What term papers or reports are assigned on what topics?
5. What special programs exist in the school such as those for the gifted or the special education students?

A third study of the individual school will be one of the student body. The media specialist will need to be aware of the following pupil characteristics:

1. Reading ability.
2. Recreational or non-study interests.
3. Propensity for higher education.

The media specialist must be aware of the multitudinous data resulting from these examinations, for it will all affect the needs of the library's users, the content of the collection, and the use of the media collection.

With the information from the studies cited above, a librarian can intelligently begin to prepare a base collection or to build a core collection upon existing materials.

The initial question in establishing a base collection is "What materials are imperative now?" The reference collection should be given first priority, followed by the purchase of instructional media for the faculty. Prostano and Prostano state:

> The school media collection must begin with as comprehensive a reference collection as is possible with the funds available. Collection building begins with such traditional media as dictionaries, encyclopedias, almanacs and other general reference tools. . . . If funds are reasonably adequate, the selection of reference tools should be coupled with the purchase of media needed by teachers in instructional situations.[3]

The next step is to develop the general collection in strength and scope within the budget limitations. A practice that is often followed is the purchasing of a commercially packaged opening-day collection. This procedure has definite drawbacks, one of which is that the media specialist has not had the opportunity to check the titles against the needs of the media center. Such a collection will usually provide some coverage in all of the broad subject areas; however, certain curricular topics requiring an indepth concentration of titles will fall short of the needed scope.

Instead of buying a pre-packaged collection, the media specialist can request a special service prior to purchase from most of the major book jobbers. For example, Baker & Taylor Co., Follett Library Book Company and Bound-To-Stay-Bound Books, Inc., three jobbers who are active in the school market, will supply upon request an availability check of the titles in specific selection tools such as the *Children's Catalog,* or the *Senior High Catalog,* or the *Elementary School Library Collection.*

The following is a listing of some of the advantages in making sure of this service:

1. Current costs are known.
2. Out-of-print titles are excluded.
3. Time and effort is saved by not having to consider unavailable items.
4. The media specialist will have a choice and will be able to plan emphasis on the subject areas which need an in-depth collection.
5. The print-out can normally be used as an order form, saving much time and money in preparing a formal typed book order.

Since these listings are retrospective in nature, the media specialist has the problem of making the collection up-to-date. Careful perusal of current reviewing tools will be necessary. Note that direct order items will not appear on the listings and will have to follow normal ordering procedures.

There are several problems which affect the establishment of a core collection; monetary limitations is one such problem. Budget restrictions influence the selection and the number of items that are purchased. Under these restrictions, the effort to provide the widest or more varied coverage in a given subject area becomes difficult, so first consideration should be given to works that are anthologies, collections, "collected works of . . .", and comprehensive treatments. These works can be supplemented by individual works or specialized treatments after the core collection is established.

To expand a limited periodical or book collection, collections of reprinted articles on broad curriculum areas can be purchased at a reasonable price. The *Social Issues Resources Series* is an example of such a service. Vertical file packets on popular report topics are available from several sources at favorable costs and will serve as supplemental material. One example is The Library Reference Service Company.

Another factor in stretching the budget is the consideration of available bindings. A certain title included as a core selection may be one that, though necessary, will not receive heavy use; paperback editions of such works will result in a financial saving.

Another problem affecting the collection is grade and/or reading levels. In the elementary grades, these levels are quite broad, ranging from the non-reader to the academically talented sixth-grader. This problem exists on all education levels to some degree. For example, a high school may have students with reading levels as low as third grade or as high as the college and adult levels. The results of the Nelson-Denny reading test which is administered nationally to the tenth grade will aid in determining the reading abilities of the high school student.

Out-of-print materials are a constant problem in collection building, and it is one that has escalated during the past few years. When the publishing industry faced a paper shortage and increasing costs for paper, smaller runs of individual titles were made. The decision in the *Thor Power Tool Case,* 1979, resulted in a dramatic decrease of publishers' inventories. These facts have resulted in a greater number of out-of-print titles and in titles going out-of-print at a more rapid rate. Because of this situation, a high percentage of titles listed in the retrospective standard selection tools will be unavailable. Remainder companies such as Barnes and Noble and University Book Service may be a source for out-of-print material.

The publishing industry conducts surveys periodically to determine characteristics and perceived book needs of the population. Since the industry is profit motivated, the types of materials published reflects what publishers believe will sell the best. For example, during the past few years, there has been a heavy concentration in easy books because of the presence of a baby boom.

A perusal of reviewing media for a period of a few years will also illustrate publishing patterns in given subject areas. For the past two years, there have been very few titles published in mathematics and the pure sciences for young adults, while there are many recommended titles in science on the elementary level. These policies present a subtle problem for media specialist in that material can not be purchased if it is not published.

There are commercial sources published by book jobbers that can be helpful to a media specialist in building a core collection. Each of these catalogs or guides has unique characteristics.

The Follett Library Book Company publishes two catalogs entitled *Guide to Good Reading;* one on the elementary level and one on the secondary level. The titles included are selected by a librarian on the company's staff, all titles are available or can be supplied at the time of the catalog printing, reading levels are cited, and review sources are given. Note that these review citations are *not* necessarily favorable reviews. It should also be noted that this company supplies library bindings only.

Bound-To-Stay-Bound's catalog covers grades K–12 and includes approximately 17,000 titles. Favorable review citations and the appropriate age level are given for most titles. Only Library Prebound bindings are available. This tool is especially useful for retrospective purchasing.

The Baker and Taylor School Selection Guide for Grades K–12 has several unique features that are useful to a school librarian in maintaining a core collection. Purchase priorities 1-2-3 are assigned to each title, all titles are annotated, all titles have been published in the last three years, and paperback titles are given in a special section. Another special feature in this tool is the core collections. These core collections are representative of topics of interest in today's schools and list current titles that are available and suitable for media centers. Forthcoming titles from publishers' Spring lists are also included. A committee of practicing school librarians, representing various areas of the nation, select the titles and core topics for this guide.

The bibliography included in this paper is a selective one. Factors involved in the selection of these titles include cost, focus of the collections, availability to most small media centers, and currentness. Many of the larger, standard selection tools are therefore not cited.

By using these commercial guides, this selective list of selection tools, and current review media, the school library media specialist can build and maintain a useful core collection.

SELECTION TOOLS: A SELECTIVE LISTING

American Association for the Advancement of Science. *The AAAS Science Book List Supplement.* Washington, D.C.: AAAS, 1978.

American Association for the Advancement of Science. *The AAAS Science Book List:* 3rd. ed. Washington, D.C.: AAAS, 1970.

Best Reference Books. Littleton, Colo.: Libraries Unlimited, 1976.

Books for the Teenage. New York: New York Public Library.

Brown, Lucy Gregor. *Core Media Collection for Secondary Schools,* 2nd. ed. New York: Bowker, 1979. 263 p.

Children's Catalog. 14th ed. New York: H. W. Wilson, 1981.

Dority, G. K. *Guide to Reference Books for Small & Medium-Sized Libraries, 1970–1982.* Littleton, Colo.: Libraries Unlimited, 1983.

Elementary School Library Collection. 74th ed. Williamsport, PA: Brodart Books, 1984.

Encylopedia Buying Guide: A Consumer Guide to General Encyclopedias in Print. 3rd. ed. New York: Bowker, 1981.

Gillespie, John T. *Best Books for Children: Preschool Through the Middle Grades.* 2nd ed. New York: Bowker, 1981.

Junior High School Catalog. 4th ed. New York: H. W. Wilson, 1980.

Katz, Bill. *Magazines for Libraries: for the General Reader and School Junior College, University and Public Libraries.* 3rd ed. New York: Bowker, 1978.

McDaniel, Roderick. *Resources for Learning: A Core Collection for Elementary Schools.* New York: Bowker, 1971.

National Association of Independent Schools. *Books for Secondary Libraries.* 6th ed. New York: Bowker, 1981.

Peterson, Carolyn Sue. *Reference Books for Elementary and Junior High School Libraries.* 2nd ed. Metuchen, N.J.: Scarecrow Press, 1975.

Richardson, Selma K. *Periodicals for School Media Programs.* Chicago: American Library Association, 1978.

Senior High School Catalog. 12th ed. New York: H. W. Wilson, 1982.

University Press Books for Secondary Schools. New York: American University Press Services.

Wynar, Bohdan S. *Reference Books in Paperback: an Annotated Guide.* 2nd ed. Littleton, Colo.: Libraries Unlimited, 1976.

Wynar, Christine L. *Guide to Reference Books for School Media Centers.* Littleton, Colo.: Libraries Unlimited, 1981.

USEFUL COMMERCIAL CATALOGS

Baker and Taylor's School Selection Guide for Grades K–12.
Bound-to-Stay-Bound Books K thru 12.
BroDart Books for School and Public Libraries.
Follett Library Book Company Elementary Guide to Good Reading.
Follett Library Book Company Secondary Guide to Good Reading.

REFERENCES

1. American Association of School Librarians, American Library Association, and Association for Educational Communications and Technology, *Media Programs: District and School* (Chicago, IL: American Library Association, Washington, D.C.: Association for Educational Communications and Technology, 1975), p. 68.

    2. Phyllis J. VanOrden, *The Collection Program in Elementary and Middle Schools* (Littleton, Col.: Libraries Unlimited, 1982), p. 40.
    3. Emanual T. Prostano and Joyce S. Prostano, *The School Library Media Center* (Littleton, Col.: Libraries Unlimited, 1977) pp. 78–79.

Business and Education

Esther Dyer

This article documents trends in cooperation between business and industry, set in their historical context. Examples of partnerships are given and their implications for collection development are explored.

The business of education is no longer simply a matter for the educational establishment. Economic productivity is impossible without educational productivity. It is the purpose of this article to document the growing trend towards business and education partnerships within the context of American education today by documenting the decline of public trust in education, sketching the history of the trend toward business and education partnerships, describing selected models of cooperation, outlining broad areas for media center involvement and lastly identifying implications for collection development.

PUBLIC TRUST AND PUBLIC EDUCATION

In his address to the 89th Congress, President Lyndon Baines Johnson characterized education as ". . . a force for freedom, justice and rationality . . . the universal force for good." The launching of Sputnik created an evironment in which the American public became increasingly cognizant of the need to spur the acquisition of scientific knowledge. Consequently, millions of dollars were made available to the educational enterprise for investment in programs, materials and equipment. Dollars for education were viewed as investment in America's future citizens and assurance of pre-eminence abroad.

The Great Society was a golden era for education. Public

Dr. Dyer is an archivist with Blue Cross/Blue Shield.

trust in education as a panacea for social problems and a legitimate mechanism for achieving scientific excellence reached a high watermark. The foundations of this belief were severely shaken by the *Coleman Report* which found, for example, that environment and teacher expectations provided better indicators of student performance than did per pupil expenditure. Contrary to the notion that money spent on educational programs can alleviate the differences in student's social, cultural, and economic backgrounds, schools, because of geographic location and homogeneity, tend to reinforce rather than counteract the initial influence of home and native culture on students. Nonetheless, advances were made in educational programs in science, mathematics and reading; and steps were taken to improve the equality of opportunity for all students, regardless of physical characteristics or mental acuity.

Unfortunately, improvement in educational programs, curriculum innovation and equality of educational opportunity could be equated to dollars spent on in educational budgets. In other words, inputting X amount of dollars did not guarantee that all students entering the schools would leave with Y level of achievement and attitude. Thus, the application of education did not assure a quality product or even a basic uniform level of competence.

As the economy weakened, more attempts were made to justify educational expenditures. Consequently, the decade that followed the publication of the *Coleman Report* has been termed the Decade of Accountability, characterized by attempts to measure whether or not the inputs (tax dollars) were well spent and to quantify output (student achievement). The educational enterprise was no longer assured of automatic funding; and educators became increasingly familiar with the terms PPBS, MBO, and zero-based budgeting systems. Schools had to prove their utility to taxpayers and validate the effectiveness of programs in order to secure tax support.

As federal support for schools decreased, local districts assumed an increasingly larger portion of the the funding burden. The passage of local school bond issues and new taxes became linked in many cases to successful public relations efforts and student improvement on standardized tests. The growing disenchantment of the American public was eloquently captured by Robert Hutchins in an article entitled "The Great Anti-School Campaign":

. . . nobody had a kind word for the institution that was only yesterday the foundation of our freedom, the guarantee of our future, the cause of our prosperity and the bastion of our security, the bright and shining beacon that was the source of our enlightenment, the public school.[1]

Although written a dozen year ago, Hutchins' words aptly summarize the current public opinion of education in the United States today.

Recognition of the educational dilemma was forthcoming in two major reports to the Nation dealing with our educational system: *A Nation at Risk* and *Basic Skills in the U.S. Work Force*. The latter study focuses on the independent initiatives of business to overcome the deficiencies of the labor force. While the former dramatically conveys that educational attainment is declining in comparison with our own historical attainments and with attainments of other countries.

A Nation at Risk dramatically conveys the judgment that educational attainment is declining in comparison with our own historical attainments and with attainments of other countries.

Our Nation is at risk. . . . If an unfriendly foreign power had attempted to impose on America the mediocre educational performance that exists today, we might well have viewed it as an act of war. As it stands, we have even squandered the gains in student achievement made in the wake of the Sputnik challenge. Moreover, we have dismantled essential support systems which helped make those gains possible. We have, in effect, been committing an act of unthinking, unilateral educational disarmament.[2]

The *Basic Skills Study* is the report of a task force of leading corporate executives and public educators which defines the problem of basic skills deficiencies from the business, union and school perspectives and seeks to devise new methods for generating cooperation between companies and school systems at the community level. Major findings of the study include the following:

1. A significant gap exists between business and school system perception of basic skills "adequacy". For example while most companies surveyed identified basic skill deficiency in high school graduates, over 75% of the school systems deemed their graduates appropriately prepared for employment.
2. Business and unions identified speaking/listening, mathematics, and science skills as most frequently deficient vs. reading skills more usually cited by educators.
3. Two-thirds of the companies and most unions noted that basic skills deficiencies limit the job advancement of employees, with resulting employee frustration and high turnover rates. While businesses think of new employees as potentially a 35 year investment, school systems seemingly educate youth for the "first job" rather than long term viability in the work place.[3]

THE CHANGING SCHOOL POPULATION

A recent (1982) Gallup Poll of the *Public's Attitude Toward the Public School* reinforced the theme that the American public is steadfast in their belief that education is the major foundation for the future strength of this country. Yet schools are facing new challenges even in the very nature of the student body they serve.

> Each generation of Americans has outstripped its parents in education, in literacy, and in economic attainment. For the first time in the history of our country, the educational skills of one generation will not surpass, will not equal, will not even approach those of their parents.[4]

In the decade from 1970 to 1980, the student population changed dramtically. Enrollment in the nation's public schools declined by over 5 million students since 1970. The next decade will see a 14% drop in the number of persons aged 14–24 and a 20% drop in high school enrollments. Further, children today are more autonomous, emerge from childhood more rapidly and have greater exposure to the world and global events then any previous generation. Television has had a marked impact on the extent of common knowledge, the attention span of children and the expectations they have of education. Changes in family structure, such as the increase in working mothers, single parent homes, and other swings in demographics have created different environments for schooling. While the Commission's report notes that the *average* citizen is better educated and more knowledgeable than his peer of a generation past, the *average* high school graduate is not as well educated as the average graduate of 25 or 35 years ago, when a much smaller percentage of the population completed high school. Some educational historians have tried to shift the burden of the blame to the popularization of education. In other words, equality of opportunity and demographic trends, not education per se, are the primary causes of the decline in student achievement. Indeed these factors are important but they are only part of the big picture of the status of American Education today.

EDUCATION IN JEOPARDY

The goals of universal education and a literate society are in jeopardy in America today. Schools are in trouble. Among the findings of the National Commission on Educational Excellence are the following indicators of risk:

1. International comparisons of student achievement, completed a decade ago, reveal that on 19 academic tests, American students were never first or second and, in comparison with other industrialized nations, were last seven times.
2. About 13 percent of all 17 year-olds in the United States are functionally illiterate. Among minority youth this percentage may reach as high as 40.
3. The College Board's Scholastic Aptitude Tests (SAT) demonstrate a virtually unbroken decline from 1963–1980. Average verbal and mathematics scores dropped 50 to 40 points, respectively.
4. National science achievement scores of U.S. 17 year-olds steadily declined in 1969, 1973 and 1977.
5. Between 1975 and 1980, remedial mathematics courses in public 4 year colleges increased by 72% and now

constitute 25% of all mathematics courses taught in those institutions.

6. Business and military establishments spend millions of dollars on costly remedial education programs, including such basic skills as reading, writing, spelling and computation.

Clearly, the education of tomorrow's decision makers is not a matter only for schoolmen, but is of vital concern for all citizens and corporations. Improvement in economic productivity are impossible without improvements in the workforce, in educational productivity. Educating youth to become part of the Learning Society and to deal with its increasing technology and complexity, places new demands on education. The educational establishment must adapt to a changing society and develop relevant and meaningful programs that meet the needs of today and equip students for the changes of tomorrow.

Much has been written about the time lag between the conception of innovations in society as a whole and their inclusion as part of the curriculum. Students of the change syndrome in education have gone so far as to estimate that 20 years is necessary from innovation to diffusion. For example, computer skills are only now becoming a vital part of the school program. Even so, there are many schools today that still do not provide the necessary training to understand this technology nor allow students access to computers. Future shock while talked about by educators has yet to really impact on the design of new curriculum and the changing needs of the workforce. Part of the blame has much to do with economies of scale and the difficulties in times of austerity to make changes. If education is to close the gap and keep up with the changes in the private and governmental sectors, then increased funds must be made available to support such endeavors.

BUSINESS AND EDUCATION

The economics and the environment of schools have created an atmosphere conducive to growing involvement of business government in helping to determine new directions for the educational enterprise. Business and governmental establishments no longer have the luxury of tending to their own affairs and simply choosing from a pool of qualified workers those best suited to the jobs available. Increasingly, education is becoming big business and of concern to business and military leaders who must choose either to spend money on expensive remedial programs or help in changing the structure of education so that students are better equipped to meet the requirements of the marketplace.

According to *Basic Skills in the U.S. Workforce*, more than a third of the corporations surveyed currently provide, indeed replicate, basic high school training for their employees. AT&T alone spends $6 million a year to train 14,000 employees in basic reading and mathematics competencies. While the Department of Defense (DOD), the country's largest employer with over 1000 installations and 4.5 million personnel spends over $13 billion in training personnel with a dedicated staff of 200,000 to supervise these activities. DOD, the country's largest employer rejects 22% of its applicants on the basis of lack of basic skills training.

Clearly the independent *Basic Skills* report adds further evidence to the indictment of American Education today. Its strength, however, is in its portrayal of the concerns of business about education and in the levels and extent of support that may be forthcoming. Few policy makers have attempted to understand the

> . . . business perspective in analyzing basic education problems of the secondary schools and to match that perspective to the views of public educators. The independent initatives of business to overcome basic skills deficiencies, whether in the existing work force, or among newly hired employees, have been largely ignored.[5]

More than 80% of jobs today are in the private sector and that percentage will increase in the 1980's. "Yet as a potential and actual employer of secondary school graduates and nongraduates, it is perhaps American business which best understands the need to improve the basic skills deficiencies."[6] The political, economic and social stability and vitality of the United States are crucially intertwined with quality education for all young people. Economic productivity is impossible without educational productivity. Good basic education provides a firm foundation for a productive society.

It is interesting to note that in response to the question of cooperation among businesses, schools and unions, 90% of respondents from all three groups expressed a desire to examine first-hand the viability of cooperation to resolve the problem. *Basic Skills* points out that both schools and business need to communicate better. Business must be willing to aid in curriculum development and classroom instruction.

Partnerships in education are now viewed as a means of moving the educational frontier ahead. Yet barriers to cooperation do exist in the form of political problems, logistics and indeed the very nature of bureaucracies. Successful programs will be those at the grassroots levels which meet the needs of particular schools and which are flexible enough to provide for the employment patterns and special demographic characteristics of the area. They must also be feasible within the political configuration.

MODELS OF INTERACTION

Historically, education has been a major beneficiary of corporate largess. Computer corporations alone donated nearly $100 million of equipment and software to educational institutions in 1983. A recent report by the Council for Financial Aid to Education estimates total corporate contribution in 1981 at $2.9 billion, of which $1.4 billion went to education. In fact, despite a drop in corporate profits of 4.2%, a survey of 712 companies reveals that corporate support of education rose 11% in 1981 over 1980, to hit a record 0.4% of pre-tax net income. To a great extent, the increase in corporate giving in the face of declining profits is due to the existence of corporate foundations.

The idea of business and education working cooperatively is not altogether new. Since the 1970's there has been a growing movement towards public-private sector partnerships. The Private Sector Initative Program (PSIP), under the aegis of CETA from 1978–1983, sought to develop creative ways of involving the private sector in employment and training programs, and improving the opportunity for disadvantaged individuals to enter the private sector workforce. The new Private Industry Councils (PIC), populated mostly with members from the business community, were a major innovation in the history of employment and training programs. Sample PSIP programs included: occupational training, on the job training, pre-employment training, placement programs. Yet the full realization of these programs was hampered by the fact that PSIP was tied to the political realities of local CETA programs.

In the same spirit there have been a number of exemplary programs that have historically tried to improve the skills of young people and have tried to provide schools and young people with the appropriate skills to enter the job market. Junior Achievement for example, currently has 9,414 business executives (26% are CEOs), committed to instructing in their programs, that number was expected to rise to 12,000 in 1984.

Illustrative of industry sponsored programs are Project InVEST, MATHCOUNTS and Medical Explorers. Project InVEST (Insurance Vocational Education Student Training) is a model insurance company office simulation that is offered as a fully accredited high school business education "capstone" course meeting two class periods a day for the entire senior year. Administered by the College of Insurance, the program is supported on a national basis by the Independent Insurance Agents of America, the National Association of Insurance Women and insurance companies. The program helps students understand the importance of their role as consumers and producers of insurance services in a private enterprise system. Using automobile insurance as a case study, the program helps students bridge the gap between office education and office work. The involvement of local insurance companies and the local chapters of the national associations together with teachers is a key element in the success of Project InVEST.

The MATHCOUNTS program is a coaching program and math competition series in operation in 45 states. Sponsored by the National Science Foundation, National Society of Professional Engineers, CNA Insurance Companies, National Aeronautics and Space Administration and the National Council of Teachers of Mathematics MATHCOUNTS hopes to involve more than seven million junior high school students by the end of 1984. Programs are administered by local chapters of the sponsoring associations and the year long program culminates in a series of local, state and national competitions. The goal of MATHCOUNTS is to ensure a technically literate population.

The Medical Explorers, on the other hand, is sponsored by the Boy Scouts of America and is designed for young men and women to become more knowledgeable about career possibilities in health care. In cooperation with local Boy Scout Explorer Councils, hospitals sponsor these programs which include weekly participation in hospital activities, training sessions, and interaction with hospital staff. Through their participation, youngsters are made more aware of health and hospital administration both as potential employees and as recipients of health care. Doctors, hospital administrators and volunteers are involved in program development. Often medical explorers participate in summer camps which have the added attraction of courses in such areas as CPR.

The success of these and numerous other programs combined with the disenchantment with educational practice and the current administration's attempts to involve the private sector in public areas did much to prompt the White House sponsorship of the National Partnerships in Education Program. In his 1983 State of the Union Address, President Ronald Reagan asked the "ratio" to unite in revitalizing American education by setting a standard of excellence. On October 13, 1983, President Ronald Reagan launched the National Partnerships in Education Program in a White House ceremony, with 150 representatives from business, schools, government and trade associations in attendance. He challenged the schools to form partnerships in education with business and directed the federal government to promote partnerships. The President described the program as follows:

> Across the country, groups of working men and women have been forming partnerships with schools—partnerships in education. To form a partnership in education, volunteers from a business, government, or other organization strike an agreement with a school to develop programs that will help the school's students in a number of basic ways. The volunteers might tutor students, estab-

lish scholarship funds, donate furniture and equipment or teach classes.[7]

The school year 1983–1984 was proclaimed "National Year of Partnerships in Education" by the President. The White House Office of Private Sector Initiatives is responsible for developing programs and encouraging increased private sector activity by:

1. increasing public awareness of the importance of public/ private partnerships by drawing attention to successful private sector initiatives;
2. developing communication networks that will provide a market for social services that will connect with those in need;
3. removing barriers to the development of effective social service programs that are administered by private organizations and individuals; and
4. strengthening the professional resources of the service sector.

Priorities of the program included: building an educational resource; conserving family and community resources; achieving full employment; and improving economic productivity.

Partnership in Education primarily promotes local Adopt-a-School programs which involve business and government in educational activities that address basic skills and job skills of students. Private sector contributions might include the following:

1. Lectures by corporate employees to classes;
2. Special skills training of selected students in a corporate environment;
3. Scholarship funds, career days, internships and job placements;
4. Supplying tutors, equipment or materials;
5. Providing internships or summer employment for teachers;
6. Advising in the development of programs, curriculum and career counseling programs.

IMPLICATIONS FOR MEDIA CENTERS

The trend toward expanding the horizon of the educational institution by involving business in planning for schooling is growing. The 1980's will see more diverse programming and efforts to improve curriculum by infusing expertise from the world of work into the halls of academe. Thus, while documenting the risk, the current concern about education provide new opportunities for schools to develop new programs and for the Media Center to become the vortex of this process by operating as a switching station for information and resource for programs.

Media centers have been casualties of educational disarmament in the past decade. Often among the first areas to experience financial cutbacks, media centers in elementary schools have been closed while those in secondary schools have limped along on austerity budgets with less material and fewer staff members. Media Centers, once proclaimed as the heart of the school, are no longer a reality in some schools in our nation. For many students, school libraries are their only access to libraries, yet in 1981 more than 7% of the nations students attended schools without libraries. Unlike a generation before, many students today are effectively denied access to the vast resources of an information society. *A Nation at Risk* highlights the need for excellence in education and for resources, materials and staff that can help students to face the challenges of modern society and develop the skills necessary for living in the Information Age.

Libraries and the Learning Society is a recent publication of the American Library Association. The papers were prepared for a series of seminars held January through March 1984 by the United States Department of Education, Office of Educational Research and Improvement, Center for Libraries and Education Improvement in five cities across the nation. The viewpoint of the private sector is not included in the published response, although the Special Libraries Association was included on the advisory board for the project. Yet the private sector will account for 80% of the jobs in the future and presently is an area where information use and the funding for information centers is expanding. *Libraries and the Learning Society,* nonetheless, is a valuable springboard for change and innovation. In order to achieve the goals of a learning society, the American Association of School Librarians notes the following competencies of media specialists in developing new programs. Media specialists and their information centers can:

1. Acquire and maintain an information base that will help students in comprehension, writing and listening skills, and offer an in-depth knowledge of the literary heritage of America.
2. Aid in the development and implementation of computer programs in the school curriculum.
3. Provide for the individual needs of students whether they are gifted, learning disabled or non-English speaking.
4. Provide for development of research skills and library skills for students and faculty.
5. Review, evaluate and recommend relevant diverse instructional materials to achieve specific objectives in the curriculum.[8]

It is this latter contribution that needs to be expanded into an information center concept. Historically the library has been the only place where students who do not fall within the norm (students too bright or too dull to move in the mainstream) could receive individual attention. Collections for school media centers have provided for the exceptional student. In looking at 1985 and beyond, media centers must add to their repertoire human resource files that document the resources of the community, and the potential contributions of corporations and government. Published literature, while still the most important factor in most collections will have to be supplemented by information created specifically for individual schools and programs. Further the library must be on the frontline in using computers and in providing students and teachers with appropriate access to software information and to ways in which to use the technology in educational practice.

Libraries must transform themselves into information centers. Media specialists must become actively involved in planning for tomorrow's curriculum needs. *A Nation at Risk* calls for increased funding for the educational establishment. Media centers should be at the very hub of this frontier in upgrading the educational program, in locating and analyzing potential programs and materials and in taking the lead to link the marketplace with the educational institution. The net effect of the changes on media center collections should be the following:

1. Expanded vocational collections, including the identification of sources for simulations, models, industry-produced materials, tours and speakers.
2. Expanded business information section to appropriately portray the free enterprise system, the contributions of and the range of professional opportunities in the private sector.
3. Increased usage of non-traditional selection sources and the increased creation of information bases to meet the needs of particular communities.
4. Location, identification and scheduling of cooperative efforts with the business and governmental communities.
5. Identification of resources and programs that will enhance teachers' knowledge of the world of work.
   Development of new programs that stress research skills and increase the use of in-house and external information resources.
6. Development of new programs that stress research skills and increase the use of in-house and external information resources.
7. Identify sources for grant funding in both the private and the public sectors.

The above program possibilities are but suggestions that barely scratch the surface of the myriad future alternatives for program development. Like the proverbial iceberg, these changes are visible but the depth and exact nature of the phenomena are as yet unknown. Clearly there is a mandate from the nation to improve education and just as clearly business is willing, indeed eager to aid in this venture. Information specialists must seize this opportunity to develop more effective means of training tomorrow's decision makers. The future is now.

REFERENCE NOTES

1. Robert M. Hutchins "The Great Anti-School Campaign" in *Great Ideas Today* (Chicago: Encyclopedia Britannica, 1972): p. 155.

2. National Commission on Excellence in Education. *A Nation at Risk: The Imperative for Educational Reform* p. 5.

3. Center for Public Resource, *Basic Skills in the U.S. Work Force,* New York, 1983, p. ii–iv.

4. *A Nation at Risk,* p. 11.

5. *Basic Skills,* p.i.

6. op. cit. p. ii.

7. Ronald Regan, *Remarks of President to the Participants of the Partnership in Education Program.* October 13, 1983. p. 1.

8. *Libraries and the Learning Society: Papers in Response to A Nation at Risk.* (Chicago: ALA, 1984) p. 2.

9. "Project InVEST" in *Today's Insurance Woman,* Winter 1981. pp. 21–22.

10. "Project InVEST helps its students find employment" in *National Underwriter,* Sept. 23, 1983. p. 78.

11. "School-Work Link" in *Personnel Administration,* April 1983.

12. Sharkey, Andrew G. "Work/Learn Program Improves Image of Business" in *Association Management,* July 1983. pp. 89–90.

13. Williams, Dennis A. "The ABC's of Economics" in *Newsweek,* May 10, 1982. p. 86.

GENERAL BIBLIOGRAPHY

Adelson, Joseph, *Twenty-Five Years of American Education: An Interpretation.* Washington, DC.: National Commission on Excellence in Education (ED), September 1982.

Astin, Alexander W., *Excellence and Equity in American Education.* Washington, DC.: National Commission on Excellence in Education, November 1982.

"Business Awakes to the Crisis in Education," *Business Week,* July 4, 1983. pp. 32–33.

"Business Must Make an Investment for Economic Stability," *Infosystems.* October 1983. p. 28.

Byrom, Lechter L., "Business and Education, A New Partnership," *Vital Speeches.* Vol. 48. No. 3 Nov. 15, 1981. pp. 73–76.

Caruso, Joseph J., "Collaboration of School, College, and Community: A Bridge to the Progress," Educational Leadership. April 1981. pp. 558–658.

Center for Public Resources, *Basic Skills in the U.S. Work Force: The Contrasting Perceptions of Business, Labor, and Public Education.* New York: Center for Public Resources, February 1983.

Coleman, James S., *Equality of Educational Opportunity.* Washington: GPO, 1966.

Corwin, Roland G., "Innovation in Organizations: The Case of Schools," *Sociology of Education,* Vol. 1. p. 48 (Winter 1975), p. 2–12.

Coyne, James K., "Partnership in Education" *Engineering Times,* Vol. 5, No. 11. November 1983.

Curran, Lawrence J., "A challenge to education," *Byte.* October 1983. p. 4.

Dyer, Esther R., "Forces Affecting Educational Change and School Media in Centers," *Peabody Journal of Education.* vol. 55, No. 3. April 1978. pp. 184–192.

"Education Does Well in Corporate Giving," *Chemical Engineering News,* February 7, 1983. p. 29.

Franklin, Grace B. and Randall B. Ripley, "An Evaluation of the Public-Private Partnership in the Private Sector: Initiative Program," *Journal of Health and Human Resources Administration.* Fall 1983. pp. 185–208.

Frederick, Rudolph, *Edcational Excellence—The Secondary School–College Connection and other Matters: An Historical Assessment.* Washington, DC.: National Commission on Excellence in Education, Aug. 1982.

Glorioso, Joseph A. "Can CEOs Improve Education?" *Industry Week.* September 19, 1983. pp. 36–42.

Hutchins, Robert M.: "The Great Anti-School Campaign," *Great Ideas Today.* Chicago: Encyclopedia Britannica, 1972. p. 155.

Libraries and the Learning Society: Papers in Response to A Nation at Risk. Chicago: American Library Association, 1984.

Melnick, H.H., "Precollege Counseling: A Unique Fringe Benefit," in *Employment Benefits Journal.* September 1982. pp. 2–3.

Miller, William H. " Can Business Cure Education's Ills?" *Industry Week.* July 25, 1983. pp. 27–30.

Molz, Kathleen Redmond. *Federal Policy and Library Support.* Cambridge, Mass.: MIT Press, 1976.

The National Commission on Excellence in Education, *A Nation at Risk: The Imperative for Educational Reform.* A Report to the Nation and the Secretary of Education. Washington, DC.: GPO, 1983.

Ozmon, Howard: "Adopt-A-School: Definitely Not Business as Usual," *Phi Delta Kappan.* Vol 38, November 1980. pp.114–115

"Public Values and Public School Policy in the 1980s," *Educational Leadership.* Vol 38, November 1980. pp. 114–115

"Reagan 'Adopts' Black School," *Washington Times.* October 14, 1983.

A Report of the Distinguished Citizens Task Force on Quality Teaching. West Hartford: University of Hartford, September 1983.

"The Struggle to Go to the Head of the Class," *Business Week.* June 1983. p. 68.

Wantuck, Mary-Margaret,"Helping the Schools Get Back to Work," *Nation's Business.* September. 1983. pp. 30–32.

Ward, Beatrice A. *The Years between Elementary School and High School: What Schooling Experiences Do Students Have?* Washington, DC.: National Commission on Excellence in Education, May 1982.

Zimiles, Herbert. *The Changing American Child: The Respective Educators.* Washington, DC.: National Commission on Excellence in Education, October 1982.

State Education Agencies' Role in Collection Development

Barbara Spriestersbach

State education agencies provide support for collection development with regulations, funding, guidelines and technical assistance to the local library media specialist. Examples of these
supports further define the state agency's role.

The other day the phone rang in my office and the librarian
from Gotebo (there really is such a place) asked what she
should include in her new career collection. That one was
easy. I dropped the list of basic career materials in the mail. It
was there because I knew that many schools in Oklahoma are
trying to improve career instruction. State education agencies
have a role to play in collection development in local schools.
A recent survey revealed a wide variety of services are being
provided to local districts.

State education agencies provide support for collection development with regulations, funding guidelines and technical
assistance. The library media section of the state agency is
charged with the responsibility of providing leadership in all
areas of library media services. The very foundation of a library media program is the quantity and quality of its collection. Students and teachers must have access to appropriate
resources when they need them.

A balanced, up-to-date collection of materials and equipment is essential for teaching and learning. This collection
must be selected to support, implement and enrich the total
instructional program. The building level library media specialist has the primary responsibility for collection develop-

Ms. Spriestersbach is Assistant Administrator, Library and Learning Resources,
Oklahoma State Department of Education.

107

ment. It is appropriate that local library media specialists coordinate the evaluation and selection of materials and equipment for the school because they know the existing collection,
faculty, students, curriculum, community and budget limitations. It is a difficult, time consuming task and library media
specialists look to many sources for assistance. The SEA can
make the task easier with realistic regulations that are enforced, guidelines, workshops and technical assistance in
areas of selection, evaluation and management.

Several factors affect the amount of support available from
the state agency. The structure of the agency itself may limit
activities to regulations and financial accounting. The organizational pattern of school districts within a state, the density
of the population, and the availability of technical assistance at
the district level also affect the need for services from the state
agency. For example, in Oklahoma, with 616 school districts
with only seven (7) district supervisors, technical assistance for
most LEAs is available only from the state agency.

REGULATION

One of the basic functions of a state education agency is to
set the regulations that will govern the operation of public
schools and to monitor compliance with the regulations. Most
states include regulations that set standards for library media
services. These regulations are monitored as part of the accreditation procedure by the library media staff or other state
agency personnel.

Some state regulations are very specific. For example, Geor-
gia's regulates minimum number of books and minimal budget. Oregon regulations require LEAs to provide "appropriate instructional materials and equipment."

Most states do not have quantitative regulations for equipment. If equipment is mentioned it usually says "appropriate"
or sufficient to support audiovisual materials or "adequate to
support instruction."

If a mimimum budget is required it is most often number of
dollars per pupil, but it may be a percent of the operating
budget of the district. For example, Ohio requires one-half of
one percent of the total general expenditure.

A clear, easy to express, set of regulations gives needed support to the building level media specialist. One problem with minimal standards is that they are minimal, not exemplary. Most state regulations are far below ALA recommendations and administrators often look at these figures and consider them adequate.

Several states have separate line item appropriations for library media resources. It is most often part of the general education appropriation bill. The public demand for computers has given incentive for special funding for this equipment. Three of the 34 states responding to the survey have state appropriation for computers and several others are anticipating it. Twenty-three percent of the states surveyed have a line item appropriation for books. Only 17% include audiovisual materials and eight percent include equipment. Most line-item appropriations are allocated on a per pupil basis, and are considered supplementary to local budgets. In Oklahoma, the state funding is for competitive grants ranging from $10,000 to $20,000. Funds can be used for books, audiovisual materials, equipment or salary. North Carolina's appropriation for instructional material and supplies average $18 per pupil. They also have 5.3 million for computers.

State education agencies aid collection development at the LEA by interpreting and monitoring regional accreditation standards. The state education agency is also instrumental in interpretating or monitoring federal funds. Since Chapter 2 funds are not categorical, they could be used in any one of the 28 previous programs. LEAs may determine where they will use their allocation. A large percentage of the funds have been used for materials and equipment, particularly computers.

Technical assistance is provided by the state education agencies to LEAs in a variety of ways—guidelines, bibliographies, reviews, traveling exhibits, workshops, inservice and examination centers. These services may be the activity of the state education agency alone or in cooperation with other agencies, professional organizations and universities.

Most states publish guidelines that give recommendations for developing exemplary library media services. They usually contain criteria for facilities, personnel, materials and equipment and services. Sometimes the same publication will contain a suggested library skills outline for instruction (Virginia). Iowa, Illinois and Oklahoma, give a two or three-phase plan for development. This enables schools to make short and long range goals. Iowa's guide *Plan for Progress . . . in the Media Center* has an accompanying planning guide. (See Figure 1.) It is designed to help school personnel plan for the development of its media center. The form could be adapted to most guides.

Some states have developed publications as part of the guidelines, procedures manual or separately to assist LEAs in the evaluation of materials and equipment. Tips on selection, acquistion procedures and weeding may be provided. Bibliographies of recommended titles for books and audiovisual materials are provided by some state agencies. Bibliographies of recommended titles for books and audiovisual materials about the state are the most often provided. Bibliographies are often a joint venture between the state agency and the state library. Special topic bibliographies may also be developed to meet needs within the state. The most requested help now is for review of computer software. Several states, notably North Carolina, are evaluating software and making the evaluation abailable to the LEAs.

The problem of censorship has been so great that most state agencies have encouraged districts to develop a selection and review policy. These publications often give sample policies and steps to take if materials are challenged. Assistance of this type is particularly valuable in states that contain schools with little or no professional personnel at the building level. Without professional personnel there is a tendency to depend on sales representatives and publishers catalogs for purchase.

Some states maintain a collection for examination and evaluation. In the past, it was limited to books, but now there will be audiovisual materials and computer software as well. Sometimes a review file is maintained. They may publish locally produced reviews. *Picks & Pans* from Montana and *Gushers & Dusters* from Oklahoma, are publications that give reviews written by building level specialists. It is probably most benficial to small schools with limited resources. Two of the 34 states responding to the survey indicated that the state agency sponsors traveling exhibits.

Both statewide and regional workshops are sponsored by

Figure 1

Collection	Goals To Be Achieved	Where We Now Stand	To Be Achieved By (date)	To Be Achieved By (date)	To Be Achieved By (date)
Books					
Magazines					
Video Recordings					
Computers					

state education agencies. Some workshops are in cooperation with other curriculum areas, professional associations or state libraries. Usually, there will be sessions
that address matters relating to collection development.
Almost every state has offered workshops on computers
and software for library management and instruction.

Most state agencies are severely limited in personnel to
prepare bibliographies, conduct workshops and develop publications. When it is not possible to provide all these activities, they often help in the dissemination of materials developed by others.

State education agencies are providing leadership in the area
of accessing data bases for LEAs. Fifty-eight percent of the
states offer this service to local districts, sometimes for a fee.
Most local districts are unable to provide this service. In some
states, this service is provided by the state library and in others it
is a cooperative effort. Most library media specialists are fully
aware of the need for up-to-date information for the faculty.

The entire concept of networking calls for cooperative
planning, inservice activities and funding. Several states have
passed legislation and provide funds for planning and implementing networking between libraries. State education agencies are usually involved.

Wisconsin's law dealing with networking details the responsibilities of the state agency. It states among other things that
the state superintendent shall: "(3) (a) Plan and coordinate

school library media services with other library services and promote interlibrary cooperation and resource sharing between school library media programs and other libraries."

Wisconsin recognizes the chief limitation to full school participation with the statement:

> The Department has been equally consistent in maintaining that such cooperative activities must be built on top of basically adequate local library, media, and information services, and not as a substitute for such services. Cooperative planning and activities extend the usefulness of existing resources; they do not substitute for them.

State agencies have responded to the need for more resource sharing with workshops and technical assistance. They could do more to highlight the many examples of cooperative efforts that take place within a community or area. The cooperation may involve selection or evaluation, children's services, community schools, summer programs, etc. One good example is the Cooperative Children's Book Center (CCBC)—an examination center for children's literature. The CCBC also provides bibliographies, workshops and traveling exhibits.

This article has only touched lightly on the complex topic of collection development. After stating in the beginning that building a collection for a local school is primarily the job of the local library media specialist, it soon becomes evident that most state agencies are involved with regulations, policies and assistance. Since no one pattern of involvement would be appropriate for all states, no attempt has been made to define what the level of service should be. It *should* fit the needs of the districts in each *state* just as a collection should fit the needs of the students and teachers in that building.

If the level of service does meet the needs of the district, the librarians in your Gotebos will be fulfilling their obligations to their patrons.

BIBLIOGRAPHY

Plan for Progress . . . in the Media Center.
Media Center Planning Guide, State of Iowa: Department of Public Instruction, 1969.
Multitype Library Cooperation 1980, Wisconsin Department of Public Instruction.

Maximize Your Collection Through Positive Public Relations

Myrtle M. Lilly
Eileen Bell
Mary Ann Holbrock
Linnea M. Bass
Esther Perica

In a time of expanding information and shrinking budgets, it is necessary to make the most of the resources available. Techniques from business and industry as well as ideas for creative promotion are the topics of this article.

Today's media programs are faced with an unprecedented need to make major adaptations in their operations. The "information explosion" has presented them with vast amounts of information to organize and make accessible to patrons. The new technology which might help control that information is costly and constantly changing. Computers are suggested as devices for solving almost every library problem from circulation to bibliographic searching. Video taping, cable television and other developments are touted as the waves of the future. Since it is impossible for any but a few libraries to acquire all of the new technology, school media directors are faced with difficult choices. To make matters worse, budgets are remainig static or are declining amidst the enticing proliferation of things to buy. The expansion of information and technology, combined with the budget crunch, has presented today's librarian with a difficult question: "How can a library offer more, yet spend less?"

Myrtle M. Lilly is Library Assistant at Elk Grove High School Library, Elk Grove, IL. Eileen Bell is Head Librarian at Prospect High School, Mt. Prospect, IL. Mary Ann Holbrock is Assistant Librarian at Elk Grove High School Library. Linnea M. Bass is Assistant Librarian at Buffalo Grove High School, Buffalo Grove, IL. Esther Perica is Head Librarian at Elk Grove High School.

There are no simple answers. However, the literature of libraries and of school administration is pointing to a method of coping with growing information and shrinking budgets. The answer is "manage better and promote more." Experts feel that many directors do not take managing seriously; they view their profession as librarianship with management as an incidental responsibility. Results of this outlook have been uneconomical division of labor, lack of focus and direction, neglect of new developments, and a variety of other ills. Libraries in other words are offering less than they could.

In order to cure the ills of mismanagement, school librarians have been urged to adopt professional management techniques from the business world. A wide variety of techniques have been suggested as being appropriate to school media programs. One of the more frequently suggested ideas is participatory or participative management. As its name suggests, the technique involves the staff in making all levels of decisions. While there is a consensus of opinion on what participative management is in theory, there is remarkable lack of agreement as to how participative management operates in practice. This lack of clarity has led some librarians to equate participative management with anarchy, while others view it as a way for administrators to escape being blamed for poor decisions! The literature of business provides insight into the way participatory management should work.

Industrial literature highlights the use of "quality circles," which are used successfully and extensively in Japan and by some major American firms. Quality circles are problem-solving groups of staff members and managers who meet regularly to find ways of improving quality control and productivity. The technique is based on the concept that the staff is one of the corporation's most valuable assets and that they have something to contribute towards improving the organization because they run the day to day operation. In Japan, the rewards for quality circle performance are primarily intangibles such as prestige and recognition. The success of the technique with industrial workers suggests that all employees, including those libraries, may be good candidates for involvement in participative management. In a library situation, then, the administrator should consider asking non-professional staff to join the certificated staff in quality planning and the decision-making process. After all, no one ever guaranteed only those with a M.A.L.S. are creative. If the Japanese analogy is applied here, the prestige and self-satisfaction staff receive will be reward enough for the extra work.

The primary advantage of participative management and quality circles is touted as being a more satisfied, willing and productive staff. However, there are other positive results of this avenue of administration. One of these is that better decisions are often made. People with varied backgrounds and expertise working together toward a common goal are stimulated to produce more and better ideas. A diverse group is also able to weed out the bad ideas and improve on the good ones. Since the responsibility falls to the entire group, individuals are free to express their own ideas. Once the decision is made, each member of the team is more likely to feel a commitment to its success. In short, the use of participative management should create an upward spiral in which morale increases each time a decision's excellence is proven.

Since participative management is based on the idea that staff members can enjoy and seek out responsibility, this method is appropriate for generating and carrying out good public relations (PR) ideas within the school library setting.

Public relations is one area in which school libraries may fall short in their "search for excellence." All librarians are interested in building good, solid, usable book collections that are up to a standard and will serve the needs of students and teachers. What needs to be considered, however, is the question, "Once the collection is established, how often and how well is it used?" A staff needs to do much more than just unlock the library doors in the morning; it needs to publicize and promote the material to both students and faculty. Since participative management is based on the idea that staff members can enjoy and will seek out responsibility, this method is appropriate for generating and carrying out good public relations ideas within the school library setting.

Two facets of public relations must be dealt with in any library. The most obvious is the area of publicity campaigns to bring patrons into the library. The second, and perhaps more important facet, is that of staff attitudes. No matter how many students are attracted to the library by slick ad campaigns, they will not become users if they sense that the staff serves them grudgingly. Staff attitudes broadcast a public relations message that is just as powerful as the best-planned publicity extravaganza. Both types of PR are likely to be most effectively improved through the use of participatory management techniques.

Attitudes of staff members are best improved through collegial interaction, rather than by prime directive. One cannot, after all, order an employee to arrive at work the next day loving all teenagers. It is possible, however, through group goal setting, to remind the staff of its service oriented function. Sometimes the goal of personal service is pushed aside because of the press of "minor" details: unshelved books, unfiled cards, unclipped pamphlet file material, etc., etc., ad infinitum. Participative management is an excellent method of attacking a staff attitude problem, since it is the management technique most likely to create staff commitment to the goals set.

Librarians cannot expect miracles. The results of negative PR cannot be eradicated in a day. Beginning with the premise that the student always comes first and must never get the impression that he is "a bother," a library staff must create positive PR. Slow, steady progress should result in gaining the confidence of the students and a good rapport with both students, faculty, and administration. Once the PR efforts turn to the positive side, a well-used library collection and intense staff job satisfaction will result.

In addition to staff attitudes, the entire atmosphere of the library must make a positive impression upon the students to make them want to return, and make the library "their own"—a familiar friend which they want to visit often. Posters, plants, good lighting, cheerful colors and uncluttered, orderly arrangement of furniture and books, all added to pleasant smiles and friendly attitudes of the people who work there, make the library an inviting place. When the setting is right and the student feels at ease and comfortable in the library, getting "into" books is easier to accomplish.

Once the staff attitude is both positive and service-oriented, publicity campaigns must be mounted. Since the old adage about two heads being better than one is at the basis of participative management theory, PR efforts planned by the entire staff should be superior to those planned by any one person alone. Utilizing staff talents for creative thinking, artistic work, even cutting and pasting, will enhance their commitment and improve the results. Let the library staff participate in everything from brainstorming ideas, to sending memos, to making banners and posters. The more manpower available, the fewer problems will be encountered. A staff, when effectively motivated, can be more industrious than ever.

Consider the following generic publicity campaigns for just about any activity the library has planned.

GENERIC PUBLICITY CAMPAIGN

• Posters
  —individually made on posterboard
  —an 8½ 11 master made then duplicated on a copier

• Press Releases
  —School newspaper
  —School Yearbook
  —Local Paper
  —Community Ad Paper
  —Principal's Newsletter

• Signboards
  —School Marquee
  —Electronic signboards in shopping malls, etc.

• Faculty Announcements

• Banners in library and school halls

• Letters written to school administrators notifying them of event

• Displays in library or in school display buildings

Remember to go back to the group for "brainstorming" ideas. There is nothing like a good, effective, cooperative "team" to put together and carry out creative ideas for projects. The following are efforts of a brainstorming session:

—Seek out the school principal in the Fall and go over plans for the year. Meet again at least twice during the year to review progress of the Media Program. Near the end of the year, summarize what happened and identify ideas for next year. Encourage reaction, discussion, and suggestions from your principal.

—Publicize everything to the maximum. Appoint a student PR director and stand back. Encourage announcements for the public address system; display unusual signs in the halls; write a release in the school or local newspaper. Remember radio is better than ever, and most stations love student made announcements.

—Wheel a cart of new books into whatever room your teachers congregate—be it the mailroom, staff lounge, or faculty library. A day or so should be long enough, and remember to change the carts often.

—Be very specific about library and personal goals and objectives. Establish goals based on input from the administration, faculty, students, and staff. Make sure everyone knows the objectives for the year.

—Develop news releases. Be aware of the five W's and an H—who, what, when, where, why and how. Answer these questions and a release is ready to send to the school or local newspaper.

—Get together with other librarians in the community, from all types of libraries, and offer training sessions and workshops for support staff members, volunteers, and aides.

—Opportunity for visibility for all library services increases where there are changing, exciting happenings at the library which can be publicized and talked about. Get good mileage from your events and exhibits by having them travel to nearby libraries.

—Sudden bursts of interest in a topic should be probed. Churn out book displays, bibliographies, quizzes, etc.

—All staff members should be lovable. Give away kisses (the candy kind), hugs, bookmarks, bibliographies, etc.

—Hold a merry moment for that student who took out the first book of the year, the student with the largest (or smallest) library fines. Honor specific groups of people each day for a week.

—Establish a reading club. Encourage all students to join

and read a book. The student reading the most books should receive a special prize.

—Make good use of "Parent Night" at school. Be as visible as possible so parents will be encouraged to visit. You may wish to run a promotion so that parents could be more involved at school, or give away coupons good for their student's free return of overdue books.

—Lets your signs tell the story. "Please interrupt me" could be placed on librarians' desks and all other staff work areas. "Please ask the librarians for assistance" signs should be mounted in areas such as the card catalog, pamphlet file, and index tables to indicate that student assistance is top staff priority.

—Bookmarks could be photocopied on card stock and distributed with books checked out. "You're a '10' in our book" or "We care enough to give you our very best" are bookmark slogans which extend a warm invitation to building a positive environment in the library.

—Since one of the primary functions of a school media center is to teach the students how to use a library . . . teach in a clear and understanding manner. The skills learned and practiced in high school and before will become valuable tools in college and beyond. Library skills must be an integral part of the modern student's survival kit!

—Conduct an annual "Senior Favorite Book/Magazine/Record/Tape Survey" to serve several purposes. It will give members of the Senior class some acknowledgment of their status in the school and it gives the library publicity. In addition, the results can serve as a guide to future acquistions.

—Encourage faculty members with special interests or hobbies to head a student club and use the library as their meeting room after school. Books and other library materials could be selected and placed on a cart for their use. Display space in the library could be made available for their projects.

One of the most permanent methods of building good public relations with both students and teachers is the irresistible duo of "service with a smile." Every member of the library staff is a representative of the library program to the user, and every contact with a user is an opportunity to promote the program. Good service is the key element in promoting the library program and it does not require any extra or added budgeting. That willingness to go an extra step and use your library connections or networks to make sure that a student gets the article he needs and you do not have will be remembered. The library staff should always present a willing and helpful attitude when students come to them with questions and problems in their research efforts.

There is also a great need for good library-faculty PR. How often has this complaint been heard? "The media center is just a dumping ground. When the teachers don't know how to handle a student, they send him to the library." Teachers who are guilty of this strategy are prime candidates for an internal PR blitz. They need to be convinced that the media center is a valuable resource and not a substitute for a detention hall.

Cure this problem through personalized PR. Develop a rapport with fellow faculty through informal discussions over lunch, coffee, etc. Obliquely slip in suggestions on the correlations into cooperatively developing a unit plan: offer the library instruction, a follow-up quiz, even grade the papers, and return to the classroom to go over the corrections with the students. Moreover, encourage teachers to assign research projects which are designed to make use of library projects which are designed to make use of library resources. The librarian can help grade by looking over notecards and bibliographies. You can thereby turn faculty members into your own PR men! If their needs are met in the media center, they'll be sure to let fellow staff know about it!

Although teachers are outside the reach of the "Quality Circle," librarians can invite their participation in some phases of management, such as collection development. Photocopy reviews of new books in specific fields and distribute them asking for purchase suggestions. Likewise at weeding time, have teachers go over the discard cart and advise on withdrawals. The teachers' satisfaction with such participatory projects is built-in PR. The results of these subtle PR efforts may be realized slowly but success will build steadily and a positive media center attitude will result. A true attitude of

"What can I do for you?" can be one of the greatest public relations promotions a library staff member can have.

The support of the school administration is imperative. Talk to the school principal at the beginning of the year and explain your management focus, publicity plans and the objectives in mind. If he concurs, he will support you. If not, proceed a little slower and try to win him over as the months go by. It is hard to imagine a school administrator not being publicity minded. If that is the case, do your best to bring him around. In these days of declining enrollment, budget cutting and closing of schools, an administrator's support can mean life or death to a program.

A library can therefore offer more, yet spend at least the same, if not less money by better staff utilization through "Quality Circle" management. A staff that is unified through shared decision-making will work more productively for each has an investment, through his ideas, of himself in the task at hand. Employing participative management thus enables all staff to be involved in PR, instead of just the administrative librarian. Thus the total staff realizes that each service they perform for patrons, whether faculty or student, should and does have positive implications. This is "maximiziing the library's collection" in the most far-reaching and valuable manner. This is "positive public relations" in its most authentic and potent form!

BIBLIOGRAPHY

Certo, Samuel C. *Principles of Modern Management.* Iowa: William C. Brown, 1980.

Goldberg, Robert L. "Participative Management—Style and Substance." *Catholic Library World*, 51 (4): 149–153, November, 1979.

Hipps, G. Melvin. "Participative Management in Libraries." *Illinois Libraries*, 60 (6): 538–540, June, 1978.

McGregor, Douglas. *The Human Side of Enterprise.* New York: McGraw-Hill, 1960.

Rummel, Kathleen and Esther Perica, eds. *Persuasive Public Relations for Libraries.* Chicago: American Library Association, 1984.

Wadia, Maneck S. "Participative Management: Three Common Problems": *Personnel Journal*, 58 (11): 927–928, November, 1980.

The Effect of Administrative Policy on the Use of School Library Media Centers and Resources

Helen E. Williams

Annual reports of heads of school library media programs are analyzed for the effect of administrative policies on activities of the center. The kinds of data reported, including descriptions and uses of collections, are detailed. Recommendations are made for effective use of annual reports.

The school media program is an integral element within a given educational and administrative structure. It "stresses" direct services to students and teachers, media collections development, and instructional design that fulfills the educational goals of the school. . . . The school media program is conducted under the direction of a media professional, usually a media specialist with a knowledge of education and with leadership and managerial competencies."[1] The size of the staff to execute the program is usually determined by the size of the school, the nature of the school organization, the allocation of program activities, and the amount of external support from district and other resources.[2]

The responsibilities of the school media program may be delineated using verbs which represent the critical nature of the multitudinous activities to be accomplished. Words such as: defining, planning, integrating, participating, developing, providing, operating, reporting, conducting, initiating, maintaining, performing, and building are indicative and characteristic service mandates.[3]

Dr. Williams is an assistant professor at the University of Maryland College of Library and Information Services.

The reporting responsibility is isolated from this list to provide an overview of services rendered within special settings and under altered circumstances. Because reports from heads of school media programs generally quantify and summarize the services offered and completed during the past year, they provide some indication of priorities and emphases within the media center and the parent institution, as well. Therefore, annual reports are used here as a basis of determining if a new policy which altered the media centers' staffing patterns also affected the use of some elementary school media centers and their resources.

This analysis of annual reports is in no way intended to reflect negatively upon the school system from which they originated. Instead, its purpose is to show how a revised administrative policy is reflected in the annual reports of the professional personnel most directly affected. It may suggest the importance of such reports in providing to a larger audience a clearer understanding of what school librarianship is about. It is hoped that the annual report might come to be viewed as an important document to be developed for information to students, teachers, and parents, as well as for use by school administrators. Its potential value as an effective public relations item has heretofore been underestimated, if considered at all.

BACKGROUND

When taxpayers in Prince George's County, Maryland, revolted in 1978 and voted to restrict an increase in tax revenue, a funding crisis resulted and services were curtailed within every county public agency. In 1982, the funding level for schools represented a shortfall of approximately $32 million. This resulted in reduced budgets for employee pay and fringe benefits, the instructional program, administration, and other areas as well. The County Executive recommended the elimination of all elementary school library media specialists and expressed the sentiment that these functions could be carried out by classroom teachers and school volunteers. Effective on June 30, 1982, more than 500 certified employees were terminated. Rather than follow the County Executive's recommendation, the Board of Education voted to provide half-time library media services to all elementary schools. This meant a reduction in force of 55 elementary school library media specialists. In response to this action, the Office of Library and Media Services provided inservice activities for the remaining elementary school library media specialists during the Fall of 1982. These activities included time management, priority setting, self-image, and other human relations activites. In addition, school principals encouraged organizations to solicit volunteers from the communities.

DATA

The data were collected from the annual reports of 45 elementary school library media specialists. Reports from two consecutive years were used in order to juxtapose full-time professional services provided in 1981–82 with the half-time services provided in 1982–83. Names of 49 schools were systematically selected from a list of the 101 elementary schools in the county. However, four schools were eliminated because of the lack of their second-year reports. A county ruling specifies that media specialists in schools scheduled to be closed need not submit annual reports at the end of the last year of operation. Therefore, the resulting sample included 90 annual reports written by media specialists who represented 45 elementary schools.

The standardized, two-page, annual report form requested: total media center attendance counts; an indication of the quantitative size of the print and nonprint collections; circulation figures for print and nonprint materials; the number of missing print and nonprint items; the number of volunteers and student assistants, and their hours worked; and the total number of hours spent by the media specialists with faculty for joint planning. Additionally, space was provided for the identification of regularly scheduled non-media classes and non-media activities which were held in the media center.

Totals, means, and medians were calculated and are reported to provide as accurate a description as possible. Where totals are inconsistent, it is due to missing data. Some reports failed to provide information for items such as missing materials, collection size, and numbers of volunteers and student assistants. Because no explanations were provided for the missing information, readers are free to assume that either the questions did not apply (i.e., that there were no volunteers or student assistants), or that the information was not developed for reporting (i.e., that no inventory of the collection was taken).

Attendance

Attendance in the media centers was greater by 283,307 during the year of full-time placement. Reported individual schools figures ranged from the low of 4,876 to a high of 72,500. Much of this attendance maybe attributed to library orientation and instruction classes which were mandated during both years—a fact which was verbally transmitted because it was not reflected as a specific report item. The second year decline, as indicated in Table 1, may well reflect the combined results of compacted instructional media center use and the further lack of access to the facility and its resources.

Volunteers and Student Assistants

Although six library media centers operated without volunteers during both years, the total number of volunteers increased by 33 percent, or from 138 to 184. They contributed a 14.3 percent increase of time. However, the corps of student assistants dwindled from 786 during 1981–82 to 696 during 1982–83, when reports also showed them contributing 2.4 percent, or 2,715 fewer hours to work in their LMCs (see Table 1). Four schools reported having no student assistants during the first year while seven reported having none during the second year.

The absence or reduced staffing by adults and student volunteers may have contributed to the reduced attendance. Conversely, the new staffing pattern may have precluded only the documentation of attendance and use. If the annual reports are to be taken at face value, however, it is evident that volunteers and student assistants did not adequately compensate for the absence of full-time media specialists.

TABLE 1

Comparison of Elementary School Library Media Center Attendance,
Volunteers, Student Assistants, and Time Spent Planning with
Faculty in LMCs with Full-Time and Half-Time Professionals

	Full-Time (1981-82)			Half-Time (1982-83)		
	Total	Median	Mean	Total	Median	Mean
Library Attendance	950,735	18,040	21,127	667,428	12,217	14,832
Volunteers	138	2	3	184	3	4
Hours Worked	12,480	150	277	14,267	240	317
Student Assistance	786	10	17	696	10	15.5
Hours Worked	14,090	240	313	11,375	180	253
Hours Planning with Faculty	2,246	40	59	1,075.5	20	25

Collections

Individual LMC print and non-print collection sizes ranged
from 5,669 to 15,150 during the first year, when five reports
failed to provide this information. During the second year, a
decline was evident in the range reported—5,679 to 14,340.
Eight LMCs failed to complete this item.

Circulation of materials dropped approximately 25 percent
during the year of half-time placement. The median circulation of 17,873 during 1981–82 fell to 12,113 during 1982–83,
with one school not reporting this information for the latter
school year.

The most noticeable advantage to be found among the data
shown in Table 2 is the decrease in the number of missing
print and non-print materials; 1,427 or 40.6 percent fewer
items were missing during the second year. The disadvantage
of limited access and availability may have contributed to this
positive outcome (see Table 2).

Non-Media Activities

Table 3 lists and compares by frequency and percentage the
activities which were reported as being non-media in nature,

TABLE 2

Comparison of Elementary School Library Media Center Collections,
Circulations, and Missing Materials in LMCs with Full-Time and
Half-Time Professionals.

	Full-Time (1981-82)			Half-Time (1982-83)		
	Total	Median	Mean	Total	Median	Mean
Collections	374,496*	8,881	8,322	328,887*	7,988	7,309
Circulations	987,590	17,873	21,946	735,856	12,113	16,352
Print	895,082*	16,159	19,891	665,909*	11,178	14,798
Nonprint	92,508*	900	2,056	64,547*	626	1,434
Missing Materials	4,941*	76	107	3,514*	57	78
Print	4,402*	63	98	2,928*	41	65
Nonprint	539*	6	12	449*	4	10

*N= fewer than 45 schools reported this information
----

and which were regularly scheduled into the LMCs during the two years of observation. Of the 22 activities reported, two increased in frequency, six different ones were added during the second year, and four maintained the same frequency. Two activities experienced reduced frequency and eight were discontinued. The overall result was a slight decrease in the use of LMCs for non-media activities. Regardless of whether one questions the categorization of book fairs as regularly scheduled non-media activities, it is apparent that a large majority of the centers did not schedule in any activities which did not relate specifically to educational media (see Table 3).

Non-Media Classes

The eleven non-media classes which were reported to be regularly scheduled into the LMCs, and which are presented in Table 4, also show a decline during the second year. Classes for the talented and gifted (TAG) showed the largest increase among the three classes which were scheduled during both years. Because five classes decreased their use of the LMCs and an equal number increased as one remained unchanged, the overall use of the LMCs for non-media classes seems to have remained unchanged (see Table 4).

TABLE 3

Comparison of Regularly Scheduled Non-Media Activities in
Elementary School Library Media Centers with Full-Time
and Half-Time Professionals

	Full-Time (1981-82)		Half-Time (1982-83)	
	No.	%	No.	%
Book Fair	1	2	1	2
4th Grade Enrichment Group	1	2	-	-
Faculty Breakfasts	-	-	1	2
Grade-level class meetings	1	2	-	-
Intermediate TAG	-	-	1	2
Lectures	1	2	-	-
Meetings of Chapter II	-	-	1	2
Newspaper	1	2	-	-
Newsteam	-	-	1	2
Patrol Meeting	-	-	1	2
Photographer	2	4	1	2
Primary TAG	-	-	5	11
Social Events	1	2	1	2
Speakers	1	2	-	-
Special Programs	1	2	-	-
Staff Meetings	1	2	-	-
Student Council	2	4	2	4
Student/Faculty Meetings	1	2	1	2
TAG	7	16	11	24
Testing	1	2	1	2
Women's Club	1	2	-	-
Workshops	1	2	-	-
TOTAL	24	53	34	76

DISCUSSION AND RECOMMENDATIONS

What do these annual reports reveal? The unaltered, standardized format suggests concern for the most basic and traditional services and activities. The actuality of the often partially completed forms suggests an effort to maintain a

TABLE 4

Comparison of Regularly Scheduled Non-Media Classes in
Elementary School Library Media Centers with Full-Time and
Half-Time Professionals

	Full-time (1981-81)		Half-Time (1982-83)	
	No.	%	No.	%
Counselors, health aide & students for nutrition & weight control	–	–	1	2
Enrichment group	1	2	–	–
English Speakers of other Languages	2	4	–	–
Intermediate Talented & Gifted	4	9	–	–
Kindergarten Volunteer Groups	–	–	1	2
Primary Talented & Gifted	4	9	1	2
6th Grade class meeting	–	–	1	2
Talented & Gifted	8	18	10	22
Teacher & Blind Student	–	–	1	2
Tutoring, small group	1	2	–	–
Vision Class	1	2	1	2
TOTAL	21	47	16	36

modicum of service under less than ideal circumstances. This interpretation is not intended to excuse partially completed reports, but rather to recognize behaviors often associated with being overextended.

Are priorities identifiable? A district-level priority of providing special classes for talented and gifted students is indicated by the relatively high proportion of LMCs which scheduled the use of their physical facilities for this purpose. Verbal verification of this as a priority was made by the district's coordinator of media services.

Did the altered staffing pattern (a reduction from full-time placement in one school to one-half-time placement in two schools) make a difference? If reduced attendance, circulation, and numbers of student volunters can be related to the half-time presence of professional library media specialists, then it can be accepted that a difference was made. Table 1 provides further verification of a negative difference by revealing that media specialists lost more than half, or 1075.5 hours of the time formerly devoted to planning with their faculties.

Finally, in making recommendations for formulating annual reports which are potent in their contents as well as in the image they promote of the profession, we might refer again to *Media Programs: District and School.* This publication provides more than discussions and lists of suggested areas of responsibilities, services, and initiatives upon which to establish and build exemplary programs. It represents, I feel, the professional image by which we prefer to be recognized. Subsequently, its consideration in the formulation of reports which may ultimately define not only a year's work but a professional image, is recommended.

Annual reports are valuable official documents because they allow us to record, measure, compare, justify, and inform. They document a level of service and support to a client group and to the overall goals of the parent institution. While they provide a basis for evaluation, they are evaluative by the very nature of their composition and, I might add, use. In his discussion of library management, Gore states the following:

> Annual reports of institutions tend to be pale, lifeless things, generally unreadable and unread. They don't have to be that way. . . . I look upon the annual report of a library as a unique and indispensable occasion to create, and re-create the complex reality of the library for the several constituencies it serves: students, faculty, and administration. . . . A library is bound to be perceived by its patrons as the elephant in the old Hindu fable was perceived by the blind men: as anything and everything but what in reality it is.[4]

School library media professionals in Prince George's County, Maryland, have clearly been jeopardized by funding cuts, as have librarians within other types of libraries who can identify with the distress and disillusionment which often result from demonstrations of diminished public support. What is required is that continuous assertive efforts be made to increase our specific public's awareness of the value of our services to the enrichment of their lives. The annual reports which provided the basis for this study were designed to capture the most traditional measures of status and services. Further, they were designed for presentation to and for use by the administration. Should this necessarily be the end use of this information?

We might dare to wonder what would result from the presentation of a less formalized and more visually appealing report to be sent as a newsletter to students and their parents. These reports might be enlivened with testimonies from students and teachers about the value of a particular media-related service to the success of an educational endeavor. Volunteers and student assistants might be invited to share some highlights experiences, and, of course, the LMC specialist might explain those outstanding events which are meaningful but which cannot be quantified within traditional categories.[5]

The public relations role of the administrative staff might then be to cull from all individual school reports those which most impressively reflect the educational philosophy of the school district. This document, when provided to parents, would continually remind them of the positive aspects of their children's educational experiences. Their increased appreciation of those services are likely to increase in proportion to their level of awareness. Again, Gore speaks to the reporting responsibility:

> Traditionally we have placed great emphasis upon reporting on what goes *into* a library: dollars, books, staff positions, and new building space—as if that demonstrated anything but our capacity to spend other people's money for them. Much less is said about what comes out, in terms of services provided . . . operating efficiencies. . . . and net performance rates. . . . Have you ever asked yourself what nonlibrarians must think of an institution that launches a barrage of statistics, but has absolutely nothing to report about the work it has done?[6]

The annual reports studied for this report were of a no-nonsense format designed to capture accomplishments in basic and traditional terms. They indicated the quantitative levels to which library media services to public elementary school students in Prince George's County, Maryland were reduced. They did not measure educational impact, therefore the questions remains to be answered by the students themselves who will demonstrate somehow that they have compensated for, adjusted to, benefitted from, or have been damaged by this reduction of an educational service during their formative years.

REFERENCES

1. American Association of School Librarians. *Media Programs: District and School.* Chicago, IL: American Library Association and the Association for Educational Communications and Technology, 1975, p. 13.

2. Ibid., pp. 30–31.

3. Ibid., pp. 13–14.

4. Gore, Daniel, "Things Your Boss Never Told You About Library Management," *Library Journal,* 1 April 1977, p. 768.

5. Ibid.

6. Ibid., 768–769.

7. See also: Howland, Patricia, "Sure-fire LMC Repots," *School Library Journal,* October 1979, pp. 126–127; Loertscher, David V. and Land, Phyllis, "An Empirical Study of Media Services in Indiana Elementary Schools," *School Media Quarterly,* Fall 1975, pp. 8–18; and Nesse, Mark A., "Annual Reports with Punch," *Public Libraries,* Summer 1980, p. 46.

Myths, Misconceptions and Mistakes in Collection Development

Bernice L. Yesner

Practical suggestions for improving collections in new and established schools are offered.

A review of the literature pertaining to school library media programs shows that in the coverage of the main ingredients—materials, equipment, space and personnel—the overwhelming emphasis has been on the first category. Thousands of pages have been devoted to the number of volumes needed proportionate to pupils or the teaching staff. Much has been written about the necessity for continuous weeding and "keeping up" especially in such subject areas as science or in types of materials such as video cassettes or microcomputer software. Library skills materials in almost any format, have been popular items for the past two decades. An often used phrase is "Basic Collection" which is never properly defined and the AASL, AASL/DAVI and AASL/AECT standards or guidelines have tried, from time to time and with qualified success, to promote quantitative recommendations for amounts and types of materials.

THE NEW SCHOOL

One area which is avoided like The Plague is what constitutes a beginning collection for a new school. Since new schools and additions to existing facilities are usually financed

Mrs. Yesner is an adjunct faculty member of the Southern Connecticut State University School of Library Science and Instructional Technology and is a consultant in private practice.

with bond issues, rather than annual budgets, much attention is paid to the furniture, shelving, carpets, etc. with the perception that these are all needed, in advance, in order to have a library media center which is operable. Yet this same perspicacity does not pertain to the collection.

More often than not the new school which opens in the fall has a library media specialist (note the use of the singular) who was hired to report to duty a few days before the arrival of the students. Announcements to the faculty, students and parents all indicate that an attempt will be made to have the library media center open by October. No consideration has been given to the time, effort or money needed to select, purchase, process, or catalog, shelve and file a multiplicity of materials in order to have a library media center that can give the services to which the students and staff are entitled. Yet the same people who are responsible for this grievous oversight have meticulously equipped and stocked the cafeteria kitchen and the custodians' supply closets. There was never a moment's doubt that the cafeteria would serve food from the first day that the students returned to school, so plans were made well in advance for the materials, equipment, space and personnel adequate to the task.

Perhaps an enlightened administrator, knowing the problems connected with book orders and deliveries, tried to help out the lone library media specialist by ordering sets of encyclopedias, "packages" of audiovisual and micro software, or biographies, "standards" and "classics" promoted by some publishers and supply houses. I don't think I need to dwell on the likely quality of these "Boy, have I got a deal for you" types of offers. Now the solitary professional, even if blessed with a full time paid aide, starts the school year with a mountain of cartons to be opened and their contents checked, authorized for payment, processed, cataloged, etc. The enormity of the task is manifest to anyone who walks by. If the library media specialist is not new to the profession and is not fearful that failure to spin gold out of all this flax overnight will mark him/her as an incompetent, a cry for help may reach the principal and the result will most likely be an appeal to the PTA for volunteers. Just how this inundated media specialist will find the additional time to train and oversee these volunteers is not taken into account. Nor is there any acknowledgment of the fact that women are entering the work force of the nation at ever-increasing percentages of their numbers and are not available for volunteer work.

The students, constantly reminded that this is "their school" and "their school library media center," had no say in whether they wanted to go to this new school with its un-opened and inadequately stocked library media center. On Back-to-School Night or Dedication Day the parents and tax-payers are taken on guided tours, and, when they pass the nonoperating facility, they are told, "Of course, since this is a new school, the library isn't open yet." Compounding the crime is the fact that most parents accept the statement as gospel.

Long after this initial year, when other tour guides on sub-sequent annual Back-to-School Nights are asked by citizens dismayed by the sparsely covered shelves the reason for this, they will often respond, "Well, this is still a new school and it takes a 'while' to build up a collection." Since there is seldom any further clamor from the parents, the "while" goes unde-fined and the condition unchanged. In school systems where there is a timetable whereby the new school will have an appropriate collection in 5, 7 or 10 years, it never occurs to the planners, the staff, the students or their parents that the school children, during that interim, are being shortchanged. If the responsible adults were aware of this injustice, they must have been perfectly willing to sacrifice that group of pupils.

THE BALANCED COLLECTION

Another phrase subject to a wide range of misinterpreta-tion is "The Balanced Collection." Some library media spe-cialists deem this to mean coverage of all areas of the Dewey Decimal System. Many administrators think it ought to be an equal number of materials for each of the subject disciplines of the school. This might be carried out as 1,000 volumes supporting the Language Arts program/1,000 supporting the Physical Education program or, if the student has 3 classes of Language Arts per week vs. 2 classes of Physical Education the ratio would be 3,000 to 2,000. A survey of actual collections would show that Social Studies and Language Arts programs are better supplied than the other subject disciplines.

Most school systems have goals and objectives which avow they serve all students according to their individual needs and abilities. Those schools which have published statements affirming the purposes of the school library media programs, similarly espouse the dedication to having enough materials to cover the curricular needs of each pupil at his/her level of interest, understanding and ability. But does the collection really support this claim? Twenty books, one hour-long TV special taped off-the-air, two sets of filmstrips and a large wall map of Ancient Greece (from earliest times to the fall of the Roman Empire) scarcely supports that part of the curriculum for one class, much less the whole sixth grade which will also be studying it at the same time. If only the books can be taken home, even if they are put on overnight circulation, how well is the problem of supply/demand addressed? Even students with minimal math skills quickly figure out their poor chances. Theft, vandalism and overdue materials are often the result of the pressure placed on pupils by demands for materials they cannot get by proper means.

When an administration is appraised of this problem, often the complaint is parried by "Well, they can always use the public library." The role of the public library is to serve the entire public *not* to try to do the job the school system has failed to do. An attempt to do so robs the public of the services which they have a right to expect from the public library, and the basic problem of the failure of the school to carry out its mandate remains unsolved.

If the beginning collection was inadequate, the annual budget can never make up the differential. The initial purchases will wear out at a faster rate than they can be replaced either by title or similar content. Also, students who have become good users of libraries need and use greater numbers and varieties of materials. Teachers who trained in, and subsequently were employed to teach in, schools with inadequately supplied collections soon learned to "make do," teach from the textbook, xerox like mad, or order paperbacks from the school bookstore to support the required reading. The statement "If the kids can spend $4 for a movie, they can buy the paperbacks they need," *must* be countered with the simple truth that private schools are not obliged to supply required materials BUT PUBLIC SCHOOLS ARE. There are millions of school children not going to $4 movies or wearing designer jeans and the United States is dedicated to an equal educational opportunity for all.

Faced with a budget that cannot possibly do what it should for the curriculum, how can we ever win the support of teachers who have never experienced the joy of teaching with the range of materials needed both for their instruction and for their students' learning? One way is to choose a specific area or unit, such as the American Civil War, and use a very large proportion of the budget to cover that area as it should be covered. This would enable one or two teachers in the school to know, at last, what sufficient curriculum support really means. It would then present a working model to showcase to other faculty members, administrators and parents. Given a planned progression, drawn by lot, in which other areas of the curriculum or grade levels would get the same support, we would have a better chance to improve everyone's situation at a more rapid rate.

NOT JUST THE BEST BOOKS

One of the goals of the public library is to have in its collection the definitive titles in various subject areas. Another is to have as many copies of a title (such as a bestseller) as the patrons require. The school library media collection must also reflect its goals and those of the school itself.

Part of the instructional program is involved with teaching students to discriminate amongst and to evaluate materials, to recognize writing style, bias, authoritative writing which supports its own theses, etc. In order to perfect these skills students must have a number of materials. To learn to pick the best from a wide range of materials, pupils need access to these multiple materials.

Another goal of the school library media program is to prepare students for a lifetime of self-instruction and learning, long after the formal school years are past. The large role that computers play is well accepted, but the amount of software that is needed for those computers is very poorly understood.

And the need to be able to separate the wheat from the chaff of what is offered in the software market is even less appreciated. Learning to search a database efficiently, which means more economically as well, cannot be done if the library media center is not tied into a variety of databases.

Becoming familiar with the immense range of periodicals published, and what they cover, is vital not only to every pupil going on to higher education but to everyone who will enter the work force. The skills of using periodical guides to seek out information must be attained, whether the collection houses the original publications, microforms or laser read discs.

MANAGEMENT OF COLLECTIONS WITHIN COLLECTIONS

There are sizable subdivisions of the collection which have restricted use, are geared to the needs of certain patrons, or have particular problems of housing/shelving. Often the management of these materials has not been planned carefully or thoughtfully.

The primary collection materials for preschool children, primary grade students, prereaders and beginning readers are not just picture books. The total collection for these younger children in an elementary school should be housed together, whether in an alcove, an ell or at one end of the facility. The labels on all the materials in this collection clearly indicate that they belong to this specialized collection, i.e., PRIMARY or EASY. This does *not* mean that the use of this collection is limited to PreK–2 pupils. What it does mean is that the younger children know this area is for them even though they may browse through and borrow materials used by older boys and girls. Storytelling areas, puppet theaters, floor cushions, picture book tables and lower shelving belong in the primary level area and so do the full range of materials for younger children.

Many schools still separate out the primary level nonfiction thus curtailing the use of these materials by the very age group for whom they were intended. As for the upper grade pupils who may find some of the primary materials suit their needs and abilities, they are free to use them. The important thing is to make sure that ALL children, teachers and parents understand the nonrestrictive intent of the primary collection.

Outsized Books

Those magnificent volumes (sometimes called "coffee table books") on such subjects as military uniforms, Georgian houses, Renaissance art, firearms, tools, Native American pottery, etc., pose problems in housing. Shelves may have to be lifted four to five inches to accommodate their height. Many libraries label them Q and place them at the end of the entire collection. This means that, all too often, this collection is forgotten by the patrons who go to the shelves where they expect the titles to be and, not finding them there, assume they are in circulation.

A better method is to label these materials "+" and house them, on their sides, on the bottom narrow shelf left for this purpose in the section of shelving where they would have been if they were not outsized. Even the youngest students learn that the plus sign means "more than" and a + label on those shelves reinforces the concept. Many university libraries utilize this same technique but put their + volumes on a top shelf rather than a bottom one. Since their patrons are full grown it works very well, but elementary/secondary students do better with the lowest shelf.

Short Story Collections

An oldtime method of identifying books which contained short stories (story collections) was to put S.S. on the label and house all of them at the end of the fiction collection. Like the oversized book treated as a separate collection, they tended to be overlooked. These books will be found more easily and better used if they are labeled SHORT STORIES above the call number and interfiled with the fiction. It will also put an end to the misinterpretation of S.S. as Social Studies materials. Patrons needing a book of short stories can quickly scan the fiction shelves and spot those so marked. Those pupils in search of a novel are alerted that the books marked SHORT STORIES are just that.

Local Materials and Authors

Many schools have collections which are of local or regional interest such as histories of the town, country or state.
These are of great value and interest to historians as well as to
the students. Sometimes this collection also includes books on
all subjects written by people from the area. Depending on
the size of this collection and its worth, plans should be made
for its housing, hours of use and accessibility with considerations for increased protection and security measures.

College Catalogs

Although there is a collection of college catalogs in the
Guidance Department, the school library media center of the
secondary school needs to have as complete a collection as
possible with ample duplication of the most requested catalogs. In some schools this may turn out to be a very large
collection which is housed in its own designated area or room.

Audiovisual Software

The desire to shelve together all materials of like subject
content, regardless of format, can cause difficulties. To place
filmstrips, record albums and TV cassettes on the same shelf
with the book because they are all on the plays of Shakespeare may be to the advantage of students and teachers in
terms of one-stop shopping, but it is extremely wasteful of
space. Intershelving can use between 1/4 and 1/2 more book
shelving for the nonfiction collection. Some library media specialists try to place as much AV software as possible in a
standardized box (audio and TV cassettes, filmstrips, etc.)
which stands upright on the shelf and is labeled on the bottom
as if it were a book. All records are routinely recorded on
cassettes and the originals do not circulate, only the cassettes
do.

Other library media specialists prefer to keep the original
boxes that the individual materials or kits were shipped in.
This devotion to the sacred original container necessitates
much mending. Unfortunately, in the case of kits, it also restricts the use of the materials for often the whole box circu-

lates when one part could be loaned leaving other parts to be used by other students or teachers.

Materials on Permanent and Semipermanent Loan

Hardware and software used in the classrooms the entire school year are still part of the library media center which is responsible for at least an annual inventory and examination of the condition of the equipment and materials. Classroom collections, however, should be changed at least once a month. As teachers become more accustomed to taking their classes to the library media center to investigate topics and search out answers to questions, or sending in teams of students as information seekers, the traditional use of the classroom collection becomes narrow, restrictive and obsolete.

Textbooks

In those schools where the school library media collection consists of all materials of learning, regardless of format, that the school owns or has access to there is provision for added space and personnel for textbooks. Circulation of textbooks is greater at the start of each semester, of course, and the textbook clerks, after those hectic early days, serve the rest of the library media program.

In multitext disciplines the students do not need all their textbooks for the entire year. Calling the texts back when they are no longer in use lessens the amount of damage and loss. In those disciplines where some textbooks can be used at the beginning of the semester by one class and later in the semester by another class there is a substantial saving of needless duplication.

Collections of paperbacks used in English, Social Studies or Foreign Language classes may need to be circulated for just a month (until after the exam) and then they are bundled and returned to the library media center for loan to other classes.

Materials Not Owned But Available

Resource people and their possessions which they are willing to share with the school are also part of the library media collection. So are the materials museums will loan on request and the field trips open to the students. For these valuable resources to be useful they must be cataloged so that students and teachers know what and where they are and how they can be accessed.

PATRON RECOMMENDATIONS

For the philosophy of service to students, staff and parents to be sincere, and not mere lip-service, there must be continuous evaluation of the collection in terms of satisfying patrons. Collections must grow, reflect the changes in curriculum, and meet teaching/learning needs of the faculty and student body. Who knows best how well this is being done if not the patrons themselves? Try to devise several ways of eliciting that information other than a suggestion box (you know what will be inside) or a once-a-year questionnaire. People of all ages like to know their opinions are respected and valued.

SECTION II
NETWORKING AND
COLLECTION DEVELOPMENT

The politics of multi-type library cooperation are explored from three points of view.

Regional Networking and Collection Management in School Library Media Centers

Dale W. Brown
Nancy A. Newman

The barriers to school participation in networks are discussed. The potential contributions of and benefits to schools of network participation are explored. Metropolitan Washington Library Council is included as an example of cooperation.

All types of libraries share the common goal of providing appropriate materials to meet their users' needs. A network concept based on the principle that all types of libraries and users stand to benefit from cooperative efforts should be embraced by school library media specialists. Although networking programs which include school library media centers have increased during the past few years, there continue to be barriers, particularly in the area of collection management. However, these barriers must be overcome in order to develop and support more comprehensive services to school-based users. The availability of microcomputers in most schools has greatly enhanced the potential for resource sharing with other institutions and agencies.

The National Commission on Library and Information Science (NCLIS) defines a network as "a formal arrangement whereby materials, information, and services provided by a variety of types of libraries and/or other organizations are made available to all potential users." (9, p. 6) Cooperating institutions, which have established communication links and procedures to provide common services, make up a network.

Dale W. Brown is Director of Libraries and Instructional Resources for the Alexandria (VA) City Public Schools. Nancy A. Newman is a library consultant in Washington, D.C.

Although most of the barriers to networking relate to all types of libraries, some are unique to school library media centers. The common barriers include such behavioral characteristics as resistance to change, fear of the unknown, and concern for autonomy. Lack of commitment to technological innovation and change has also impeded progress inplementing cooperative efforts. Also, librarians in academic, special, and public libraries sometimes underestimate the value of school library collections. Sive (10, p. 1) states that school libraries are the "unseen majority" and that out of 100,000 libraries in this country, two-thirds of them are in schools.

The barriers that could be considered unique to school libraries are isolation from other information professionals, exclusion from planning, and inadequate communication technologies. For example, a majority of school libraries still do not have telephones in their facilities. There are also bibliographic barriers created by the absence of juvenile and curricular materials in the national bibliographic databases. A further problem is created by the fact that some school library media specialists are not committed to cataloging by national standards. Immroth (6, p. 18) suggests that the training of school library media specialists does not provide skills or positive attitudes toward networking. Fleming (5, p. 25) quotes from *The Olney Experiment: a Progress Report* that "the dichotomy in library education that contributes to the basic orientation of individual librarians is an additional problem. One begins to think like a public librarian, or to approach problems from the perspective of the school, resulting not infrequently, in professional pride that precludes a working-together attitude." This type of parochialism and institutional bias does not contribute to cooperative efforts in networking for collection development and resource sharing.

Lines of communication must be established as a first step to overcoming some of the barriers to networking. Initiatives should be taken by school personnel to assure their inclusion in regional and state planning meetings. Publicizing these activities in the community encourages the demand and support for such projects. Woolls (13, pp. 282–84) pointed to a need to ascertain the views of librarians in the field, not just those at systems headquarters, to learn more about the background principles of resource sharing. She states that the information needs of both librarians and the clientele served by schools are little researched and vastly unknown. School library media collections can contribute greatly to resource sharing. A study by Drott and Mancall (4) found that low use of school library media centers does not indicate lack of holdings, but lack of instruction and guidance. Other librarians need to be aware of these findings and should not assume that school library resources are inadequate. School library media personnel, in particular, have developed skills in media evaluation, selection, and utilization. Schools embraced the multi-media concept far in advance of other types of libraries. As a result audiovisual media collections in schools are extensive. The general collections of children and young adult literature, as well as professional education resources, can be used effectively by other types of patrons outside the school setting.

Materials for special learners, ethnic collections, foreign language books and audiotapes, and career education materials are part of school library collections which could be shared. High interest/low vocabulary books can be used by adults who are marginal readers and for adults who are members of ethnic populations learning English. Books could also be loaned to public libraries for summer and night service reading programs.

Doll's (2, pp. 196–97) research indicated that school libraries can make significant contributions to a network, whether it is a school-based or a multitype library network. In her research, when book titles from one elementary school were compared with another elementary school, there was a thirty percent overlap. When public library titles were compared with school library collections (the collections for the entire school system), there was also about a thirty percent overlap. Therefore, only about one-third of the titles in public library collections will be in school library collections.

Other libraries have much to offer students and faculties in K–12 settings. Advanced learners should also have access to college and university collections. The visually impaired could use large print books and periodicals available through public libraries. Mancall and Drott (8, p. 103) reported that students show a strong tendency to go beyond their school libraries when working on independent study papers. This library use extends to local public libraries, regional public libraries, academic libraries, and to a variety of special collections. Students reported high success rates in all of the libraries which they used.

Planning for collection development and management precedes and determines the success of network efforts. Kolb and Morse (7, p. 53) suggest network planning as a three phase process. The phases are awareness, understanding, and action. Resource sharing could begin with periodicals and audiovisual materials, with a joint materials examination center, a co-sponsored exhibit which would provide a common selection opportunity, or simply visiting other libraries. Selection tools could be shared. A newsletter announcing new mateials and services of all libraries in the community would be helpful. Joint ordering of materials by public and private schools often proves to be economical, particularly with expensive items such as computers.

Many school systems do not even share materials within their own system. In these days of budgetary constraints, much emphasis and effort needs to be placed on sharing resources between schools in each system. At minimum each library media center should have a telephone for inter-library communication, an adequate delivery system, and a union list of periodicals and audiovisual materials. Another small beginning that should be considered is a local or regional storage library for low-use items. This facility would contain usable materials which could be loaned to libraries on demand.

The increase of technology and use of microcomputers in school library media centers greatly enhances the capacity to manage and share collections. Not only are these activities less time consuming with this technology, but there is also a possibility that a new impetus for networking may result from the implementation of an on-line capability. Multi-media bibliographies and inter-library loan records could be stored in the computer. Records for weeding the collection and for inventory of existing resources could be online.

An increasing number of states have developed comprehensive networking programs which include school library media centers in the total plan. Others are in a more formative stage. In the Commonwealth of Virginia, the state library and the regional public libraries cooperated in a retrospective conversion project which led to the formation of CAVALIR in 1979. CAVALIR is a union catalog of approximately seventy libraries in the state. Although a number of public, university, and special libraries in Virginia are linked together by OCLC, Henrico County school libraries were the first to be involved in a retrospective conversion project in preparaion for participation in OCLC.

Through special state funding, the Library Networking Committee of the Consortium for Continuing Higher Education in Northern Virginia held resource sharing workshops in 1978 to identify the strengths of constituent collections and for the first time provided a key to total library resources in the region. This effort was followed by a series of training events to assist local librarians in locating and using regional resources. Such efforts have set the stage for more substantive networking efforts when the technology is in place. This Library Networking Committee represents all types of libraries and has been meeting for the past six years to generate cooperative efforts. It has been the major goal of the Committee to identify those resources which are available in the participating institutions and to make the availability of these sources known to the entire community. Sharing of resources is also represented by the establishment at participating libraries and resource centers of borrowing privileges for faculty and students at Consortium institutions.

The Metropolitan Washington Library Council is a multitype cooperative of 240 member librarians in the Washington, D.C. area. The Library Council coordinates library activities in the region and offers librarians and their staffs continuing education courses, cooperative programing and delivery services, and a jobline of library openings. The Library Council is a part of the Metropolitan Washington Council of Governments, the regional organization of the Washington area's major local governments.

Established in 1975, the Library Council has maintained a continuous program of service to local library and information agencies. Through the Council, library and information needs are addressed across political, geographical, and institutional boundaries. Public, college and university, government, special and school libraries all participate in the organization. Publications such as MAGS, a union list of serials, is published by the Council. The universal borrowers card allows citizens to borrow materials from participating libraries.

On the local level Alexandria City Public Schools Library, Media and Information Services has been involved in the Council from the beginning. The Director of Libraries and Instructional Resources has served as school library representative on the governing body of the Council for many years. Through involvement on the Council the school's system has been able to participate in the mainstream of cooperative library development in the region. Training programs and workshops have been especially useful.

Much effort is being made by library media specialists on the state, regional and local level in Virginia to continue this trend in effective cooperative efforts. In linking school libraries to these networking activities, there is much potential for their connection to the larger world of information. The ultimate result of resource sharing by school libraries will be to end their isolation and bring them into the mainstream of library service to all learners.

To emphasize the importance of resource sharing, Sorenson (11, p. 310) believes that the future users and producers of information in our country are enrolled in our elementary and secondary schools where they are forming attitudes, not about information, but about how able they are to find the information they need. Another challenge was offered by Berry (1, p. 19) when he warned that if schools and public librarians do not get together and begin to develop cooperative services, the citizens and politicians will do it for them.

BIBLIOGRAPHY

1. Berry, John. "School/Public Library Service." *Library Journal* 104 (May 1, 1979): 19.

2. Doll, Carol A. "School and Public Library Collection Overlap and the Implications for Networking." *School Library Media Quarterly* 11 (Spring 1983): 196–97.

3. Driver, Russell W. and Driver, Mary Ann. "Automation in School Library Media Centers." *School Library Journal* 28 (January 1982): 21–25.

4. Drott, M. Carl and Mancall, Jacqueline C. "Materials Students Use: a Direct Measurement Approach." In David V. Loertscher (Ed.), *School Library Media Centers: Research Studies and the State-of-the-Art: Six Research Briefs*, pp. 21–30. Syracuse, New York: ERIC Clearinghouse on Information Resources, 1980. ED 195 287.

5. Fleming, Lois D. "Public and School Libraries: Partners in the 'Big' Picture." *School Media Quarterly* 7 (Fall 1978): 25.

6. Immroth, Barbara. "Networking and the School Library Media Program." In Shirley L. Aaron and Pat R. Scales (Ed.), *School Library Media Annual, 1983, Volume One,* p. 18. Littleton, Colorado: Libraries Unlimited, 1983.

7. Kolb, Audrey and Morse, Jo. "Initiating School Participation in Networking." *School Media Quarterly* 5 (Fall 1977): 53.

8. Mancall, Jacqueline C. and Drott, M. Carl. "Tomorrow's Scholars: Patterns of Facilities Use." *School Library Journal* 26 (March 1980): 103.

9. National Commission on Libraries and Science. Task Force on the Role of the School Library Media Program in the National Program. *The Role of the School Library Media Program in Networking.* Washington, D.C.: Government Printing Office, 1978, 6.

10. Sive, Mary Robinson. *School Library Media Centers and Networking.* Syracuse, New York: ERIC Clearinghouse on Information Resources, 1982, 1. ED 226 764

11. Sorenson, Richard. "The Role of School Media Programs in Library Networks.: in Barbara Markuson and Blanche Woolls (Ed.), *Networks for Networkers,* p. 310. New York: Neal-Schuman, 1980.

12. Virginia. State Council of Higher Education for Virginia, The Library Networking Committee of the Consortium for Continuing Education in Northern Virginia. *Resources Identification: a Report.* Richmond, Virginia, 1978.

13. Woolls, Blanche. "Warp, Woof and Loom: Networks, Users, and Information Systems." In Barbara Markuson and Blanche Woolls (Ed.), *Networks for Networkers,* pp. 282–84.

Northern Area Network:
School and Public Library
Cooperative Collection Management

Judith B. Palmer
Jeanne Domville
Laura Shelly

The Northern Area Network is a joint computerized database project of North Allegheny School District and Northland Public Library, including all holdings of Northland Public Library and, eventually, all of North Allegheny School District's secondary school holdings. The impact of the network on all areas of collection management will be discussed as well as the long term benefits of the network.

The Northern Area Network is a computerized joint database project of the North Allegheny School District and the Northland Public Library, both of which are located in the northern suburbs of Pittsburgh, Pennsylvania. The network was begun during the winter of 1983 using federal and foundation grants, and it includes all of Northland's collection plus portions of north Allegheny's secondary school libraries' collection. Eventually, all of the secondary schools' collections of print and nonprint materials will be online, creating a database of some 195,000 items.

The school district covers 48 square miles in the northern suburbs of Pittsburgh and has an enrollment of 7,180 students. Its four secondary library media centers house over 90,000 volumes, plus an extensive collection of audio-visual materials. Northland Public Library serves a population of 68,751 in four municipalities. Though the two agencies over-

Judith B. Palmer is the high school librarian, North Allegheny School District, Pittsburgh, PA. Jeanne Domville is Head of Children's Services, Northland Public Library. Laura Shelly is Director, Northland Public Library.

155

lap service areas, tax funds are appropriated separately. The Northland Library owns approximately 100,000 volumes which circulate to its users; Northland ranks ninth in Pensylvania for circulation activity, and at any given time, half of its collection is checked out to patrons.

In 1978, as part of a building program, Northland acquired an in-house computer which automates all bibliographic and circulation functions. Using Universal Library Systems' software (ULISYS) which features a modified MARC entry, this DEC PDP 11/34 system allows staff to search by call number, author, subject, title, series, added entry, and ISBN. Northland made its collection available to users in North Allegheny secondary schools in May 1979 through on-line searching. Terminals were installed in the library media centers of the intermediate school (grades 9–10) and the senior high school (grades 11–12). This arrangement was extremely useful in allowing students and staff at the schools to access the public library collection through their own buildings. The availability of specific titles could be easily determined, and teachers could plan curriculum assignments with a wider range of accessible materials.

This arrangement, along with a consistently healthy climate of interaction and cooperation between the two agencies, led representatives from each to begin seeking ways of helping users—both students and the general public—take full advantage of collections developed with their tax dollars. Two-way computer access was a desirable possibility which would make it easier for each library to refer patrons to an exact location for requested materials. The audio-visual collections developed by the school district could become available to the general public, as well as reference works not purchased by every library. Each school could access not only Northland's collection, but also the collections of the other secondary libraries in the school district. All participants could begin working toward a cooperative purchasing plan, permitting collection development funds to be spent with more specialization and less duplication.

As these possibilities were examined the absense of cohesiveness in cooperation became apparent. While the two major agencies are in close physical proximity to each other and serve essentially the same users, no list of joint holdings existed. Even with previous coopeative efforts, no comprehensive plan for resource sharing had been developed. National networking was already a sophisticated reality, but at that time localized computer networks appeared to be an unexplored arena. (A Dialog search of ERIC and LISA files revealed no reported ventures of this kind.) A pilot project to form a combined on-line database could provide an excellent tool for local resource-sharing plans to be formalized. Further support was taken from Ballard, who reports in *Library Journal* that most users prefer to choose their reading from what they find on the shelves or know is locally available, and not from the universe of literature.[1]

Although the school district and the public library each approached the project's outcome with different goals in mind, these differences in expectation and in service philosophy were directly addressed by the planning personnel, and were incorporated into the project design. Such candid assessments paved the road to a successful project. No agendas were hidden.

After extensive research and planning, an L.S.C.A. Title III proposal for inter-library cooperation was submitted in July 1982 through the State Library of Pennsylvania. Funds totaling $43,320 were solicited for the development of a multi-type library database consisting initially of Northland's full holdings, designated portions of the collections at the four North Allegheny secondary libraries, and an online community information file. The proposal outlined expansion of the network to include the participation of a hospital medical library, a local technical school library, and portions of the Allegheny County Law Library. An additional $5,000 was awarded by the Gannett Foundation. The Northern Area Network was underway.

PROJECT GOALS

A primary goal of the project involved expanding the hardware of Northlands then-present system to allow for additional disk storage required by the new ULISYS software that

---

[1]Tom Ballard. "Public Library Networking: Plausible, and Wrong." *Library Journal.* April 1, 1982. p.680

would make the shared database possible. Additional specialized activities were outlined in a second goal, with specific
objectives providing for: 1) the development of an on-line
community resource/local information database for the North
Pittsburgh area; 2) the initiation of a system for cooperative
purchasing, allowing certain collection sites to become comprehensive in designated subject areas; and 3) the growth of
auxiliary services to the schools through use of the computer,
such as computerized catalog card and magazine label production, automated acquistions, and inventory control.

The implication of these goals and objectives was guided by
an Operations Committee comprised of: The librarian coordinating the project for the school district; the director, the
technical services librarian, and the computer systems manager from the public library; and the project facilitator (a
full-time para-professional librarian hired with grant funds to
perform the data entry and conversion from the schools). The
grant was awarded for a one-year period, but step-by-step
implementation of the program was slowed by a variety of
factors beyond the control of the participating agencies. The
L.S.C.A. funds dispersal did not correspond well to the time
table specified for equipment purchase. The new software
system was not installed on schedule, causing a ripple-effect
of related problems. When the software was finaly installed, a
bug in the conversion program caused small portions of the
existing data to require re-entry. Some details of the schools'
data-entry were not foreseen, such as appropriate shelf list
organization and notation; this made it necessary for the project facilitator to perform some time-consuming steps in as-
suring smooth data entry. And finally, the value of a standardized online Subject Authority File was realized only as
the project gained momentum, and procedures had to be established for the revision of the existing Authority.

In many ways, however, these setbacks worked to the project's advantage. Initial skepticism on the part of some personnel was overcome as the passage of time allowed them to
gain a more thorough understanding of how the database was
constructed. We were extremely fortunate that the project
facilitator was a M.L.S. librarian with data processing experience. She could explain in detail the impact of the network
and make professional decisions regarding the conversion.

The standardization of a cluttered Subject Authority proved to be a tremendous aid to quick and accurate cataloging by participating agencies.

The Northern Area Network is now beginning to function in the way its originators had projected. A staff in-service training was conducted for the school library media personnel, instructing them in the mechanics of search strategies and data entry in the Northern Area Network. Students and teachers are now using the system daily and data entry from the schools continues to progress. In-service instruction was also conducted for Northland staff to answer questions and outline changes in database procedure necessitated by participation in an online network.

COLLECTION DEVELOPMENT AND THE NETWORK

Each agency which participates in a network develops a collection designed to meet the needs of its own users. There is very limited expectation regarding support from other agencies.

The public library user population is the most diverse of the participating agencies. It ranges from pre-school to golden age and is made up of students, parents, home repairers, workers of all kinds, retirees, and homemakers, all with changing needs and interests. Students are a vocal portion of the public library's patrons.

Students from kindergarten through twelfth grade as well as students attending one of the two colleges in the service area or living in the area and attending one of the seven colleges located in the city of Pittsburgh use Northland Library. These patrons are served by other libraries as well and therefore their needs are not Northland's first priority in collection development. Northland's first priority is to serve the public that does not have access to another library.

These considerations in developing priorities are not always clear to the public library user. Students often have such acute informational needs that they forget the information needs and interests of people who are not involved in formal education, and who also require materials.

The school library media centers have a limited population

and a specific curriculum to support. This should and does make collection development easier. However, the school library media center's collections must cover the wide range of student interests, needs and abilities that exist within the school. They must also try to provide information in different formats (audio-visual materials) to accommodate the various learning styles of the students. Special students are now a part of the school population and in many cases they require special materials. The school library media center must anticipate classroom, teacher, and student needs so that the educational experience is not interrupted and is always enhanced. The days of a book, a slate and a teacher are gone forever. The tools necessary to provide a basic education change as the information explosion and increased technology continue to change schools and libraries.

The school library media centers do maintain collections designed to help meet the requirements of assignments that are developed around student interests, to answer personal needs, to teach library competencies, and to encourage library (information) use in decision making. Unfortunately access to this material is limited, as access to the school is limited. This lack of access has an effect on the public library's need for additional materials to support its program when school is not in session. Swanton, writing in the March, 1984 issue of *School Library Journal,* quotes a recent study which found that the greater a child's use of the library in the summer, the more language arts skills the child retained when school resumed in the fall. In this same article Swanton urges school and public librarians to cooperate in their efforts to encourage and provide positive reading experiences for children.[2]

The hospital library serves a specific population and supports a particular area of information. It is a medical library with few resources in other areas. The user population is made up of doctors, nurses, and hospital administrators. The collection is made up of the combined resources of what was a nurses' library and a separate docctors' library with some materials for laypersons. Health education has become impor-

---

[2]Susan Swanton. "Minds Alive: What & Why Gifted Students Read for Pleasure." *School Library Journal.* March, 1984. p.102

tant in the schools and in the community, and as public awareness continues to develop, people are demanding the information that enables them to make informed health decisions. They want background information to help them discuss medical care with health professionals. Providing access to additional health and medical materials is a service the other agencies could not achieve without the network.

There are other special libraries that fall into this category. They have materials that could be very useful to members of the public school library populations but are not ordinarily available or affordable. These materials can be added to the network and made available to network users. Materials found in the collections of special libraries that would only be useful to a few professionals due to their technical nature need not be included in the network. The network plans to add portions of the Allegheny County Law Library and the Alfred M. Beatty Technical School Library. Other collections are presently under consideration.

COLLECTION MANAGEMENT AND DATABASE USE

The primary goal of networking in 1984 remains the same as that given by Bender in *School Library Journal* in 1979. Networks are formed to meet the needs of users now and in the future through the sharing of resources and services.[3]

The inclusion of materials in the Northern Area Network not only makes them accessible to Network users but also develops an increased awareness of information sources for users. This is an important teaching tool for the school library programs. It is likely that some of the materials found through the network will become so popular with new users that they will have to be duplicated by other participating libraries.

There are other advantages to the Northern Area Network worthy of mention. It proves very helpful to have a union catalog readily available when looking for useful materials on

---

[3]David R. Bender. "Networking & School Library Media Programs." *School Library Journal.* November, 1979. p.31

a particular subject to add to the collection of one of the libraries. The database becomes an additional selection tool. It can even provide some information regarding material use. Examination of particular items is also possible. There are times when duplication of material can and should be avoided. For example, one of the libraries looks to the network for seldom used back issues of *Current Biography* it might otherwise have purchased. Must every library in the network have the most recent edition of *Who's Who,* or worse, does each library buy it every five years and all in the same year leaving the whole network without a current edition for a time? Schedules are now being developed to insure that this situation does not occur. Increased service is always considered when making these collection decisions. There are some titles that every or almost every library should keep current. Each library will continue to duplicate these titles. There is nothing in our arrangement that keeps any library from buying any title. Each library is unique and must make its own collection decisions. Communication is the key to a successful network. All materials must be put online and if something prevents one of the libraries from following a jointly determined buying plan, the network needs to be informed in order to make other arrangements. Communication, effort and intent are important. If the network is to reach its full potential, each participating library must consider its place in the Northern Area Network as an integral part of its several functions.

The network also provides cataloging information and may eventually provide catalog cards for participating libraries. Inventory and weeding are both made considerably easier by the technical aspects of the network. Through the use of portable equipment the books on the shelves can be inventoried by passing a wand over the barcode. The libraries that use the computer for circulation have data regarding material use that provides information for weeding, purchasing, and ongoing inventory.

Storage of materials is a major problem for many of the participating libraries at present and is of course, a potential problem for all libraries. The program of the school library media center and the types and numbers of materials have grown to such an extent that most of the schools face an immediate space problem. Periodical indexes are used as a major research tool in all of the libraries and competency in their use is part of the curriculum in the middle schools. All of the libraries, therefore, keep back issues of magazines that support their particular periodical indexes. These include *Abridged Reader's Guide to Periodical Literature, Reader's Guide to Periodical Liteature,* and *The Popular Magazine Index.* Space is an important consideration as each library decides how many years of back issues to keep and which magazines to buy on microform. The network is working toward an organized plan for a shared microform periodical library. New technology makes this a logical plan. It will be a major step forward in service to be able to fill all requests for magazine articles accessed through the indexes we provide. Nothing is so frustrating to patron and librarian alike as to spend considerable time and effort to locate an information source through a periodical index and then find the magazine missing or the article gone from the journal.

School library media centers are often forced to withdraw or discard materials because of curriculum changes or space consideration that otherwise might have been retained. These materials can now be sent to another library or stored as additional copies with ease. Biographies and some fiction might be discarded for those reasons but be useful in another collection.

Special collections in each library will provide additional resources in particular areas. Each library in the network will select at least one area or subject to maintain as a special collection. This will mean that the library agrees to: keep all the material it considers to be worthwhile; examine and add to the collection all worthwhile materials discarded by other participating libraries; purchase what its budget allows of new material; make the materials accessible to the users of the network. The subjects for the special collections will be areas such as science fiction, community history, public education, Pittsburgh history and culture, business resources, Pennsylvania history and other subjects of particular interest. Once these collections are established, we will make their existance known to our users.

USE OF THE NETWORK COLLECTION

It was known as the project began that each library and each librarian would have to overcome some feelings of what has been called institutional territoriality. It must be kept in mind that as service is provided to another library's patrons, we are increasing service to our library's users. As the project unfolded and we began to see the full potential of the service we could offer, a sense of belonging to the Network began to develop. The obligation to serve all of the users in the Network must be realized and fullfilled by all of the participants if we are to be truly successful.

The Network will provide on site use, interlibrary loan and on site borrowing by the patrons of all of the participating agencies. Because of the physical proximity of the members of the network and the overlapping user groups it is difficult to evaluate the extent of increased use that has resulted from improved access. School library users use the computer terminal in their school libraries to access materials from the public library collection. They then go to the public library and use the materials or take them out. Parents locate materials housed in the school library media centers and have their children borrow them. This means that better access is getting more materials into the hands of users, but it is hard to count the numbers. As awareness and demand increases, and as the technology advances, there will continue to be changes in how information is provided to patrons.

The need exists to supplement the public library collection during school vactions. Assignments are often given that involve research and that are due after a vacation during which many useful books are locked away in the school. With materials being accessible through the public library terminal it will be a relatively simple matter for the public library to gather requests and the school to send mateials for on site use or circulation.

Searching the database has also helped users build an understanding of the various libraries and of the importance of having wider access to information. At present, the technology itself is a motivational factor. This condition will not last forever; it will undoubtedly fade as computers become commonplace. However, we will use it to our advantage while we can and at the same time provide our users with computer-readiness experience.

A recent much publicized technological innovation has been OPAC (On-line Public Access Catalogs). This means that the card catalog of the future will likely be a computer terminal used by the library patron. People will access library holdings from terminals in the library or from their homes, if dial-up capabilities are available. This is already happening in scattered instances. The Northern Area Network provides to its member libraries the potential of beginning to use this new method of making collections accessible. In fact OPAC is now available in each of the four school library media centers. Students and teachers are encouraged to make their own independent searches. This educational training in turn will provide guidelines for the public library as it plans the training of its adult population in use of the public library's terminals or their home terminals to access the collection. The experiences in the schools will also prove helpful in determining the number of terminals which will be needed to provide adequate service in the public library.

The use of OPAC in the schools allows staff to examine student search strategies. This opportunity was discussed by Cheryl Kern-Simirenko, writing in *Library Hitec*. Librarians have always wondered what techniques were employed by patrons when they were trying to find material through the card catalog. Now by examining the printouts from the computer terminals used by students searching the Northern Area Network database, it is possible to see the subjects used and the strategies employed by those students.

Librarians can use this information in catloging materials and it is very valuable in developing ways to instruct students in the use of card catalogs, indexes, and databases. Documented search strategies are also helpful to the student in trying to develop his/her own techniques for using these information retrieval-tools, including costly databases. The ability to develop strategies to search an information database is fast becoming an important information skill, and using the Northern Area Network will give users valuable experience.

LONG RANGE PLANS

Even though the Northern Area Network is still in its infancy, plans are already underway for the future. Retrospective data entry will continue for at least the next twelve months, until the entire collections of the four schools are online. During the same period, extra features and services will be added. These include serials management, resource files, and catalog card production. Future plans would not be complete without looking at the potential software enhancements planned by the vendor, Universal Library Systems. They are developing Boolean and KWIC searching procedures for their system as well as an acquisition program. In addition to enhancements, the Network will look to future growth through the addition of other libraries.

Serials management, already in use at Northland, is a semi-automated method of journal control. The school library media centers will begin using this in the near future. All serials titles taken by each library will be entered into the computer with coding indicating which library receives it, from whom, date of renewal, price, whether it is indexed and where, and frequency of publication. Each month, self-adhesive labels will be printed out. These labels will carry the name of the magazine, name of the library, the control number (barcode) and the issue date. The labels will then be placed on the magazines as they arrive; extra labels at the end of the month will indicate which magazines were not received. The full computer data can be used to issue periodic holdings lists for each library, thus providing a union list of serials.

Resource and community information files have become very important "home made" media in both the school district and the public library. These manually maintained resource files include a variety of information concerning areas such as daycare facilities, local government, speaker's bureau, and local association and club directories. A software program has been written to allow for a database consisting of these local resource files, although no data entry has yet taken place.

Catalog card production via the computer is a feature much anticipated by all members of the Network, especially the hospital library. It will not have dramatic effect on students

nor on patrons in the public library, but it will have an enor-
mous impact on the workloads of each library's staff, especially in the schools where clerical assistance is limited. This
software program is available but will need some modifica-
tion. The computer will produce cards in requested quantities
for any item entered in the database. With the use of a high
speed printer, this could cut processing time by as much as
50%.

Software enhancements which will be available in the next
twelve to twenty-four months include Boolean and KWIC
search. Boolean is the searching technique which allows the
user to enter several descriptors at the same time connected
by "and" or "not," providing a high degree of search sophistication. KWIC or Key Word In Context searching allows the
accessing of titles by any major word in the title entry, not
just the first word. Both search techniques will add to the
Network's capabilities. In addition an acquisition program
will be available for purchase within the next six months. This
program will handle the ordering process for member libraries
and will lessen staff workloads.

A description of the potential future of the Northern Area
Network cannot be limited to a discussion of the computer
enhancements; it must include the growth of the Network
through the addition of other libraries. As soon as the bulk of
the data entry in the schools is completed, the Network will
be ready to take on other collections. The first is the local
hospital library which is waiting for the appropriate time.
Their collection of approximately 4,000 volumes would give a
new dimension to the Network. In addition, discussions with
the County Law Library, a vocational school library and several other very small special collections in the area such as the
Audubon Library have yielded positive potential for the Network's expansion. The Northern Area Network should continue to grow at a controlled rate. This slow development is
necessary to allow for the careful training and healthy merger
of the other agencies into the network. As the system develops, Network participants can evaluate its strengths and
weaknesses. They can invite other libraries or agencies with
small collections to join as the need is identified.

The future of the Network could include the addition of all
of the school district's elementary collections and/or the

schools' initiation of the system's circulation functions as the public library does. These possibilities for the future differ from those mentioned previously in that they will require considerable enhancements to the public library's computer hardware. This would mean that the school district or an outside funding body would have to provide additional money.

CONCLUSION

A network is an on-going changing entity. The future of the Northern Area Network looks bright, but only because of its history, which was one of open sharing of ideas and a learning process.

To make a network feasible, the host library needs to have positive experiences with its own computer use. Northland Public Library's five-year background with the computerization of its collection and services would seem to have had an important impact upon the schools. Without that track record, problems could have been seen as insurmountable. No database can ever be completely error-free, but the host must make it as clean as possible. There must be general agreement by all members of the network on the makeup and format of the database, especially the Subject Authority File. Consistency is crucial, as it allows the database to grow in an organized manner. The files can be accurately maintained and easily searched by all participating library users if the same procedures are used uniformly throughout the network.

Data entry can be done at the rate of 200 to 250 items per day. This statistic is important in terms of planning for the addition of other libraries. Detailed notes should be taken during early entry stages so that clear guidelines can be drawn up to insure consistency in entry. These guidelines should be developed with input by all member agencies so that all individual libraries feel their needs are met. In this manner the Northern Area Network project facilitator created a procedures manual for database use.

Another important lesson learned during the initial startup period was that the planning for such a network should include a full analysis of hardware and software needs. The knowledge gained during the first eighteen months has made planning for further enlargements of the network much simpler and more realistic. Hardware changes made in order to implement the grant were adequate, but additional system enhancements were not properly considered or taken into account. For instance, no plans were made in the original grant proposal for a larger tape drive used to back up the system. As the database has grown, the number of update tapes run daily has increased. The situation is not impossible, but it would have been better if a larger tape drive had been built into the system during upgrade for the grant.

Similar problems have been encountered in the areas of software. We found that each individual school also had requirements which varied in small ways, and which could not be immediately met by the existing software program. Thus, the original planning document must be open to change and revision as the network begins to take shape.

The key reason for the success of the Northern Area Network was the time and care taken initially to develop a strong framework for the Network's implementation. This framework insured consistency and agreement among the participating agencies, while at the same time allowing for each agency to maintain its autonomy.

A localized computer network can succeed with each member having different goals. It was discovered that all of the libraries were willing to join in a cooperative arrangement, but not necessarily for the same reasons. Northland librarians desired the combined database in order to gain access to a larger pool of materials. The school library media specialists saw the advantages of such enlarged resources but were also interested in secondary benefits such as its teaching potential and inventory control capabilities. The hospital librararian indicated a major interest in the production of catalog cards. As long as individuals goals are outlined and the network is capable of satisfying different needs, a local network can make a strong impact on its members and on the users it serves.

BIBLIOGRAPHY

Ballard, Tom. "Public Library Networking: Neat, Plausible, and Wrong." *Library Journal*. April 1, 1982. pp. 679–683.

Bender, David R. "Networking & School Library Media Programs." *School Library Journal.* November, 1979. pp. 29–32.

Kern-Simirenko, Cheryl. "OPAC User Logs: Implications for Bibliographic Instruction." *Library HiTec.* (Winter, 1983). pp. 27–35.

Swanton, Susan I. "Minds Alive: What & Why Gifted Students Read for Pleasure." *School Library Journal.* March, 1984. p. 102.

SECTION III
SCHOOL AND PUBLIC
COOPERATION

Four essays explore the rich possibilities of school-public cooperation.

The Use of School Libraries and Public Libraries and the Relationship to Collection Development

Blanche Woolls

The ways in which differences in clientele and services account for differences in collection development strategies between public and school libraries are explored. Suggestions are made as to how strengths of each can be used to maximize service.

In order to discuss the relationship of use to collection development, the use of school libraries* and public libraries will be placed in the context of the similarity and differences between their buildings (facilities), their management, their clientele, and the types of services offered. Cooperative efforts can be suggested acknowledging the similarities and differences and relating these to collection development strategies. The necessity of addressing buildings, management, clientele, and services in relation to collection development is easily justified when comparing two types of library situations because the major differences in clientele and services define the major differences in collection development strategies and the differences in buildings and management affect the possiblities for cooperation between school librarians and public librarians.

---

*The author is aware of the alternate choice of title, "school library media center." The nature of this article made it seem preferable to refer to both as "libraries" rather than to use two rather different titles for a similar operation.

Dr. Woolls is a professor at the School of Library and Information Science, University of Pittsburgh, Pittsburgh, PA.

BUILDINGS (FACILITIES)

The school library is often placed at the center of the school building. When the library is placed near the classrooms, it is easily accessible by all students in the school during the school day when they leave their classrooms to visit the library. Since a library serves the students attending that school, the size of the library and its furnishings are provided for an identified age and ability level.

The public library may also be located "centrally" on the main street of the local community, but it is not always conveniently located or easily accessible to its adult users. It may be some distance from any school or, in other cities, public libraries or their branches are located very near school buildings. Larger cities with many branches have placed service in residential neighborhoods, and some have established library branches in shopping centers. Because the public library serves all ages in the community rather than a specialized clientele, decor and furnishings are designed for many users, not just for children and young people. When public library buildings are large enough to separate collections and users, the children's room is in an area as far away as possible from the other areas of public use. Traditionally it was placed in the basement of Carnegie buildings, and this model has been followed in designing other public libraries.

MANAGEMENT

Management as it pertains to these two types of libraries has been defined as governance, budget, personnel, and public relations. The governance structure is very different between these two types of libraries. Public librarians usually answer directly to a Board of Trustees who have been appointed by the Mayor or the City Council or the County Commissioner. This means that they have a direct line to their governing board. This is not true of the school librarian. This person must address all requests to the building principal (and/or to the school library supervisor, if such a position exists) who in turn presents them to the superintendent who then seeks school board approval. Since the school board is made up of elected officials, these persons must answer more directly to community pressures. This poliltical situation adds to a sense of helplessness on the part of the school librarian who feels little control over policy decisions which effect the library, e.g., the librarian, art teacher, music teacher, and physical education instructor's classes will relieve the teacher for the union contract "free period" each day.

In some cases the school librarian may appear to be more autonomous as the manager of the school library. A certain air of academic freedom pervades the decision-making process within that area of the school. On the other hand, the principal may demand hall passes for children outside of the classroom making it difficult for students to move freely to the library, or the central administration personnel may insist upon a fine system for overdue books. Because most situations have only one professional per building, school librarians feel isolated from other professionals, and have no one to discuss matters or to assist in choosing alternatives for solving problems. One problem common to both librarians is budget.

Budgets for schools come from the state allocation for public education and from local tax effort. School boards are usually able to levy taxes while public library boards must seek funding from city councils or county commissioners or attempt to pass referendums. While school librarians lament being in competition with other departments of the school such as the athletic department, the band, or the drama club, the public librarian must stand in line with the police department, the fire department, and the garbage collectors. School librarians may appear to receive higher "per capita" income than the public librarian. School librarians in some states receive state mandated minimum per pupil allocations for the library materials account. Thus, for one particular age level in schools the "per capita" may be a higher figure than the public librarian receives, e.g., if school librarians receive $6.00 per pupil and public librarians receive only $1.56 per capita, it may seem that public libraries have a larger funding base, because the per capita figure for funding the public library includes the population of the entire community. However, public librarians must finance salaries and building maintenance from this budget while school librarians only purchase materials and supplies from their funding.

Personnel differences exist between these two institutions. The first is related to the educational background of these librarians. While not all states require an MLS from an ALA accredited program to be a school librarian, most require an applicant to have a bachelor's degree with library science courses. Public librarians who manage large public library systems are required to have the MLS degree. However, a university degree may not be required of the person who works with children, and in small public libraries, the library director may be certified by the state library by some means other than achieving a masters in librarianship of even any education beyond the high school diploma.

Certainly public librarians have been shown to hire many more clerical staff than do schools. The results of a study published by the National Commission on Libraries and Information Science shows that the proportion of clerical staff to professional staff in the public library is 1:1.2, while professional to clerical in schools is 1:.63.[1] Smaller school districts may hire one librarian to serve in three or even more elementary schools; a clerk may or may not be assigned to the building. In these situations it is not likely that the school library collection has been developed with interaction between teacher and librarian.

A final difference has to do with the salary of these persons. School librarians are a part of the teacher bargaining unit and receive the same salary as other teachers. School personnel are required to be at school during the hours school is in session and on days when pupils are in attendance. This means longer holiday vacations for school librarians. Also, the school year is only nine months. Teacher salary is often higher than the public librarian's who receives a specified vacation of two to three weeks, a limited number of holidays each year, and who must also work evenings and weekends.

The public librarian must initiate more public relations activities to encourage use of the library than is necessary for the school librarian. The public librarian must advertise in the local newspaper to encourage attendance at book fairs, spe-

---

[1]Ladd, Boyd. *National Inventory of Library Needs,* 1975: Resources Needed for Public and Academic Libraries and Public School Library/Media Centers. [Washington, D.C.]: National Commission on Libraries and Information Science, March, 1977, [p.. 19]

cial programming for children and youth, book talks, and other events. For emphasizing special events, the school librarian need only send a message over the school's loud speaker system or place an announcement in each teacher's school mail box.

CLIENTELE

The school library serves the students in a single attendance center. It is the only type of library which serves a captive audience. Children are taken to the library by their teachers whether they wish to go or not. In contrast, the public library must reach out to attract its clientele, and that clientele includes everyone in the area served by the public library. While the public library may serve some of the same children as the school, it may not serve all children in the school. One reason is that not all children attending any school may choose to visit the public library or be allowed to go. It may be too distant for children to go alone. The differences in governmental boundaries may restrict use of the public library to children within the city limits while the school serves both city children and county children who are bused to the school. If several schools exist in a community, the public library will be serving children from all schools rather than teachers and students with a single curriculum.

SERVICES OFFERED

Both libraries offer book and media collections to their clientele. However, the collection at the public library is both for recreational use and for research with the emphasis perhaps more on the recreational aspect. The collection at the school is designed to meet curriculum needs with much less recreational reading provided. Because of its curriculum emphasis, the school library may have a more specialized subject-oriented collection.

The public library media collection is seldom as extensive as that of the school, and the public library collection may contain fewer subject-oriented educational materials. The variety of formats is also different. Public librarians concentrate on recordings and videotapes while school librarians purchase transparencies, kits, filmstrips, and 16mm films. The advent of the microcomputer and the consequent adoption by the education community has seen much more microcomputer software available in the schools than is found in the public library.

The school library is open during hours school is in session while the public library is open after school, on weekends, and during the summer months. This means the public library collection may seem more accessible to some students because they have little time during the school day to visit the school library. Certainly those school libraries which are closed the three months of the summer are inaccessible to students. This is especially critical in the case of the reading retention of elementary students. Recent research has shown that summer reading programs help students retain their reading skills.

> The single summer activity that is most strongly and consistently related to summer learning is reading. Whether measured by the number of books read, by the time spent reading, or by the regularity of library usage, reading during the summer systematically increases the vocabulary test scores of children. Although related to differences in parental status, summer reading has a substantial effect on achievement that is largely independent of family background. Although unstructured activities such as reading do not ordinarily lend themselves to policy intervention, I will argue that at least one institution, the public library, directly influences children's reading. Educational policies that increase access to books, perhaps through increased library services, stand to have an important impact on achievement, particularly for less advantaged children.[2]

A second major difference in the use of the school library is that most schools have a bell system which rings at the end of

---

[2]Heyns, Barbara. *Summer Learning and the Effects of Schooling.* New York: Academic Press, 1978, p. 161.

a specified period of time. Students using the library must leave when the bell rings whether or not they have completed their research. Students who go to the public library may have longer periods of time when they can work.

The age orientation of the school collection limits the span of materials which may be available to the student in the school, while access to the adult collection for students wishing to expand their research is available to them at the public library. On the other hand, materials available in a children's collection may help introduce a high school student to a more difficult topic. These would not be available in the typical high school library.

The most recent gap in service between schools and public library has been in the area of advanced high technology for interlibrary communication. OCLC for interlibrary loan and the use of databases in the retrieval of citations have been available in mid-sized and larger public library systems for some time, although they are seldom used for retrieval of information for children or young adults. Few schools have been able to join OCLC thus hindering the use of the OCLC database for locating materials. Very few schools have been able to subscribe to an online database to expand the search capabilities of teachers and students. This greatly reduces access to information for students.

IMPLICATIONS FOR COLLECTION DEVELOPMENT

The chain of command in both institutions may cause some problems in trying to share in collection development. If the school board members consider that *their* money bought the materials and these materials must be used only by the students for whom the tax money was collected, sharing these materials with another agency may be restricted. School librarians also face the chance that a teacher will become very angry if they discover that material requested for a class is in the hands of someone outside the school population. It is the proposition of this author that material removed by a user from any collection is unavailable, and it doesn't really matter who has it. If the school librarian does not explain where the material is, how will the teacher know it is away on interlibrary loan rather than in the hands of a student or teacher in the school? Using the excuse that any material might be unavailable if needed implies that school librarians cannot help teachers plan far enough ahead to reserve materials, an often mentioned need.

The lack of budget in both locations makes sharing collection development strategies desirable as well as practical. Neither librarian is able to purchase all the materials needed to serve their clientele, and duplication in shared areas of interest could add unneccessarily to already strained budgets.

The hours the school and public library are available to students have great influence on use which should influence who selects an item. An example might be a very expensive microcomputer program which schools should buy such as a tutoring program for the SATs. This program would be requested by guidance counselors who would wish it to be available in the school during the school day. Many students have very limited time to go to the school library during the day, and these students would appreciate having the SAT program available at the local public library during the evenings, the weekends, and throughout the summer. Such a transfer of materials can accelerate two-way sharing. Determining which library should purchase which periodicals, how much duplication of titles is necessary in both libraries, and which periodicals should be retained for more than five years are also shared decisions. Access to periodicals will also be as constrained by hours of service as it will be by periodicals available. It may be that microfilm copies of popular periodicals will be sent to public libraries over vacations when peak use is anticipated.

Size of staff in libraries also has implications for shared collection development. The school librarian who is serving in more than one school will not have knowledge of the collections, the needs of the teachers, or the time to discuss sharing scarce resources. The small public library may be managed by someone in the community who has volunteered or been paid a very small salary over time. This person will have had little if any incentive to gain the appropriate education for being a skillfull collection developer. On the other hand, if a trained librarian exists in either location and no such person exists in the other, assistance with collection development policies is essential. Public and school librarians should share information concerning special collection strengths and in deciding to develop new areas. These are further shared collection development policies.

The school librarian can be very helpful in advertising the collection strengths of the public library as well as in encouraging the use of the public library programming by students in the school. Public librarians can point out collection strengths in the school library to adult patrons needing such information. Vocational materials and job related information are examples of such school library strengths.

Because public librarians are more likely to have communication links among libraries, the assistance of the public librarian in locating materials, the willingness of this agency to help students use interlibrary loan for book materials, and the sharing of purchase of periodicals may help make a much wider variety of information resources available in even the smallest city. Helping expand this service to non-urban areas is also essential. The rural areas of any state are most likely to have very small public library collections, to have consolidated schools which still serve under 400 students in grades K–12, and to be the greatest distance from a college or university. These students who are in the most need of expanded resources are the most distant from larger collections so that communication costs to locate and request materials are the highest. They may be the least able to afford the cost of communication and postage or other forms of delivery of material.

Certainly beginning to understand the similarities and differences in the management and the services offered can help all librarians make competent choices in selecting between alternatives which may increase the use of school libraries, which may help initiate collection development policies which will serve to alleviate the pressures on declining budgets, and make more resources available to the clientele in both locations, the school and the public library. The next step is to meet and talk with librarians to see exactly the use being made of current collections and to discuss ways user needs may be met by sharing strategies to maximum resources between both agencies.

School and Public Library Cooperation: A Prerequisite for Cooperative Collection Development

Betty V. Billman
Patricia Owens

In this age of information overload and decreasing funds for acquiring information sources, it is essential that cooperation in meeting users needs be maximized. The authors provide a taxonomy for cooperation among different types of libraries and explore the results of various cooperative activities.

It's here. The past two decades have ushered our society out of an industrial age and into one of information and high technology. As John Naisbitt states in *Megatrends,* "We have for the first time an economy based on a key resource that is not only renewable, but self-generating. Running out of it is not a problem, but drowning in it is."[1] This new age has created the all too familiar "I have some good news and some bad news" situation for librarians. Information is what libraries are all about. They select, acquire, manage and somehow make sense of the deluge of information that is generated. Bumper stickers even declare, "Connecticut Libraries: They're in the Answer Business." In addition, elaborate automation networks and sophisticated bibliographic retrieval systems are available to help us provide the answers more quickly than ever before. That's the good news. Libraries and librarians of all types are critical in providing resources in an age of information.

Betty V. Billman is Library Media Consultant in the Connecticut State Department of Education. Patricia Owens is Director, Division of Library Development, Connecticut State Library.

183

But, then there is the bad news. To continue Naisbitt's thoughts, "This level of information is clearly impossible to handle by present means."[2] Unfortunately, the potential for providing information to meet the ever changing and often demanding user has not been undergirded with appropriate financial, and/or sometimes philosophical support necessary to carry out the task. The same two decades that have brought us to the age of information have been accompanied by inflation, resulting in reduced buying power, curtailed local budgets, and decreased or discontinued funding for library services (in particular, the questionable continued status of Library Service and Construction Act funds and the discontinuation of the Elementary and Secondary Education Act, Title IVB). Some school library media specialists and public librarians have thrown up their hands in dispair as the gap between the potential for library service and their reality seems to widen. Fewer and fewer libraries can even dream of meeting patron needs with only their own resources.

The majority of the professional librarians are aware of the potential and equally aware of the reality. They are searching for ways to provide better library services, taking steps, no matter how small, toward that goal. Times of austerity have encouraged an openness to attractive options and alternatives for service as it becomes increasingly evident that almost all libraries must abandon their "stand alone status" in favor of working together to satisfy the information needs of the patrons they serve. In addition to "networks" and "automation," "cooperation" has become a buzz word of the 80's. It is the cooperation between school library media centers and public libraries and its relationship to collection development that will be the focus of this paper. Much of what will be said is based on the status of cooperation among school and public libraries in Connecticut.

For the past four years the Connecticut State Library and the Connecticut State Department of Education have joined forces to promote better communication and cooperation among school library media specialists and public librarians at the local and regional levels and at the same time strengthen and define the unique role that each plays within a community. In addition to providing better service to the citizens in the state, there was also a need to present a "big picture" of library service to legislators and taxpayers. Encouragement to cooperate has taken the form of conference presentations, consultant referral service from both agencies, a quarterly newsletter from both agencies entitled "Working Together" and a mini-grant program for cooperative ventures. As these efforts began we realized that the word cooperation could mean anything from "Don't bother me and I won't interfere with you" to a forced combining of the school and public library. Using the term in the generic sense left the specific activities associated with cooperation up to the imagination of the hearer or reader. To attempt to alleviate the confusion an attempt was made to define various levels of cooperation by activities or characteristics that typified each level, to present cooperation as an ongoing process. In addition to merely presenting a hierarchy of cooperation it was hoped that the information would provide a starting point for libraries in towns or regions to evaluate their present level of cooperation and what kinds of activities would be logical to attempt at that level. It was also a goal to have the chart used as a basis for short and long term planning for expanding the current scope of cooperative ventures. The range of cooperative activities were divided into six levels, each of which requires greater commitment of time and staff than the previous level.

Though the list is by no means definitive, it does give representative identifying activities. A basic premise for the levels is that communication is essential for any cooperative venture. The quality, frequency and opportunity for communication is a major determining factor in the activities or projects that can normally be achieved, including cooperative collection development. The established level of communication that exists between school and public libraries must be fairly high in order to pursue substantial cooperative collection development projects.

Before proceeding any further it is important to define what is meant by the term collection development. For the purpose of this paper, collection development will be understood as the process and accompanying activities that are used to analyze, acquire and maintain resources that will meet the information needs of a defined group of users. Collection development may occur within a single institution or cooperatively between or among institutions.

	Level I No Involvement or Cooperation	Level II Informal Cooperation	Level III Formal Communication	Level IV Formal Cooperation	Level V Resource Sharing	Level VI Formal Planning
General Description	At this level, libraries exist as separate and independent institutions, either by choice or by lack of any precedent for cooperation. Many times, staffs have never met together.	At this level, libraries are still quite independent entities but experience sporadic communication. Some libraries may communicate more than others but all still rely primarily on their own resources to satisfy user needs.	At this level, communication becomes more purposeful and on-going in nature, focusing on a specific event or issue. Staffs may meet together on an irregular basis.	At this level, mutual goals or objectives guide the cooperative activities. Though actual materials may not be exchanged, there is an increased awareness of the town's total information resources. Much of this activity can still be conducted by interested individuals. Library staffs and administrators have an understanding of the services and mission of the other libraries involved in the cooperative group.	At this level, cooperation becomes more planned, systematic and on-going as the commitment to the whole of library service grows. Involvement of school administrators, town trustees, etc. increases as many resource sharing activities involve policies or finances. Short and long term goals and plans may be developed.	At this level, cooperation exists on a frequent and regular basis and involve more people. Short and long term goals and objectives for library service are developed and approved by the appropriate governing boards.

Characteristics of Activities	Level I No Involvement or Cooperation	Level II Informal Cooperation	Level III Formal Communication	Level IV Formal Cooperation	Level V Resource Sharing	Level VI Formal Planning
	-There has been no history of cooperation -Formal contacts have not been made between the two institutions -There is no public library in town -There are no library media personnel in the school or school system -There is a competitive or antagonistic behavior on the part of the professionals or boards -There are no phones in the school library media center	-Assignment alerts are given to public librarians by the school media specialist -Occasional phone calls for reference by either school or public librarians -Joint publicity of special library events	-Plan scheduled class visits to the public library -Public librarians visit school library media centers or school classrooms -Mutual planning and promotion of summer programs for children -Social contact through professional associations or workshops -Carpooling to professional events or workshops -Sharing of professional development opportunities	-Joint celebration of library events such as National Library Week -Union Lists of periodicals or other materials -Exchange of bibliographies -Cooperative data collection	-Shared storytelling, book talks, discussion groups, etc. -Loan of school materials to public library during the summer -School library media materials are available to public library patrons -Compatibility of hardware (video, microcomputer, etc.) throughout the town or region -Shared display of special materials or projects -Mutual exchange of materials of any kind -Intradistrict delivery of materials to all libraries and library media centers in town -Regular articles in school or local newspapers, library bulletins, etc. -Shared films or film rentals	-Some cooperative collection development -Cooperative policy development (selection, weeding, equipment, etc.) -Joint cataloging/technical processing -Cooperative equipment repair, service or purchase program -Shared goal setting for library service within the town -Shared program evaluation procedures -Exchange of catalog cards or current acquisitions -Common card catalog in one or both locations -Facilities sharing for district patron services -Extended hours at the school library media center to increase patron access

Collection development begins in individual schools and public libraries as a result of the desire to meet the needs of a specific use population and development of a policy to achieve that goal. In order to do this there must be a commitment of staff time to identify the needs of the users and the resources currently available to meet them. Though a time consuming process, especially with limited staffing patterns, a collection development policy can provide tangible benefits for the institution and, with careful planning, lay a foundation for cooperative collection development. Lucille Thomas, Assistant Director, Office of Library Media and Telecommunications, New York City Board of Education, has set forth eleven points in a rationale for a collection development policy for school library media centers. We feel that similar benefits can be realized by public libraries.

1. A collection policy forces the library media specialist to examine the goals of the library media center, as well as the goals of school.
2. Construction of a collection development policy is an excellent staff development tool.
3. A written policy communicates to others what the policy is and why.
4. A collection development policy helps to assure that the library media center is committed to serving all the students and teachers in the school. Their policy is documentation of the perceived needs of the users.
5. If the library media center is a member of a system of network, a collection development policy informs other libraries about the scope and nature of the collection. This encourages coordination of collection development among different institutions.
6. A collection development policy helps set high standards for the selection and weeding of materials.
7. A collection development policy helps assure continuity when library staff changes.
8. Personal bias on the part of the individual selector is minimized when the selection of materials is made in terms of a written policy.
9. The budgetary allocation process can be based on information included in the policy.

10. A written policy can provide a means for the staff to evaluate its performance periodically.
11. A collection development policy can provide guidelines to handling complaints.[3]

A service oriented collection development policy helps define and evaluate a library or media center's role, but at the same time provides the rationale and flexibility to change that role and the framework in which that change can occur. Collection development within an institution can be a healthy process by itself but library personnel, in view of the information age we find ourselves in, must also consider working together with other types of libraries to provide the breadth and depth of resources that users require. For this type of endeavor to be successful there must again be a commitment of staff time from all libraries intending to participate. Not only is time required for the analysis of individual collections, but also for frequent and ongoing planning activities and as acquisition, maintenance and delivery of materials is implemented. In addition to time, there are some attitudinal prerequisites:

1. There must be a mutual attitude of trust and cooperation, a willingness to abandon turf and a library's stand alone status. At the same time, cooperative collection development should be approached in a manner that does not threaten the need for or support for the individual library or media center.
2. There must be a willingness to think more globally and long term about library services. This necessitates plans for greater communications with participating institutions and library staff development.
3. There must be a willingness and ability to share the information and loan materials through interlibrary loan, bibliographic access and a delivery system.

Commitment of staff, time and attitude enables school library media specialists and public librarians to approach cooperative collection development. As with cooperation in general, there can be different levels of participation in cooperative collection development. Towns may find benefits from cooperative collection development in only one or two areas such as audio visual materials, periodicals, or computer software. Different towns may legitimately be seeking different levels of cooperative collection development based on the existing level of communication that exists and the very nature of the community and its resources. The following examples illustrate some existing Connecticut school and public library cooperative collection development efforts and activities at various levels of library service.

LEVEL 1—NO INVOLVEMENT
OR COOPERATION

The Southern Connecticut Library Council recently distributed a survey to all its members. There are 35 towns in the region. The survey was very brief, intended to find out what kinds of formal and informal collection development policies have been developed by school and public libraries in the same town. Of a total of 11 responses, 5 indicated there was no sharing of any type.

Some of the comments mentioned the lack of time; the feeling that only curricular materials would be useful for students in the public library; and that there is no point in the school purchasing a specialized set of equipment or materials when public library patrons could not have access to it in the evenings, weekends, or summers. One librarian would rather see something done in the area of cost sharing.

LEVEL 2—INFORMAL COMMUNICATION

The elementary schools on a sporadic basis provide the public library with titles on their Honors Reading program list; the public library makes every effort to acquire those titles which are not in their collection.

Both the reference and children's department address requests to all local schools asking the schools to keep them advised on possible areas of study that the schools will be concentrating on. The reference department develops subject bibliographies to complement these assignments.

As an extension of the public library's sponsorship of Literacy Volunteers, the public library also acquires high-interest, low-reading materials for students enrolled in the adult basis education program.

To date, the public library's efforts have not resulted in an equal result, but they will continue to pursue cooperative collection development.

LEVEL 3—FORMAL COMMUNICATION

The children's librarian makes an annual visit to many of the elementary classrooms during Book Week to promote the idea of getting library cards and to encourage students to use the library. Conversely, the classes make visits to the public library to take out books and learn about available resources.

Library skills are taught to elementary students by the school librarian who also promotes public library use, particularly during the summer months.

The librarians also recommend good programs to one another. Recently, a series of films on peace was shown at the public library. In attendance were teachers and their students.

LEVEL 4—FORMAL COOPERATION

Formal planning was instituted when the school housed a professional collection purchased with public library funds. A fire burned the collection; insurance money paid for replacements and the schools have maintained the collection themselves since 1975.

A second development occurred when the technical high school was about to open and had neither a librarian nor a library collection. The young adult librarian at the public library recommended a basic book collection and continues to work closely with the librarian who is now on staff at the technical school.

An outstanding example of collection development occurred to 1983 when public and school media services filmstrip holdings were inventoried and a union list produced by the school media services coordinator.

For 1984–85, the public library budget recommended and has received funds to clean the school system's 16mm collection as well as to start repairing the school system's AV equipment.

LEVEL 5—RESOURCE SHARING

The public library recently sponsored a computer seminar for interested residents. The large crowd was attributed to the notion that the hot topic was computer literacy. Included among the speakers was one of the teachers who had helped introduce microcomputers into the school system. She was assisted by some of her students who demonstrated the ways in which they were using microcomputers in the classroom. Other speakers were from the Yale Microcomputer User's Group and a representative of a local business who demonstrated how his computer aided him in the running of his company.

The results of a survey passed out prior to the seminar and collected later showed that nearly half of those in attendance either owned, worked with, or were considering the purchase of a microcomputer. The survey also indicated there was a high level of "micro-anxiety." Paramount, was the question of each person's ability to cope with the change computers bring.

The library addressed the problem of "micro-anxiety" by making it a primary goal of the library. It was felt computer literacy was a further enhancement of the public literacy problem the library was addressing the town. The library also needed to prepare its own staff for the advent of computers in the library.

It goes without saying, all of the above goals had to be accomplished with little or no money.

The library purchased two microcomputers and turned the basement into a computer lab. Equipment was added through the gift of two television sets from the Friends of the Library. Library staff was trained by the library director. The second step was to circulate the computers to the public. At the end of a week most borrowers were able to operate the computer successfully and do simple programming in BASIC.

The children's librarian expressed a desire to somehow tie in computers with the annual summer reading program. Coinciding with this was the start of a club formed to exchange computer software. All three members were regular library users and they were all 12 years old. The children's librarian had a planning meeting with the teacher for the Gifted and Talented in the middle school. The children's librarian shared her ideas, found a warm and enthusiastic response and together they developed the Compu-Kids Program.

The plan was simple and effective.

The school system was already education young people in the use of computers and computer programming. These skills were ones the public library wished to foster on a community-wide basis. The public library asked for volunteers from the pool of computer-wise youngsters to work at the library during the summer, providing one-to-one contact for those who wished to learn how to operate a micro and do simple programming.

During a six-week period, 30 volunteers helped to usher 700 people into the computer age.

The public library benefited by providing a new service. The students had an opportunity to share their knowledge and have access to the equipment, the schools benefited from townspeople witnessing the fruits of their education tax dollars at work and the town benefited by having a more computer-conscious and computer-literate populace. The library also received loans of equipment as well as donations.

They are currently exploring the possiblity of creating their own AV materials, pooling talent and equipment and sharing the results.

LEVEL 6—FORMAL PLANNING

The town Library Council was formed in 1964 as the Library-School Council. The council's name evolved in the mid-1970's to the town Library Council to better represent current goals and a broader-based membership.

The purpose of the council is to facilitate communication and cooperation between school libraries, the public library and other libraries in the community. The council promotes an understanding of the mutual problems and concerns within the participating agencies and improvement of services to the common constituents. The council also offers an opportunity for continuing education for its members through guest speakers, special programs and field trips.

The council membership consists of librarians from each public school library, public library staff, representative from the Board of Education, Library Board of Trustees, private and academic school librarians and the owner of the local book store. The council meets monthly from September to June and annually elects a President and a Secretary.

Selected projects to date include recommendations leading to establishing professional library positions in the elementary schools, book selection policy for school libraries and cooperative grant writing.

The town public library recently involved teachers in the planning for a new library building by utilizing a survey that was designed to ascertain teacher's expectations of public library service to student users. The survey enabled the public library staff to incorporate teacher input into the plan in terms of services and materials the public library should supply, staffing patterns needed and functional layout of the library building. Survey results were analyzed and workshops held to discuss the differences between expectations and services that are actually offered.

Benefits included increased cooperation between school and public library staffs, between teachers and librarians and common goal setting for library service in the town.

Even within our small state cooperation and cooperative collection development exist at many levels. There are numerous variables that currently effect what can and will be done cooperatively. We believe that new technological developments, the increase in the amount of information and resources available and potential budget restraints will make cooperation and cooperative collection development more of a necessity than a choice for the future. Yet, in spite of these factors, the success of any cooperative effort lies not in the magic of the machinery and the "things" available, but with the human communication that forms the true foundation for working together.

REFERENCE NOTES

1. John Naisbitt, *Megatrends* (New York, Warner Books Edition, 1984), p. 16.
2. *Ibid,* p. 17.
3. Lucille Thomas, "Building School Library Media Collections," *The Book-mark,* Fall, 1982, p. 16–19.

Cooperative Materials Purchasing Among School and Public Libraries: Focus on Indiana

Mary Ellen Kennedy

Cooperative acquisition of materials by school and public libraries as discussed with special attention paid to joint selection meetigs, sharing of audiovisual orders, and centralized purchasing arrangements. Research indicates that this is an area of cooperation which could be highly beneficial to the participating libraries.

Collection management has taken on a new meaning in elementary school library media centers since the time when federal money first flooded into the schools in the mid-1960s. Today, budgets are smaller and personnel scarcer, while the demand for information and service remains high. Because of the need to get materials to users as quickly as possible, when they need it, library media centers in schools have attempted to maintain collections that meet at least minimum service needs. With these collections being uneven in quality, some form of cooperation among schools and other librarians is necessary to supply patron needs. Besides interacting among themselves, schools have the possiblity of working with public and other libraries in formal or informal arrangements. The topic of this paper is cooperation rather than the merging of services, and, as an example, I will discuss cooperative purchasing of materials in the state of Indiana.

The few studies of cooperation and joint purchasing among school and public libraries include those of Woolls,[1] Fleming,[2]

Dr. Kennedy is Assistant Professor and Reference Librarian at Purdue University, West Lafayette, Indiana.

197

Baker,[3] Aaron,[4] Doll,[5] and Roderer.[6] Four of these six studies concentrated geographically within two states, Illinois and Indiana. Although describing generally local practices, these studies employ research methodology that could be replicated for investigation in other parts of the country, and they may be useful in paving the way for cooperative purchasing of materials.

Woolls, in her 1973 doctoral study, noted that cooperative purchasing yielded financial savings, avoided unnecessary duplication, and concentrated, rather than decentralized, technical processes. Despite these advantages, little evidence existed to show that school and public libraries really have attempted to undertake joint purchasing, even through preliminary efforts like planning meetings between school and public librarians. The few meetings that Woolls described were informal.[7]

Beyond these meetings, there was no sharing of book lists and audio visual orders except in the case of one school library supervisor who sent copies of audiovisual and book orders to the public libraries.[8] Exhibits of materials to induce joint ordering were prepared by less than half of the public library respondents. Further, Woolls found no centralized purchasing existed among any of her respondents.[9]

Despite the prevailing fear of librarians that their functions may be diminished by cooperative services—joint purchasing being one such venture—this issue needs to be addressed in light of the demands made on libraries today. Any unique holdings of a library provide the opportunity for offering tailored services, which in turn should prove more cost effective. Within a specific geographic area, each group of holdings can be used to answer distinctive user needs and possibly increase library use. As Fleming points out, "cooperative planning of materials . . . can enlarge resources by avoiding duplication of needed but less used expensive items . . ."[10]

In addition to those expensive materials used by librarians, teachers and children, professional materials for teachers and librarians can be obtained through complementary acquistion plans.[11] Complementary acquisition or purchasing is the building of collections that fill different information needs of the same patron or patrons. Journals critical to book selection, audiovisual, and computer materials can also be acquired effectively through joint purchase by school and public libraries. Fleming also notes (as did Woolls) that lower costs are a benefit of joint school and public library purchase. Perhaps a beginning might be made through exchanges ·in bibliographies, and creation of union lists.[12]

The INNS Project (The Indiana National Network Study) reviewed the network development in the state of Indiana. Among items presented in the report was that concerning the Indiana Department of Public Instruction. While not a network, it is a vital part of the school's participation in any network plan. Among the responsibilities of this agency are development of standards for school library programs, coordination of school library media programs with the other libraries in the state, and the administration of federal funds under ESEA Title IV-B.[13]

The Indiana Department of Public Instruction also works with the Indiana networking system to promote greater participation of the school library media centers in the network activities and services.[14] With regard to activity that promotes materials acquisition the Area Library Services Authorities (ALSA), as one network group, offer opportunities for cooperative purchases and thereby financial savings to all libraries.[15] The ALSAs assist in reference, and resource sharing, generally, and count among their several achievements since their creation the work in cooperative acquisition. INCOLSA, (The Indiana Cooperative Library Services Authority) through technological developments has made the job of cooperative purchasing easier through more accurate and complete bibliographic records. Both of these networks in different ways have been effective agents in bringing the public schools of Indiana into resource sharing. Research in the INNS Project did note some barriers to cooperation. These are associated primarily with lack of dependable funding and equitable distribution of resources.[16]

Shirley Aaron covered literature on school and public library cooperation, and cited the effect of early legislation in the 1960s, as the ESEA Title II funds were used for building school library collections.[17] Aaron stated that "the task of cooperatively developing or adding to existing resources has not been pursued as vigorously as that of cooperatively developing devices to locate and mobilize existing collections for use."[18] Complementary purchasing has not been exploited to its fullest as much as has interlibrary loan.

Carol Doll's study on overlap in school and public library collections reflects another research method applied to assessing school library collections, and one that, as mentioned previously, could be replicated elsewhere. This research should have pertinence to shared purchasing, as well as to other operations under the rubric of resource sharing. Doll's data were gathered from collections in four Illinois communities of roughly 30,000 population each. She assessed the collections of two elementary school libraries and one public library in each community. In this survey, overlap in collections was considered to exist among material in several formats—filmstrips, sound recordings, magazines and books. One object of the research was to study the amount of collection overlap between public and elementary school library collections.

Among her findings, Doll noted that average overlap between school and public libraries approached nearly 50 percent.[19] In some nonbook areas, as spoken fiction and magazines, the public libraries in this study had stonger collections, while school libraries had larger collections of science film strips, for instance, than did public libraries.[20] Doll had noted in a previous discussion of overlap research, including that in her own doctoral dissertation, that overlap may be as much as 45 percent between two libraries, meaning that percentage of the collection will be held in common by the two libraries, while 55 percent will represent titles held by only one of the libraries. Doll emphasized that "libraries could evaluate the pattern of overlap and use results of the study to set up a cooperative selection policy."[21]

Nancy Roderer in her report for King Research on the Indiana Networking System discussed all of the networks in the state as they existed in the early 1980s. Specifically, the report cited cooperative purchasing as a function within the purview of the ALSAs[22]—Area Library Service Authoriites created under the Library Services Authority Act of 1967.[23] However, another agency which also contributes to cooperative purchasing is the Indiana Library Film Service, which does so by making 16 mm films available to other libraries. Its members provide financial support to the agency.[24] These two agencies then contribute most directly to this form of cooperation. The King Report defines this form of cooperation as

> an extension of resource sharing concept inherent in interlibrary loan; it applies to materials not required in the local collection . . . (and) it contributes to the collective provision of information resources across the state of Indiana in a cost-effective way.[25]

Any lack of formal cooperative purchasing is due to the fact that libraries have not structured the means to undertake the operation in any large scale. That some cooperative purchasing does indeed exist is shown by activities of the Area Library Service Authorities, and the Indiana Library Film Service.

In 1982, a new project was undertaken by Blanche Woolls and the author. Data were gathered by questionnaires constructed to draw impressions of cooperation in any form that existed between public libraries and school library media centers. School and public libraries in this study were a selected sample based on Woolls' 1973 research. Not all libraries from the 1973 study participated in 1982 either because they did not wish to, or because they were excluded due to changes in their structure. Data obtained in the new project deal with cooperation in several senses, but for this discussion, only those data concerned with cooperative acquisitions will be considered.

With few exceptions, the data did not reveal the existence of cooperation between school and public libraries in purchasing. Specifically, a survey of 22 school librarians (library supervisors) showed that only one had a joint materials selection meeting with public library staff. No one sent the public library staffs copies of book orders or of audiovisual orders. All but one of the 22 school librarians surveyed answered "no" to the question "Do you centrally purchase library materials with public library?" One responded with "don't know." Among some open ended responses to this part of the questionnaire, one school librarian suggested that knowing new titles purchased by the public library would be helpful. This respondent felt that should the public library approach the school library regarding cooperative selection, the school would gladly cooperate. Another school librarian felt that budget limitations in public and school libraries should make cooperation imperative and, furthermore, would enhance book selection with a greater variety for patrons of both types of libraries.

Public librarians on the other hand, had a slightly higher degree of positive perception of the amount of cooperation that existed between public and school libraries. Of 19 total responses, 16 librarians said they did not hold joint meetings with elementary school librarians. Three of those answered "not applicable." Two public librarians replied that they sent the schools copies of their book orders and audiovisual orders. Thirteen said they did not. Four of the 19 surveyed did not answer those questions. To the question "Does the public library provide exhibits of materials for selection purposes?" Five public librarians said "yes"; one said "Occasionally"; and one said "sometimes." Twelve of the responses were "no." All of the 19 respondents said "no" to the question, "Do you centrally purchase library materials with elementary schools?"

In summary, recent investigation indicates that very little formal arrangement for cooperation in purchasing is being undertaken in Indiana. The case for such cooperative acquisitions or shared purchasing is borne out in the two investigations done in Indiana, wherein cooperative library services were discussed. The necessity for cooperative services overall, and within them, cooperative purchasing, is recognized. One investigation recognized the need for enhancing cooperative services within the state. Other research presented rationales such as collection overlap among libraries used by essentially the same clientele and general fiscal savings through this method.

Notwithstanding the benefits of cooperative purchasing, the practice is not widespread. Perhaps inertia is also a causitive factor in the lack of visible and planned joint acquisitions, in addition to fear of loss of autonomy. More research should be done on this area of library cooperation to determine if any successful programs have existed in the past or present. The little literature available on the topic indicates that this method of library cooperation is viable, fiscally positive, and service oriented.

REFERENCES

1. Esther Blanche Sutton Woolls, *Comparative Library Services to Children in Public Libraries and Public School Systems in Selected Communities in Indiana* (Ann Arbor: University Microforms, 1973).

2. Lois D. Fleming, "Public and School Libraries: Partners in the Big Picture," *School Library Media Quarterly* 7(Fall 1978): 25–30.

3. Harold E. Baker, *The Development of a Plan for the Integration of Indiana Libraries into the National Program for Libraries and Information Science: The INNS Project, Final Report* (Indianapolis, Indiana: Indiana State Library, 1979).

4. Shirley L. Aaron, *School/Public Library Cooperation: A State of the Art Review* (Syracuse, New York: ERIC Clearinghouse on Information Resources, 1980). Contract No. 400-77-0015. ERIC ED 192-810.

5. Carol A. Doll, "School and Public Library Collection Overlap and the Implications for Networking: An Analysis of Collections in School and Public Libraries," *School Library Media Quarterly* 11(Spring 1983): 193–199.

6. Nancy K. Roderer and Carolyn J. Goshen, *An Evaluation of the Indiana Network of Cooperative Services: Final Report* (Rockville, Maryland: King Research, 1983).

7. Woolls, *Comparative Library Services to Children*, 100.

8. Ibid., 101.

9. Ibid., 101–102.

10. Fleming, "Public and School Libraries," 26–27.

11. Ibid., 28.

12. Ibid., 27–28.

13. Baker, *Development of a Plan for the Integration of Indiana Libraries*, 85.

14. Ibid., 86.

15. Ibid., 104.

16. Ibid., 106–107.

17. Aaron, *School/Public Library Cooperation*, 9.

18. Ibid., 11.

19. Doll, "School and Public Library Collection Overlap and Its Implications for Networking," 196.

20. Ibid., 197.

21. Carol A. Doll, "Overlap Studies of Library Collections in School and Public Libraries," (Dissertation Research at the University of Illinois). *Public Libraries* 21(Spring 1982): 33–34.

22. Roderer, *An Evaluation of the Indiana Network of Cooperative Services*, 22.

23. Ibid., 16.

24. Ibid., 29.

25. Ibid., 60.

Collection Development and Resource Sharing in the Combined School/Public Library

Lawrence Lewis Jaffe

The elements which affect shared collection development and resource sharing as they relate to the combined school/public library are identified. Suggestions from librarians in such situations are included.

The combined school/public library refers to a library that is operated for both school and community patrons, often with coordination of services and collection development. Libraries employing a combined structure have usually received negative treatment in library literature with recommendations to abandon such service arrangements. Despite this unfavorable treatment, the interest in and use of combined libraries persists, primarily due to lack of funds and community desires to maximize the use of physical facilities. School libraries are frequently closed during evenings and summers with frequent community pressures to open for public use.

The author's dissertation, completed in 1982, considered past and existing combined school/public libraries in Pennsylvania. Among components of this study were collection development and resource sharing. It is the purpose of this article to relate findings concerning collection development and resource sharing without promoting or discouraging the use of the combined concept. Difficulties and solutions to problems

Dr. Jaffe is a librarian in the Downingtown School District of Pennsylvania and serves as an adjunct faculty member of the Villanova University Graduate School of Library and Information Science.

in combined libraries often have an application to other forms of cooperative arrangements and even those who oppose their use may benefit from understanding their processes. Additionally, the topic continues to receive attention in the literature.

The dissertation was divided into three major sections. The first section related information on combined school/public libraries that had stopped functioning since 1965. The primary purpose of this examination was to determine reasons for cessation. Findings in this portion of the study were determined principally by employing the techniques of historical research. The second and third sections considered the eleven combined school/public libraries in Pennsylvania. These libraries were located and visited in East Lansdowne, Harmonsburg, Jersey Shore, Kane (two), Leechburg, Linesville, Millersburg, Pennsburg, Perryopolis and Royersford. The towns and surrounding service areas were primarily rural or suburban. Categories for data collected in field visits to combined school/public libraries were service area, staff, facilities, collection, resource sharing and governance. The methodology for this portion of the study employed principally the procedures of survey or descriptive research. The categories of collection and resource sharing have been reconsidered for this article and suggestions for addressing difficulties will be included.

MATERIALS SELECTION

Collection development is a complex and challenging function for all libraries and combined libraries may, because of their form, have unique circumstances and procedures. Combined school/public libraries often acquire materials by dissimilar methods in the school and public sectors. This variance may result from a school and public librarian selecting materials with different funding sources or for varying patron groups. For example, the study determined that in five libraries, the school librarian served students chiefly while the public librarian worked primarily with other patrons. In such arrangements, cooperative selection may not be possible as the school and public librarian may not have common working schedules. Incidentally, selection for a particular patron group may overlap as is often the case with children who have the potential to fall into both student and public service categories. In six libraries, one librarian served both school and public sectors. One librarian may also be responsible to two governing boards (e.g., school board and town council) and subsequent funding sources.

As with all aspects of managing a combined library, there must be sustained cooperation and consultation to avoid duplication of resources and materials. Differing budgetary sources may present accounting difficulties as purchases may involve dissimilar procedures. Efforts to combine ordering in the school and public sectors may be useful as higher discount schedules from jobbers or publishers may be achieved. School libraries including those that are combinations have often been required to order books and materials once a year. Public libraries have had a better opportunity to expend funds throughout a year and thus meet demands and react to special offers and "sales" as they occur. No library or sector (i.e., school or public) should be required to order books and materials only once a year.

Budget constraints and collection development decisions have often restricted the purchase of audiovisual materials by public libraries. This is particularly evident for instructional software such as filmstrip/records or filmstrip/cassettes. Schools have traditionally led the way in the purchase of non-book materials, partially due to the influx of Elementary and Secondary Education Act funds. Adult patrons of combined school/public libraries may have a unique advantage in gaining access to such collections.

Audiovisual collections are not the only specialized collection that can contribute to public, academic, and special libraries. *The Role of the School Library Media Program in Networking*[1] expands potential school library media collection strengths to include the following:

> Professional Libraries
> Specialized Ethnic Collections
> Career Education Collections
> High Interest/Low Reading Level Collections
> Foreign Language Materials
> Collections of Children's and Young Adult Literature

Collections for Special Students (handicapped, gifted, etc.)

Where present, such collections are directly available to the public library patron in the combined school/public library.

Combined school/public librarians invariably cited their need for additional space. As noted in their observations, the lack of space may or may not be directly attributable to the combined nature of the library. A combined school/public library does not lessen the demand for adequate facilities, either in size or layout. In fact, the special problems of serving a diverse patron group from one facility increases the need for advanced planning of design. Space shortages and inability to isolate a particular service area (e.g., display of adult fiction, storytelling) may have direct effects on collection development.

The storage of periodicals is another frequent difficulty for small libraries and combined school/public libraries are no exception. Many small libraries house back issues that are coordinated with the *Abridged Readers' Guide to Periodical Literature*. The cost of a small microfiche reader is low and the retention of periodicals on microfiche might be explored where space is lacking.

Combined school/public librarians did not report an unusual restraint on selection due to the combined nature and access of children to adult books. However, many librarians observed vigilance in restricting the adult collection to adults. Correspondingly, public patrons were obliged to wait for school-owned materials if they were being used by students with a school related assignment. In most cases, school and public books were intershelved and one card catalog used for both sectors. In such cases, the librarian may be the only individual who can determine ownership from the shelflist or memory.

The use and scope of written selection policies varies greatly in combined school/public libraries. The study determined that more public sectors are without formal selection policies than school sectors. Only one library had a unified policy for both the school and public sectors. It is recommended that all libraries have a written selection policy that considers philosophies, objectives, procedures and problems of selection in both the school and public realm. Since a combined library may be governed by both a school and public library board, a selection policy should be approved and adopted by each agency responsible for administration.

Divisions of staff, responsibilities and governance suggest consideration of one selection policy for school and public sectors. Review of a hypothetical situation may help in understanding how one policy can assist in a coordinated response by two sectors. A school student may check out a public library title which is subsequently questioned by a parent for appropriateness. The procedures for reviewing a challenged title should serve the school and public sectors with equal effectiveness and this is best accomplished by a shared selection policy which carefully deliniates operational procedures and decision-making authority. One policy must be approved and adopted by all boards responsible for governance.

Most combined school/public libraries studied did have a functioning interlibrary loan system. Almost all libraries were part of a public library system and obtained (and offered) materials on interlibrary loan. Most libraries had access to films through an intermediate unit (county-wide school support unit) or district center. Small collection size increases the need for an efficient interlibrary loan system. To facilitate interlibrary loans between small libraries, librarians must develop and acquire union catalogs in bound or machine-readable formats for use directly by patrons. The high cost of purchasing films and nonprint materials compel the use of a film circuit or low-cost rentals. Combined school/public libraries, as most libraries, must engage in activities that share costly resources.

Part of the survey instrument in the author's study involved the identification of strengths and weaknesses that had been commonly noted as associated with combined school/public libraries. A major identification tool for this effort was a checklist that had been developed from an overview of the literature and revised during an earlier pilot study of the interview testing instrument. In addition to the checklist, respondents were given the opportunity to expand the list. The following selection relates only the findings within the scope of this paper although strengths and weaknesses were identified in other areas.

Of the sixteen persons interviewed, eight indicated that the combined library had enabled students to cultivate a greater appreciation for the potential importance of the public library after their graduation from the school system. Eight also indicated that the combined facility had enabled them to meet the needs of students with adult reading and reference requirements, while twelve considered that parents with children in their schools had been more likely to discover the library for their own (parental) reading needs. Ten individuals indicated that parents were more apt to take an active interest in the reading of their children because they could visit the combined library togehter. Two respondents felt that the public librarian could respond quickly and efficiently to assignments by teachers due to the close relationship with the school. Ten respondents also considered that the combined arrangement facilitated the return of materials to the library. For example, the school librarian may request and pressure students to return overdue public library materials.

Respondents were also asked to indicate any problems that originated or were more pronounced because of the combined nature of their libraries. One respondent noted that differing goals of the school and public library may preclue substantial coordination of purchases, programs and services. As noted previously, overcrowding of storage and shelving was considered a significant problem and cited by seven respondents. In conclusion, most librarians noted the special contributions combined libraries made in their communities. Fewer librarians cited weaknesses in their libraries due to their *combined* nature. Problems were frequently noted but were not attributed to the *combined* structure.

FRAMEWORK OF SUCCESS

One of the primary products of the study was the development of a framework of success for a combined school/public library. The analyses for formulating this framework were based on the author's review of both the literature and survey data. Additionally, although a standardized survey instrument was used in each interview, information was frequently shared by respondents outside the *specific* realm of the survey instrument. These explanations, frequently confidential, were not discouraged. Openness by respondents may have been nurtured by noting to respondents that the researcher was not involved in evaluating a specific library. These frank revelations were significant factors to consider and the framework provided a vehicle to relate practical suggestions without violating confidence. The framework of success may serve those considering the establishment of a combined school/public library as well as those involved in reevaluation of an existing combined library. Since most of the elements in the framework are composed of or have an impact on collection development and resource sharing, all are included.

The categories in the framework were staff, facilities, collection, resource sharing and governance. There are many constraints in developing and using such recommendations. First, only five factors have been studied in a service institution that could include many other factors. It is not without risk to generalize from a small population and it is extremely difficult to judge the success of a library in a standardized and comparative manner. For example, collection size and circulation records in village of 2000 cannot be contrasted to the services offered by a library with a potential service population of 20,000. A smaller library may have greater activity with interlibrary loans from a nearby district center, and this may obscure comparisons and generalizations made just on collection size. Because of the variety of responses, partly due to the lack of standardization of record keeping, development of ordinal scales was considered inappropriate for this research. Even the quantitative measurements such as collection size, facility dimensions and circulation records do not address the human factors of a service profession. These qualities are complex but must be considered as critical operational factors in the success or failure of a library program. Many of the communities with combined school/public libraries would have minimal or no public library service without the combined arrangement.

The framework developed for this research is not prescriptive nor is it associated with the successes or failures of any one library. This subjective framework is a generalization of many factors and may require adaption or exclusion to a particular circumstance. The framework is composed of five summary statements called elements. To enhance understanding, brief preliminary statements are offered for staff, facilities and governance. Collections and resource sharing elements have already been considered in this paper and stand alone. Further discussion and specific suggestions relating to each element can be found in the author's dissertation.

Staff

Adequate staffing is a problem reported by most libraries and combined school/public libraries are no exception. In many instances, volunteers are functioning in key positions and it is doubtful that services could continue without their assistance. Also, a combined school/public library with one librarian may be spreading the efforts of one individual over an intolerable threshold of expectations. The importance of sufficient clerical staff cannot be overstated for any library. The combined school/public library requires the further need of coordinating training for staff that may be working with the same equipment and accessories (e.g., card catalog, shelflist) at different times under different librarians. In addition, efficient means of communication between support personnel is necessary.

Element one. The combined school/public library requires as a minimum, one school and one public librarian working with adequate support personnel in a framework that permits mutual planning and application of goals and services.

Facilities

Combined school/public librarians invariably cited their need for more space. As noted in their observations, the lack of space may or may not be directly attributable to the combined nature of a library. A combined school/public library does not lessen the demand for adequate facilities, either in size or layout. In fact, the special problems of serving a diverse patron group from one facility increases the need for advanced planning of design. The geographical location of a combined school/public library is a consideration that involves a need for compromise with a location serving both school and public patrons.

Element two. The combined school/public library should be

designed in advance of use with adequate space and selected separate areas for school, public and staff use.

Collection

Element three. The combined school/public library must strive to select and acquire a balanced collection for all patrons and establish the most simple and useful means of access to materials.

Resource Sharing

Element four. The combined school/public library must aggresively develop and participate in formal mechanisms for resource sharing (e.g., networks).

Governance

Combined school/public libraries may have one or two governing boards. Although two boards, school and public, generally indicate employment of both a school and public librarian, there are instances of one librarian responsible to two boards. The number of boards does not seem as significant as the ability to develop means of communication and cooperation when dual governing bodies are in place for one library. A useful method of coordinating an exchange between two boards has been used with success by one combined school/public library and involves one member sitting on both boards.

A formal agreement must exist when there is the slightest possiblity that one funding source might withdraw support and place total library service in jeopardy. Since board members change and community attitudes toward taxation can change, some agreement should be made for a contractual obligation relating to funds. Legal council with appropriate experience should be retained for such arrangements.

Element five. In the combined school/public library, governing structures and channels of authority must be formally established in order to permit efficient decision-making and resolution of conflicts without abandonment by any party of financial support without due and proper notice.

A simplified visual for the framework previously developed appears at the conclusion of this article.

The decision to establish or retain a combined school/public library may be extraordinarily difficult. Many objective and subjective considerations must be formulated and weighed in making such a decision. The current literature has begun to present practical suggestions and caveats for an agreement of library service that will seemingly persist. Those facing determinations involving the status of combined school/public libraries are referred to the selected bibliography at the conclusion of this article.

COMBINED SCHOOL/PUBLIC LIBRARY ELEMENTS OF SUCCESS

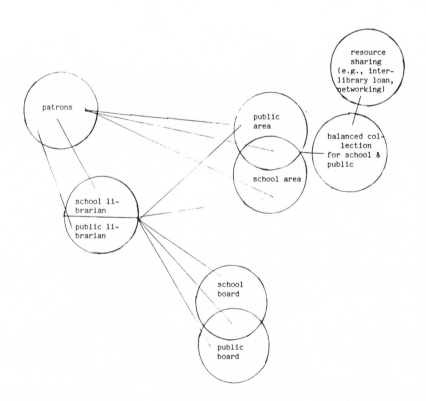

REFERENCE NOTE

1. Task Force on the Role of the School Library Media Program in the National Program, National Commission on Libraries and Information Science. *The Role of the School Library Media Program in Networking.* (Washington, D.C.: National Commission on Libraries and Information Science, 1978.)

SUGGESTED READINGS

Aaron, Shirley L., and Sue O. Smith. *A Study of the Combined School/Public Library, Phase I.* Tallahassee, Florida: Florida State University, 1977.

――――. *A Study of the Combined School/Public Library, Phase II.* Tallahassee, Florida: Florida State University, 1978.

――――. *A Study of the Combined School/Public Library, Phase III.* Tallahassee, Florida: Florida State University, 1978.

Jaffe, Lawrence L. *The Combined School/Public Library in Pennsylvania.* Ann Arbor, Michigan: University Microfilms International, 1982.

Woolard, Wilma Lee Boughton. *Combined School/Public Libraries: A Survey with Conclusions and Recommendations.* Metuchen, N.J.: The Scarecrow Press, 1980.

SECTION IV
COLLECTIONS MANAGEMENT
IN PARTICULAR AREAS
AND FORMATS

This section includes subject areas such as mathematics (Blazek) and religion (Howard) as well as collecting in particular formats such as periodicals (Bury), government documents (Jay), films (Hunt), video (Short and Gothberg) and computer software (Swigger).

Reviewing Journals in Mathematics for School Librarians and Teachers

Ron Blazek

Based on reviews of mathematics materials published during 1983 in general review journals as well as more specialized journals of science and mathematics, reviews of books and media were compared. Numbers of reviews, and their uniqueness or overlap were studied. A summary of findings and recommendations regarding selection of mathematics materials conclude the paper.

CURRENT REVIEWS IN MATHEMATICS
FOR SCHOOL MEDIA SPECIALISTS AND TEACHERS:
A COMPARISON OF JOURNAL UTILITY FOR SELECTION

Nearly ten years ago, this investigator identified the lack of communication between mathematics teachers and school media specialists as the chief factor in limiting the library media center's contribution to the mathematics instructional program.[1] Mathematics had been designated a minor user of the library in an earlier study conducted by the National Education Association,[2] and we felt, at the time, that the potential for the media center would be realized only if teachers and media specialists become more familiar with the work of one another in creating and nurturing the learning environment. A mathematics bibliography course, common to both parties, was recommended to provide much needed awareness of the great variety of instructional media available and to afford an opportunity for both teachers and media specialists to work out strategies of service. It was felt that building a useful

Professor Blazek is at the School of Library and Information Studies, Florida State University.

219

collection of subject materials was integral to the ultimate success of the enterprise.

Since then, much has been written on the necessity for systematic collection development, with at least some attention being given to the subject of mathematics at the pre-college level. Barber and Mancall, in the pages of this journal, reported their study examining the citations used in high school student papers with respect to their presence (or absence) in nineteen retrospective-type selection tools and best book lists. Noting a lack of coverage in these subjects, they stated that "Both librarians and the compilers of those tools seem to feel uncomfortable with books on science and math . . . underscores a demonstrable weakness in the compilation of these tools."[3]

Bonk and Magrill, in their well-known text, reaffirm the difficulty for any type of library in selecting sound, up-to-date appealing materials in science since most librarians have no background in the subject and feel alien and uncomfortable in it. The authors concluded that good selection tools were needed here even more than they were needed in the familiar areas of the curriculum.[4] Gardner, in a later publication, praised the role of the National Council of Teachers of Mathematics (NCTM) in taking responsibility for aiding retrospective collection development in school libraries with its well-known lists, *The High School Mathematics Library* and *Mathematics Library: Elementary and Junior High School.*[5]

The process of collection development for media specialists has been aided considerably with the publication of three recent texts by Cabeceiras, Taylor and Van Orden, all of which focus on the school library media center. Although these titles do not target the subject of mathematics as a line of inquiry, their concern for a systematically developed well-balanced collection should prove useful in this regard.[6] Some of their concerns are also found in the writings which treat school libraries as one of several fields of study. Dudley's model of school library operations would include the appointment of a faculty library committee or the help of interested teachers and the creation of evaluation centers and coordinators in large systems.[7] Katz recognizes the importance of cooperation with his emphasis on the well-established dictum for school media specialists to work first with teachers to influence students.[8] Bonk and Magrill detail the need for cooperation between faculty, staff, and students with the media specialist acting as coordinator in the process of selection. Teachers know the subject and their students' capabilities; students are the final judges of what benefits them and the media specialists are aware of the composition of the collection.[9]

The selection aspect of collection development was the concern of the present study, therefore, it is revealing to note the more recent bibliographic efforts in mathematics. In addition to the previously mentioned NCTM publications, there are the *AAAS Science Book List Supplement*[10] and the annual lists of mathematics media from the North Carolina State Department of Education.[11] Tabler's article enumerates basic math skills and suggests titles of books that can be used to develop them further.[12] Also, less directly concerned with mathematics but giving it some attention are additional listings and reports emanating from state and city departments of education for purposes of curriculum improvement.[13]

Most important to us at this time, however, is the literature which addresses the subject of current journal reviews as opposed to retrospective lists. Hamlin establishes reviews as one of nine categories of selection sources. Reviews appear in the library press, specialized subject journals, general interest periodicals, and newspapers, and they are considered the best source of information for current popular items.[14] Taylor's nation-wide survey of school media specialists reported the titles of the most frequently used selection tools. As we might expect, all but two, (*Wilson Catalog* Series and *The Elementary School Library Collection*) were periodical in nature. Only one (New York Times Book Review) was not from the library press.[15] Katz recommends a number of journal titles for reviews, seven of which do not appear on the Taylor listing.[16] Van Orden describes the utility of review journals designed either for teachers or media specialists working with students of different grade levels. *Mathematics Teacher* is recommended for junior high school to college teaching and *Arithmetic Teacher* for elementary school.[17] It was felt that in using recommendations from Katz, Taylor and Van Orden, a relatively complete listing of journals considered useful for reviewing purposes was compiled.

Given the difficulties attendant the provision of high caliber library service to the mathematics component of the curriculum in both elementary and secondary schools, and the dearth of literature, especially research reporting, on the topic, the area of collection development offers a fruitful field of investigation. The purpose of this study was to examine the performance of well-known recommended journals for library media specialists and teachers by comparing their capacity to deliver reviews of mathematics books and audio-visual media relevant to the teaching/learning situation from elementary through high school age.

The investigator's earlier study relied on the existing collection in a junior high school to develop a strategy of curriculum support, and labeled teacher influence as the motivating force in creating or encouraging student use. Now it is incumbent to determine how useful and up-to-date those existing collections might be by examining the utility of review journals and review departments in journals with respect to their potential for selection. In concentrating on selection, this study is seen as a first and necessary step in the development of a collection management policy for school library media centers. In effect, it tests the efficiency or effectiveness of those tools which might be used by media specialists and teachers to develop and maintain an up-to-date working collection. It must, by necessity, represent also the first stage in a successful media center service program in its support of mathematics instruction.

RESEARCH QUESTIONS

The following research questions were posed:

1. How do general journals compare to specialized subject journals in frequency and proportion of reviews of relevant mathematics books and audiovisual media?
2. How do general journals compare to specialized subject journals in frequency and proportion of relevant mathematics titles reviewed?
3. How do books compare to audio-visual media in mathematics with respect to frequency of titles reviewed only

once and those reviewed more than once, and what is the proportion of such duplication?

4. How do general journals compare to specialized journals in proportion of total review file given to relevant mathematics reviews?

5. How do general journals compare to specialized journals in uniqueness and duplication of relevant reviews of mathematics books and audio-visual media?

METHODOLOGY

The identification of reviews represented the use of documentary research techniques within a descriptive methodology. We focused on the totality of reviews considered relevant to the discipline of mathematics from elementary grades through high school as found in seventeen leading journals for one calendar year, 1983. The journals were determined through the use of collection development texts mentioned earlier, and represent titles commonly found in schools and available to both media specialists and teachers. Thirteen of these titles were placed in the category of "general journals," that is, their reviews were not limited to any particular subject discipline. Four of these titles composed a category of "specialized journals," in which the reviews were limited either to science/mathematics items or mathematics alone.

The two categories represent excellent points of comparison in terms of their utility for collection building in the subject area. In general, it was felt that school media specialists do not examine specialized publications in the same systematic and routine manner in which they do the general journals. If we are to believe Bonk and Magrill as well as Barber and Mancall, there is a distinct possibility that school media specialists may purposely avoid the NCTM efforts, *The Mathematics Teacher* and *The Arithmetic Teacher,* due to their aversion to the subject. Thus it becomes a matter of importance to examine the value of such publications in providing useful reviews.

Since this study was designed to examine the "totality" of relevant items, it embraced reviews of both books and audiovisual media for both professional and student audiences. Reviews of textbooks were included as well since they would be of interest to teachers especially, but columns devoted solely to reference books were not examined. The focus then, was on trade books, either student or processional, for the media center collection and text books for the teachers. Audio-visual media represented six categories of reviews with "multi-media kits" defined as a packaged combination of any two or more formats. "Software" included both concept building games and expository programs, while "games/aids" were of the non-computer variety. Four of the seventeen journals (three general, one specialized) excluded media reviews and were limited to book reviews only. The reverse was true of only one general journal.

One limitation to the "totality" or breadth of the observations was the exclusion of all books and media on the subject of computers alone. Although the mathematics journals were inclined to review these items, those reviews were considered irrelevant unless they represented titles specifically intended to improve mathematical instruction awareness. This decision was justified somewhat by McGrath's finding that although computer science people are heavy users of mathematics books, those who follow mathematical inquiry are seldom, if ever, users of computer books.[18]

The procedures utilized were quite simple, once the journal titles had been determined. All issues of all seventeen journals appearing in the calendar year 1983 were examined for reviews of mathematics items only in those columns which were deemed suitable in terms of audience and subject coverage. The total review file for each journal, then, was determined by counting all reviews in those columns or sections deemed pertinent in having the potential to render a relevant review. This excluded from our count those review columns restricted to fiction, reference books, humanities and social science works and college level audiences. When titles in these areas and topics were part of the same reviewing department as were the relevant entries they, however, were counted as irrelevant file components. Thus, total file figures given for some journals were somewhat less than acutal number of reviews. In these cases, percentages of relevant mathematics items would have been even smaller. Simple percentages were considered appropriate in reporting the differences between journals in establishing their relative effectiveness in producing relevant reviews.

ANALYSIS AND INTERPRETATION OF DATA

Frequency and Proportion of Relevant Reviews

Tables 1 and 2 provide a ready answer to Research Question 1 with respect to the comparison between general and specialized journals in number and proportion of relevant reviews. Table 1 represents a total of one hundred and ninety four reviews of mathematics books, out of which one hundred and sixty four (85.5%) come from three of the four specialized journals. From the list of thirteen general journals, seven titles produce only thirty reviews—or 15.5% of the total. Of these, *Booklist* is the biggest contributor with twelve reviews, while the six other contributing journals range from one to five reviews each. Although one might have expected better treatment of the subject in some of the journals, it may not be particularly surprising that six of the thirteen general journals chose to avoid mathematics books altogether. *Lander's Film Review* is the only journal to exclude books, but *Top of the News* and *Hornbook Magazine* are considered more literary in their interests.

Most surprising to us was the failure of *Appraisal: Children's Science Books* to render a single review. Obviously, mathematics is not a priority here even though the journal is sponsored by the Department of Science and Mathematics of Boston University. *Arithmetic Teacher* and *Mathematics Teacher,* the NCTM publications for elementary school, and junior high school through college respectively, outdistanced all other journals even if textbooks were not considered. With the inclusion of text books, their superiority as reviewing tools, was incontestable. Almost 100% of the textbooks came from the specialized journals, these titles in particular. Again, this is not surprising since the library press restricts itself to library books (tradebooks and reference), nor do teachers expect to find textbook reviews in the selected general education journals. At any rate, it should be pointed out that many of the textbooks

TABLE 1

JOURNAL REVIEWS OF MATH BOOKS BY TYPE

General Journals	Library Books Student	Prof.	Textbooks	Total
1) A-V Guide	0	0	0	0
2) Booklist	9	3	0	12
3) Bull of Center for Chil. Bks.	4	0	0	4
4) Chil. Bk. Rev. Serv.	2	0	0	2
5) Hornbook	0	0	0	0
6) Instructor and Teacher	0	4	1	5
7) Kirkus Reviews	0	0	0	0
* 8) Landers Film Reviews	0	0	0	0
9) Media and Methods	0	0	0	0
10) School Library Journal	2	0	0	2
11) Top of the News	0	0	0	0
12) WilsonLibrary Bulletin	4	0	0	4
13) VOYA	1	0	0	1
Subtotal:	22	7	1	30
**	(33.3%)	(13.5%)	(1.3%)	(15.5%)

Specialized Journals				
14) Arithmetic Teacher	10	14	11	35
15) Mathematics Teacher	26	28	58	112
16) Science Books and Films	8	3	6	17
17) Appraisal	0	0	0	0
Subtotal:	44	45	75	164
	(66.7%)	(86.5%)	(98.7%)	(84.5%)
Total:	66	52	76	194
	(100%)	(100%)	(100%)	(100%)

* Excludes books from reviewing scope

** Percentage figures in subtotals to be added vertically

would prove to be useful supplementary items for any school media center trade book or reference book collection.

Table 2 demonstrates again the superiority of the specialized journals, especially the NCTM efforts. Of a total of 165 reviews of the six categories of audio-visual media, 106 (64.2%) come from the specialized journals with *Mathematics*

Teacher and *Arithmetic Teacher* contributing 100 of them. *Appraisal* may be excused here for it is limited to books only. It is apparent that computer software is the leading medium for mathematics with 73 of the 106 reviews in specialized journals. This picture is repeated in the general journals with software claiming 31 of the total 59 reviews for the grouping. Altogether, it represents 104 of the total 165 reviews. The

TABLE 2

JOURNAL REVIEWS OF MATH AV MEDIA BY TYPE

General Journals	Soft-Ware	Film/Video	Kits	FS/Slides	Games	Audio	Total
1) AV Guide	0	1	0	0	0	0	1
2) Booklist	14	4	1	0	0	0	19
* 3) Bull. of Center for Chil. Bks.	0	0	0	0	0	0	0
* 4) Chil. Bk. Rev. Serv.	0	0	0	0	0	0	0
5) Hornbook	0	0	0	0	0	0	0
6) Instructor and Teacher	11	1	2	0	1	0	15
* 7) Kirkus Review	0	0	0	0	0	0	0
8) Landers Film Review	0	5	3	0	0	0	8
9) Media and Methods	6	0	1	0	0	0	7
10) School Library Journal	0	2	6	0	0	1	9
11) Top of the News	0	0	0	0	0	0	0
12) Wilson Library Bulletin	0	0	0	0	0	0	0
13) VOYA	0	0	0	0	0	0	0
Subtotal:	31	13	13	0	1	1	59
	**(29.8%)	(68.4%)	(86.7%)	---	(4.3%)	(33.3%)	(35.8%)
Specialized Journals							
14) Arithmetic Teacher	16	0	0	0	14	1	31
15) Mathematics Teacher	57	0	2	1	8	1	69
16) Science Books and Films	0	6	0	0	0	0	6
* 17) Appraisal	0	0	0	0	0	0	0
Subtotal:	73	6	2	1	22	2	106
	(70.2%)	(31.6%)	(13,3%)	(100%)	(95.7%)	(66.7%)	(64.2%)
Total:	104	19	15	1	23	3	165
	(100%)	(100%)	(100%)	(100%)	(100%)	(100%)	(100%)

* Excludes media from reviewing scope

** Percentage figures in subtotals to be added vertically

games medium also is heavily dominated by specialized journals with 22 of the 23 reviews.

General journals provide more reviews than do specialized journals in only two categories of media, film/video (with *Lander's Film Reviews* and *Booklist* the leading contributors, although *Science Books and Films,* a specialized journal, is the best individual provider) and multimedia kits, with *School Library Journal* the leader. Interesting here is the near-complete absence of published film strips and recordings which reflects the greater interest in multimedia kits by publishers today. Again *Booklist* with nineteen reviews, is the most productive general journal for audiovisual media as it was for book reviews. *Instructor and Teacher* is next with fifteen. Clearly, however, dominance in reviewing belongs to the specialized NCTM publications.

Frequency and Proportion of Relevant Mathematics Titles

Table 3 responds to the second research question regarding the comparison of number of titles reviewed by general and specialized journals. Tables 1 and 2 have indicated the existence of 194 book reviews and 165 reviews of audio-visual media for a total of 359. In table 3 we are able to see that these 359 reviews represent 314 titles, 173 books (55.1%) and 141 audio visual items (44.9%). (If we were to eliminate the 71 textbooks as being outside the realm of normal interest of the school library media center, this would then skew the distribution in favor of audio-visual reviews for the media specialist.)

It is clear from examining the table that the specialized journals far out-distance the general journals in number of titles as they did in number of reviews. Only 24 book titles (13.9%) were reviewed solely in general journals while 146 (84.4%) were reviewed only in specialized journals. Somewhat surprising is the fact that only three titles (1.7%) were reviewed by both groups. The total of 76 library books reviewed only in specialized journals shows dramatically the wisdom of including these journals in the normal collection-building routine of media specialists. Indeed, it is sheer folly to do otherwise.

Much the same is true of audio-visual media except that the

TABLE 3

COMPARISON OF GENERAL AND SPECIALIZED JOURNALS
IN MATH TITLES REVIEWED - SUMMARY DATA

	General Only		Specialized Only		Titles Shared		Total	
	#	%	#	%	#	%	#	%
Books								
Library Books/Students	16	*28.1	38	66.7	3	5.2	57	100
Library Books/Prof.	7	15.6	38	84.4	0	0	45	100
Textbooks	1	1.4	70	98.6	0	0	71	100
Subtotal:	24	13.9	146	84.4	3	1.7	173	100
	**(37.5%)		(62.1%)		(20.0%)		(55.1%)	
A-V MEDIA								
Film/Video	6	50.0	4	33.3	2	16.7	12	100
Multimedia Kits	1U	83.3	1	8.3	1	8.3	12	100
Filmstrip/Slides	0	0	1	100.0	0	0	1	100
Software	22	24.4	59	65.6	9	10.0	90	100
Games/Aids	1	4.3	22	95.7	0	0	23	100
Audio	1	33.3	2	66.7	0	0	3	100
Subtotal:	40	28.4	89	63.1	12	8.5	141	100
	(62.5%)		(37.9%)		(80.0%)		(44.9%)	
Total	64	20.4	235	74.8	15	4.8	314	100
	(100%)		(100%)		(100%)		(100%)	

* Percentage figures in columns should be added horizontally

** Percentage figures in parentheses in subtotals should be added vertically

amount of duplication or number of titles reviewed by both groups is greater with 12 items (8.5%) shared between them. Otherwise 89 of the 141 titles (63.1%) were reviewed only in specialized journals while only 40 (28.4%) were reviewed solely in general journals. It is clear that the school media specialist must include specialized journals in his/her selection process to develop the mathematics collection fully for 235 (74.8%) of the total number of 314 titles of books and audio-visual media were found only in this grouping. Even if textbooks were omitted totally from scrutiny of the media special-ist (which in our opinion is not wise) the specialized journals still have considerable dominance in the book area.

It is conceivable that a case could be made for eliminating general journals altogether since the 235 titles reviewed only by specialized journals when added to the fifteen titles re-viewed by both groups equals 250 titles or 79.6% of the total. To ignore general journals would not be wise in our opinion, however, since they produced 64 unique titles or 20.4% of the total. It is our feeling that collection building would be hampered if intellectual access was not provided to this large a segment of the potential acquisitions base.

Single and Multiple Reviewing of Books and Audio-Visual Media

Table 4 responds to the third research question in providing a comparison of books and audio-visual titles with respect to number of times reviewed by all journals. We are able to see that of a total of 173 books reviewed, 20 (11.6%) were re-viewed more than once for an average of 1.1 reviews per title. Most heavily reviewed of the book categories was that of professional-type in which seven titles (15.6%) were reviewed more than once while this was true of only five titles (7.0%) of 71 textbooks.

Three of the six audio-visual categories received multiple reviewing with film/video the most heavily reviewed with an average of 1.5 reviews per item. The categories of filmstrip/slides, games/aids, and audio received no duplication. In all, 20 items (14.1%) of the total 141 audiovisual titles received more than one review for an average of 1.2 reviews per title. In general, there is little distinction to be made except to say that along with film/video, titles of multimedia kits with an average 1.3 reviews per item stand out as those receiving most attention by reviewers. Only 40 titles of books and audio-visual media (12.7%) of the total of 314 received more than one review for an average of 1.1 reviews per item. This shows multiple review-ing is not characteristic of mathematics, making it even more important for the collection builder to understand the nature of the available reviewing journals.

TABLE 4

TITLES OF MATH BOOKS AND MEDIA REVIEWED
BY TYPE AND FREQUENCY IN ALL JOURNALS -- SUMMARY DATA

	Reviewed Once	Reviewed More	Total	% Dup.	# Rev.	Avg.
Books						
Library Books/Students	49	8	57	14.0	66	1.2
Library Books/Prof	38	7	45	15.6	52	1.2
Textbooks	66	5	71	7.0	76	1.1
Subtotal:	153	20	173	11.6	194	1.1
*	(55.8%)	(50.0%)	(55.1%)		(54.0%)	
AV Media						
Film/Video	6	6	12	50.0	19	1.5
Multimedia Kits	10	2	12	16.7	15	1.3
Filmstrip/Slides	1	0	1	0	1	1.0
Software	78	12	90	13.3	104	1.2
Games, Aids	23	0	23	0	23	1.0
Audio	3	0	3	0	3	1.0
Subtotal	121	20	141	14.1	165	1.2
	(44.2%)	(50.0%)	(44.9%)		(46.0%)	
Total:	274	40	314	12.7	359	1.1
	(100%)	(100%)	(100%)		(100%)	

* Percentage figures in subtotals to be added vertically

Proportion of Relevant Reviews and Uniqueness/Dupliction

The remaining tables address the fourth and fifth research questions in terms of proportions of relevant reviews to the totality, and uniqueness/duplication of the reviews. The total file represents reviews in potentially relevant columns and departments. It was felt that media specialists would not waste their time looking in separate columns devoted to fiction, humanities, etc., if they were interested in developing the mathematics collection; therefore, these departments, when isolated, were not included in our total file. Of course, when separate departments were not utilized and mathematics was a potential area of review, then the entire file was counted. In some journals, the total file does, indeed, represent the entire review output.

Table 5 clearly shows that of the sixteen journals which carry book reviews, pertinent to our mission to build school media center collections in mathematics with 35 of 40 book reviews in the *Arithmetic Teacher* and 112 of 159 book reviews in *Mathematics Teacher*. They were highly unique and represented low relative duplication. The only reviews judged irrelevant were focussed on computers, and in the case of the latter journal, on college level audiences. Of the general journals, *Instructor and Teacher* and *Wilson Library Bulletin* (remember we were not including the "Current Reference Books" department of the latter since we limited ourselves in that respect) proved to be of highest relevance but did not compare favorably with the specialized journals. *Instructor and Teacher* did have a low duplication level, for its five titles were not picked up elsewhere.

The general journals provide us with a total file of 8177 book reviews out of which only 30 are relevant to our mission (.4%). The specialized journals provide us with a total book review file of 1375 items out of which 164 (14.4%) are relevant. Combining the two categories we have 9552 book reviews appearing in potentially relevant columns and departments for the year 1983, with 194 (or 2.0%) being pertinent to our purpose. The utility of specialized journals is further confirmed with its higher uniqueness and lower duplication rate in reviewing.

Table 6 shows much the same situation with respect to the twelve journals which review audio-visual media, with the NCTM publications demonstrating highest relevance, and relatively low duplication. *Instructor and Teacher* ranked highest of the general journals in relevant media reviews with a respectable 18.5% level, but in this case, 7 of its 15 reviews were duplicated by others. General journals render a total file of 2914 media reviews with 59 (2.0%) being relevant. Of the 59 reviews, 24 or 40.7% are duplicated. Specialized journals provide a total review file of 552 entries with 106 of them relevant (19.2%). Duplication is only 18.9%. Combining the

TABLE 5

RELEVANCE AND DUPLICATION IN REVIEWING
OF MATH BOOKS

| | RELEVANT REVIEWS | | | | TOTAL | % |
	Unique	Dup	Total	% Dup	File	Relevance
General Journals						
1) A-V Guide	0	0	0		33	0
2) Booklist	11	1	12	8.3	2602	.5
3) Bull of Center for Chil. Bks.	1	3	4	75.0	797	.5
4) Child Book Rev Serv	1	1	2	50.0	665	.3
5) Hornbook	0	0	0	--	137	0
6) Instructor and Teacher	5	0	5	0	129	3.9
7) Kirkus Reviews	0	0	0	--	1014	0
8) Media and Methods	0	0	0	--	30	0
9) School Library Journal	0	2	2	100	2130	.1
10) Top of the News	0	0	0	--	17	0
11) VOYA	1	0	1	0	576	.2
12) Wilson Library Bulletin	3	1	4	25.0	47	8.5
Subtotal:	22	8	30	26.7	8177	.4
*	(14.4%)	(19.5%)	(15.5%)		(85.6%)	
Specialized Journals						
13) Arithmetic Teacher	25	10	35	28.6	40	87.5
14) Mathematics Teacher	96	16	112	14.3	159	70.4
15) Science Books & Films	10	7	17	41.2	972	1.7
16) Appraisal	0	0	0	--	204	0
Subtotal:	131	33	164	20.1	1375	11.9
	(85.6%)	(80.5%)	(84.5%)		(14.4%)	
Total:	153	41	194	21.1	9552	2.0
	(100%)	(100%)	(100%)		(100%)	

* Percentage figures in subtotals to be added vertically

two categories gives us a total of 3466 audio-visual reviews
with 165 (4.8%) relevant entries. Forty four of these duplicate
each other for a rate of 26.6%.

Table 7 provides summary data in combining book and
audio-visual reviews. *Instructor and Teacher* has the highest
relevance rate of general journals although *Booklist* is the
most productive in terms of total reviews in mathematics.

TABLE 6

RELEVANCE AND DUPLICATION IN REVIEWING
IN MATH - AV MEDIA

	RELEVANT REVIEWS				Total File	% Relevance
	Unique	Dup.	Total	% Dup.		
General Journals						
1) A-V Guide	0	1	1	100	61	1.6
2) Booklist	14	5	19	26.3	695	2.7
3) Hornbook	0	0	0	--	8	0
4) Instructor & Teacher	8	7	15	46.7	81	18.5
5) Landers Film Review	3	5	8	62.5	812	1.0
6) Media and Methods	5	2	7	28.5	89	7.9
7) School Library Journal	5	4	9	44.4	1057	.9
8) Wilson Library Bulletin	0	0	0	--	24	0
9) VOYA	0	0	0	--	87	0
Subtotal:	35	24	59	40.7	2914	2.0
	* (28.9%)	(54.5%)	(35.8%)		(84.1%)	
Specialized Journals						
10) Arithmetic Teacher	24	7	31	22.5	37	83.8
11) Mathematics Teacher	58	11	69	15.9	88	78.4
12) Science Books & Films	4	2	6	33.3	427	1.4
Subtotal:	86	20	106	18.9	552	19.2
	(71.1%)	(45.5%)	(64.2%)		(15.9%)	
Total:	121	44	165	26.6	3466	4.8
	(100%)	(100%)	(100%)		(100%)	

* Percentage figures in subtotals to be added vertically

Third in productivity is *School Library Journal* although its large total review file renders its relevance rate below average even for general journals. Again the superiority of specialized journals is dramatic in all respects with the NCTM publications being outstanding.

Specialized journals provided 270 or 75.2% of the total 359 relevant reviews with a duplication rate of 19.6% and a 14.0% relevance rate. In contrast, the general journals rendered only 89 relevant reviews (24.8% of the total) with a duplication rate of 36.0% and an 0.8% relevance rate. *Mathematic Teacher* and *Arithmetic Teacher* were clearly the best possible choices in all respects.

TABLE 7

RELEVANCE AND DUPLICATION IN REVIEWING
OF BOTH CATEGORIES OF MATH MATERIALS

		RELEVANT REVIEWS				Total File	% Relevance
	Books	A-V	Total	Dup.	% Dup.		
General Journals							
1) A-V Guide	0	1	1	1	100	94	1.1
2) Booklist	12	19	31	6	19.4	3297	.9
3) Bull of Center for Chil. Bks.	4	0	4	3	75.0	797	.5
4) Chil. Bk. Rev. Serv.	2	0	2	1	50.0	665	.3
5) Hornbook	0	0	0	---	---	145	0
6) Instructor & Teacher	5	15	20	7	35.0	210	9.5
7) Kirkus Reviews	0	0	0	---	---	1014	0
8) Landers Film Reviews	0	8	8	5	62.5	812	1.0
9) Media and Methods	0	7	7	2	28.6	119	5.9
10) School Library Journal	2	9	11	6	54.5	3187	.3
11) Top of the News	0	0	0	---	---	17	0
12) VOYA	1	0	1	0	0	663	.2
13) Wilson Library Bulletin	4	0	4	1	25.0	71	5.6
Subtotal:	30	59	89	32	36.0	11091	.8
	* (15.5%)	(35.8%)	(24.8%)	(37.6%)		(85.2%)	
Specialized Journals							
14) Arithmetic Teacher	35	31	66	17	25.8	77	85.7
15) Mathematics Teacher	112	69	181	27	14.9	247	73.3
16) Science Books & Films	17	6	23	9	39.1	1399	1.6
17) Appraisal	0	0	0	--	--	204	0
Subtotal:	164	106	270	53	19.6	1927	14.0
	(84.5%)	(64.2%)	(75.2%)	(62.4%)		(14.8%)	
Total:	194	165	359	85	23.7	13018	2.8
	(100%)	(100%)	(100%)	(100%)		(100%)	

* Percentage figures in subtotals to be added vertically

FINDINGS AND CONCLUSIONS

Based on the total reviewing practices of the selected journals for the year 1983, the following was found to be true:

1. Specialized journals are far more productive in terms of number of relevant reviews for mathematics books and audio-visual media, accounting for 270 (75.2%) of the total 359 reviews.

2. *Mathematics Teacher* and *Arithmetic Teacher,* both publications of the National Council of Teachers of Mathematics, are the most productive specialized titles, while *Booklist* is the most productive general journal. *Instructor and Teacher* has the highest relevance rate of general journals.

3. Almost 75%, 235 of the total 314 mathematics titles, were reviewed only in specialized journals with 15 titles reviewed by both groups. Not quite 21%, 64 of 314 titles, were reviewed by general journals alone.

4. Specialized journals devote a far greater proportion of their total review file to materials considered relevant to mathematics at the elementary and secondary school levels. The relevance rate for reviews was 14.0% of the total file in specialized journals and only 0.8% of the total file of general journals.

5. Specialized journals have a higher proportion of uniqueness and a lower proportion of duplication in their reviewing than do general journals. Uniqueness of audio-visual reviews in specialized journals was 81.1% (duplication 18.9%) while uniqueness of reviews in general journals was 59.3% (duplication 40.7%). For books, uniqueness of reviews in specialized journals was 79.1% (duplication 20.1%) as compared to 73.3% (duplication 26.7%) in general journals.

6. Multiple reviewing is uncharacteristic of mathematics since 247 (87.3%) of the 314 titles received only one review. Audio-visual media was reviewed an average of 1.2 times while books were reviewed an average of 1.1 times. The only appreciable differences in categories were those of film/video (1.5) and multi-media kits (1.3).

7. Individual filmstrips, slide sets, and recordings have virtually disappeared in mathematics reviewing, in favor of multi-media kits, while computer software is the dominant format for audio-visual media in the subject.

Implications for Collection Building

After examining over 13,000 reviews in the 17 journals, certain aspects of the selection process became quite clear. *Mathematics* and *Arithematic Teacher* are priority tools for media specialists and teachers in building collections in the subject. Although their performance is not surprising, we were somewhat shocked and disconcerted by the failure of general journals to keep pace in this area. *Booklist, Instructor and Teacher, Media and Methods,* and *School Library Journal* should all be used, but only as auxiliary vehicles in the mission. (The media specialist will utilize *Booklist* and *School Library Journal* primarily for other components of the collection and incidentally will discover materials of use to mathematics.) The fact that there is so little duplication of title coverage between groups (only 15 titles or 4.8%) makes it that much more important to utilize both general and specialized journals. It is obvious that journals aimed primarily at the teacher must be utilized by the media specialist.

In examining the content of the textbook reviews, it became apparent that many of these titles have information which would be of much value to the students using the media center. Therefore, it is felt that the use of various titles in this category both as supplementary items in the tradebook collection and even in the reference area would be warranted. We feel that such titles cannot or, indeed, should not be ignored by the serious collection builder. Even if we were to eliminate the 76 textbooks in this study as being outside the realm of library media center consideration, however, the NCTM publications still retain their dominance as collection building tools.

The Future

Studies of this type should be considered the first step in collection building and eventual service provision. Subsequent research should analyze the context of reviews to determine the utility of information provided in making decisions regarding the needs of patrons. This research should examine the length of reviews, the descriptive vs evaluative or analytical character, and the identification of grade levels. To evaluate effectively would require an understanding of the content of the mathematics curriculum in order to help minister the correct instructional resources.

If this can be done, then we may effectively focus on types of books and audio-visual media as part of a complete instructional system with firm ideas as to how individual titles will fit the requirements of individual users within the learning environment. Thus, planning will precede selection, which will be followed by evaluation. If we comprehend enough about the mathematics instructional program in order to anticipate the needs of its participants (both teachers and students) we are able to produce an efficient and effective collection.

How school library media specialists acquire this knowledge or comprehension depends upon their situations and their inclinations. Workshops, short courses, long-term courses, inservice programs all can be useful. The best way to start, however, is with a firm personal resolve to become more informed and more interested in the welfare of the mathematics program and its faculty. Seek out those teachers, show them you are willing to learn, and the results may be surprising.

REFERENCE NOTES

1. Ron Blazek. *Influencing Students Toward Media Center Use: An Experimental Investigation in Mathematics.* Chicago: American Library Association, 1975, p. 137.

2. National Education Association, Research Division. *The Secondary School Teacher and Library Services,* Washington, D.C.: The Association, 1958, 37 p.

3. Raymond Barber and Jacquelyn Mancall. "The Application of Bibliometric Techniques to the Analysis of Materials for Young Adults," *Collection Management* 2 (Fall 1978): 233.

4. Wallace Bonk and Rose Mary Magrill. *Building Library Collections,* 5th ed. Metuchen, N.J.: Scarecrow Press, 1979, p. 84.

5. Richard K. Gardner. *Library Collections, Their Origin, Selection, and Development.* New York: McGraw-Hill, 1981, pp. 175–176.

6. James Cabeceiras. *The Multimedia Library: Materials Selection and Use,* New York: Academic Press, 1978, 275 p.; Mary M. Taylor, *School Library and Media Center Acquisitions Policies and Procedures,* Phoenix: Oryx Press, 1981, 272 pp.; and Phyllis Van Orden, *The Collection Program In Elementary and Middle Schools: Concepts, Practices and Information Sources,* Littleton, Colo: Libraries Unlimited, 1982, 301 p.

7. Norman H. Dudley. "Organizational Models for Collection Development" in *Collection Development in Libraries,* ed. by Robert D. Stueart and George B. Miller, Jr. Greenwich, Conn.: JAI Press, 1980, p. 31.

8. William A. Katz. *Collection Development: The Selection of Materials for Libraries.* New York: Holt, Rinehart and Winston, 1980, p. 15.

9. Bonk and Magrill, *Building Library Collections,* p. 43.

10. Wolff, Kathryn and Jill Story. *AAAS Science Book List Supplement.* Washington, D.C.: American Association for the Advancement of Science, 1978, 457 p.

11. *Advisory List of Instructional Media for Mathematics,* Raleigh, N.C.: North Carolina State Department of Public Instruction, Division of Educational Media, annual

12. M. Bernadine Tabler. "Using Books to Learn Mathematics Skills," *Indiana Media Journal* 2 (Spring 1980): 19–20.

Video in the Collection

Jack Short

After discussing the role of video in the classroom, the author suggests subject areas of particular value in school collections. Examples of resource sharing to extend the collection are provided.

Studies conducted over the past few decades have consistently concluded that when educational films are correctly used in the classroom, they constitute a powerful teaching tool. The Wendt/Butts study of 1960, for example, showed that twice the number of books were read if the students had first been stimulated by related films. While most imagery comes from experience, films can provide an extension of personal, or first hand, experience. The printed word in turn can take on a deeper significance and meaning after exposure to films.

Although the studies which concluded that there was an increase in reading after the viewing of a film were valid, the studies were conducted on teachers who had available to them large numbers of films correlated to the texts they were using. The reality of the average school district in America is that few school boards make available the necessary funding to develop such a viable collection. The cost of 16mm film has been simply too prohibitive. Considering that a student should have viewed over 1800 educational films through the K–12 years, we must assume that there are large gaps of missing imagery in the experience of millions of American students.

A strategy to allow access to a greater number of 16mm titles was implemented through the development of regional and state collections. Some states, like New York, developed Bureaus of Cooperative Educational Services which service a

Mr. Short is a senior sales representative with Coronet Films.

county or multi-county base of students for each collection of 16mm film. Even in these cases the demand on the collection was such that only a limited number of films were available for use in the classroom at the most effective teaching moment. Limited funding often dictated that the collection be developed with additional prints of the same title to meet total teacher requests. That process limited the range of titles available relating to any specific educational concept.

The answer to these distribution and cost problems has arrived with the development of the 1/2 inch video tape. It is now possible for even the smallest school to develop core curriculum collections in a cost-effective manner.

Educational video tapes, although lower in cost than 16mm prints, will probably never be as low in cost as video tapes covering general topics which can be sold to a larger home and/or public library market. The number of units sold dictates pricing. Even though the cost of developing a local school building or district video collection will be lower than it would be for identical material in 16mm, there will still be a need for regional, county and state collections of lesser use titles. Apart from the core curriculum collections that individual buildings and districts would develop, regional collections should be structured to include enrichment titles. State collections could be designed to carry only the very limited-use titles.

In an elementary school video tape collection, basic titles would be those related to school bus safety, lunchroom manners, following instructions and playground safety. If a school has these topics in the collection quick response to stimuli is possible. If an incident occurs on the playground or school bus, the involved group of students could be viewing a related title within five minutes. The immediate response time frame would maximize the impact of the tape's content.

When a school district adopts a particular textbook, tapes correlated to specific chapters and concepts could be added to the collection. Considering that the school district has invested thousands of dollars in the textbook adoption, this would be a small additional investment of dollars which greatly strengthens the educational impact of the textbook. Individual schools could develop core curriculum development blocks of video tape focusing on specific skill areas. For example, a group of reading skills tapes could be correlated to a reading textbook with guidelines indicating that moment in the teaching process when a visual teaching tool would have a particularly strong value.

Unlike 16mm regional collections which require a highly structured distribution system, a number of school districts have developed a video consortium approach with minimal overhead. Most commercial producers and distributors have a very flexible approach on duplication rights and costs, and are willing to adapt to local needs as long as reasonable profit margins are retained.

Even with the development of local video collections, a need will remain for regional 16mm collections. Many teachers still prefer the full screen for teaching in certain academic disciplines. Also, with thousands and thousands of 16mm projectors in the schools, you can be sure that school administrators will not simply toss them out the window. It will be a melding of the two technologies. In like measure, in the years to come there will be other new technologies, but by then there will be thousands and thousands of video tape players and again it will be a slow transition. Dollars invested in video tape now constitute an excellent use of taxpayers' monies.

The educational film reference publication *FILM FILE* identifies over 23,000 titles which are generally related to K–12 curriculum, and are available in 16mm or video tape. Thus, even with the lower cost of video tape, cooperation is essential in making the maximum number of titles available to the students. Increasingly more video players are now found in the homes of students. The circulation of video tapes for home use should be encouraged. This provides an excellent opportunity to send home a related bibliography with each tape, building on the tape's stimulus.

Resource sharing between the school library and the public library has often been a relationship of strain and concern. With lower duplication costs of tapes, replications of collections could be considered. There is a major need in America to encourage our teen population to use the public library. Offering popular video titles could be the necessary "carrot."

Public libraries that moved swiftly into developing video collections are now reaping the benefits. They are already experiencing a higher circulation of books. Also, their new video tape users (who are often also voters) have made a significant difference in securing new and increased funding. Public library and bond millage issues have been lost in the past by small margins, so this new segment of community support has been 'beneficial.

Perceiving video tapes as expensive and fragile, some librarians have tended to put these tapes under "lock and key" or have circulated them at the desk on a "patron request" basis. As the collection grows in size, these librarians are experiencing a large drain of staff time to this task.

One New York State public library director with a sizeable collection came to the conclusion that his shrinkage on an open stack approach would cost less dollars than paying staff to open and close cases. He found that not only was his loss experience extremely low, but also that his circulation tripled as patrons could "paw through" the collection.

A State of Washington library director has found that as the scope and range of his collection has increased, the circulation of those materials has increased at an even faster rate of acceleration. Where some highly print oriented librarians have resisted any move toward new technology in accessing information, they are finding the community pushing them into meeting community needs.

A major shift occurring in the content of public library collections is the move from completely feature film video tapes into the "how to" and informational type of titles. At the early stages of video tape in the public library, as well as with the first 16mm film collections, the staff member assigned the title of "film librarian" was often a "film buff" and had the assignment for that reason. As more library professionals take on the responsibility of developing a video tape collection, the feature film emphasis will lessen a bit, and a more balanced collection will evolve to meet total community needs. Certainly with the increased focus on continuing education, video utilization will be a natural part of that development.

With only few exceptions, it has held true in the past that where you have a strong school library system, there is a higher utilization of the local public library. Professionals in the school library and the public library can use the development of their video collections as a basis for increased communication on total library needs for the entire community.

Selecting Video Materials for the Secondary School Library Media Center

Helen M. Gothberg

The basic information necessary to the purchase of video materials for secondary school library media centers is covered. Videotape and videodisc formats are explained. Trends in transferring 16mm film, sound-slide, and sound filmstrip programs to videotape are discussed and their comparative costs are noted. The strengths and weaknesses of both film and video are explored, along with a brief description of resources which are useful in the selection of video programs.

The argument over whether a school library media center ought to be more than a collection of printed materials was concluded some time ago. The question in today's modern school is not whether to purchase audiovisual materials or not, but rather how to make intelligent and cost effective choices in deciding which formats to buy. There are many A-V options from which to choose including slides, filmstrips, motion picture films, and video tapes. Which one is best? There is no one simple answer to this question, for each medium serves different purposes, and decisions made at the local school level depend on the educational needs to be met. What is important is that the school library media specialist make selections based, not just on cost or convenience alone, but on a thorough understanding of the strengths and weaknesses of each available format. Although there is some variety in almost any of the audiovisual formats available, video materials are the most varied, changing, and confusing. Mak-

Dr. Gothberg, Ph.D. is Associate Professor at the Graduate Library School, University of Arizona.

ing effective use of today's limited materials' budgets means targeting two areas of understanding: What are the possible options available within the video format, along with their strengths and weaknesses; and second, when is it most appropriate to purchase video programs?

VIDEO FORMATS

The best way to begin a discussion about the selection of video materials is with a description of the two basic formats and how they work. Video materials are currently available in two broad categories of format—tape and disc.

Video Tape

Video tape is a thin plastic material coated with iron oxide particles. These particles are sensitive to the magnetic fields on the audio and video heads on the video player which pick up the signals. Both audio and video as well as cue and control tracks are played from one side of the tape only. Video tape is flexible yet tough enough so that it is not easily broken. Tape can develop creases if improperly handled which can result in loss or distortion of the visual image. Pre-recorded video tapes have variable playing times from a few minutes up to two hours, depending on the format selected. Video tapes are available in several widths and two types of packaging.

Two-Inch Reel

This format is the original video tape which was developed for broadcast purposes in 1955. It is primarily the tool of broadcast stations, and even here its use is rapidly decreasing in favor of smaller, more compact formats.

One-Inch Reel

One-inch tape followed the development of two-inch tape and was viewed as a revolution of sorts in that it made the first "portable" video possible. Its primary use today is in broadcast TV, cable, and some other types of closed circuit distribution of video information. It is not a format which will be found in the school library media center except in very unusual circumstances.

Three-Quarter Inch (U-Matic) Cassette

This format has been the predominating one for pre-programmed use in schools and libraries for the past decade or more. It was the first color cassette developed, and it provided users with easy care and handling and at relatively low cost when compared to 16mm film.

Half-Inch Reel or Cassette

The first half-inch reel tape was developed by Sony in 1969 for use with black and white portable equipment. It meant that video taping became an activity which could be carried out by large numbers of untrained persons, both for fun and for educational purposes. The half-inch format was further refined by packaging it in the cassette format which is about the size of a paperback book or half as large as the three-quarter inch cassette. Color video in the half-inch format was possible with the half-inch reel, but it did not come into its own until the half-inch cassette, designed for home taping of broadcast programs, came on the market. Half-inch video cassette is available in two non-compatible formats—VHS and Beta. VHS provides up to two hours of prerecorded commercial/educational programming whereas Beta provides up to one hour. Both formats have longer recording/playing times for home use.

Quarter-Inch Cassette

This format is the newest and most compact on the video cassette market. Its narrow width means that it can be packaged in a box about the size of an audio cassette. Does this mean that there may be an eight-inch cassette the size of a match box in our future? Perhaps, but only time will tell, and for now at least, quarter-inch video tape is the end of the line.

Videodisc

Videodisc is the other type of video format available. Presently there are two competing non-compatible formats on the market, reflective optical and grooved capacitance.

Reflective Optical Laser Disc

This disc is twelve inches in diameter, has no grooves, but is read by a laser beam as it rotates at 1,800 rpms. Microscopic "pits" pressed into its hard surface contain the "frames" of information, with a capacity of 54,000 images possible on one side of the disc. The optical disc contains pre-recorded information on both sides unlike video tape which plays on only one side. The laser-read disc floats on a cushion of air as it spins, so it can be accessed digitally and instanteously. This format of disc has dual sound tracks, can store still as well as moving images, and can be used with a microprocessor or computer for various kinds of sophisticated display.

Grooved Capacitance Disc

This disc is similar to an audio recording in that it must be played in linear fashion, thereby providing options similar to videotape. It does not have much of the sophistication of the laser-read disc. The grooved disc comes packaged in a plastic playing caddy, and both caddy and disc are inserted into the player. The capacitance disc is more subject to wear than is the optical.

Advantages and Disadvantages of Formats

In looking over this array of software, the school library media specialist must decide which one of these formats is best suited to the school's needs. Where video tape is concerned the issue is between half-inch cassette and three-quarter—and in the case of the former, between Beta and VHS. Two-inch, one-inch, and one-quarter-inch formats are not of much use in the school. They are mentioned here because the larger formats are noted as options in some of the tools for acquisition which are noted later, but they are intended for broadcast or wider distribution purposes than an individual school. One-quarter inch tape is too new to have much available in the way of pre-recorded material, and it seems to be more of a novelty item just now—however, in the world of video change can come about quickly.

There are several points which should be considered by the potential purchaser of one or more of these video formats:

1. The picture quality of three-quarter inch materials is somewhat better than half-inch, but these differences are not always that noticeable.
2. Currently, there are more educationally oriented video materials available in the three-quarter inch size than in the half-inch cassette. The latter is largely geared to the popular home-use market. However, this picture is gradually changing. Increasingly we find producers of audiovisual materials offering the same title in many options.
3. There are cost considerations. There can be anywhere from $20.00 to $100.00 difference between the purchase price of the two formats, with half-inch video cassette being the less expensive.
4. Half-inch cassette materials may be checked out of the school library media center for home use. Three-quarter inch video cassette is almost always used within the library media center, since few individuals own the more cumbersome and expensive equipment needed for playback. Many households have a home video player.
5. Videodisc is the least expensive of the video formats; however, there is much less available in the way of pre-programmed materials suited to secondary school use.
6. The laser optical disc appears to be the most promising of the two discs for educational and library uses. The optical disc can store a large number of still frames. The Library of Congress is experimenting with book preservation by using the laser-read disc. The storage of large collections of slides and photographic prints is also feasible using the optical disc. Because it can be accessed digitally when used with a player which has a microprocessor, or in combination with a microcomputer, single frames can be quickly located. Individualized instruction on disc is enhanced by instant replay when a wrong

answer is given or new material added for clarification. Motion pictures, photographic stills, printed information, and dual sound tracks, combined with the branching capabilities of the computer have made the optical disc an exciting new technology for storage and for individualized instruction. Business, industry and medicine have all pioneered in the use of the disc in this latter area.

7. Mastering an optical disc is an expensive and complicated process even though the individual discs themselves are less expensive than tape. Video discs cannot be recorded locally in the same way that video tape can, but there are indications that a breakthrough in this area may be just around the corner.

8. The future of disc technology remains uncertain, and there are many problems yet to be resolved if it is to be truly competitive with video tape.

Trends and Costs

Video is the trend of the future. We find producers of audiovisual materials offering the same title in a number of format options. For example, Time-Life lists for many of its titles in the current catalog, 16mm film, ¾ inch video cassette, and one-half inch video cassette in both VHS and Beta options. Their 90 minute presentation, "Making of the President, 1972" lists the various costs for each format as follows:

16mm film	$950
3/4-inch (u-matic) video	250
1/2-inch video cassette	200

The difference in the cost of 16mm film and video tape is major; however, the difference between the video formats is not as large. Yet, where tight budgets are concerned it should be taken into consideration. Time-Life offers materials sold in video format only as well. Other companies are making similar offers, and the ones noted here are only by way of example. Some companies such as Aims, offer 16mm film and video cassettes at the same price for a given title.

Slides and filmstrips, along with 16mm motion picture film, are also making their way into the video tape market. The Center for Humanities, a major producer of sound slide programs, now lists many of their programs on video cassette at a reduced cost. For example, a 53 minute sound-slide presentation may cost $169.50 but $149.50 in video. Guidance Associates has filmstrips as well as films on video tape. One of their 16mm films will list at $530.00, while the three-quarter and half-inch cassettes are priced at $179.50 and $159.50 respectively. The program, "Death and Dying: Closing the Circle" is made up of five filmstrips and five audio cassettes. Each one is a separately contained presentation. The filmstrip format is priced at $189.50; the half-inch video cassette of the same set of filmstrips costs $199.50; and the three-quarter inch video, $299.50. The latter requires two cassettes because of program length, and this accounts for its higher cost.

In cooperation with the Center for Humanities, Guidance Associates offers some programs in sound-slide, sound filmstrip, and video format options. A comparison of the costs for a program on writing paragraphs for English composition are as follows:

Sound-slide	$219.50
Sound Filmstrip (6 cans & cassettes)	199.50
3/4-inch video cassette	179.50
VHS or Beta video cassette	159.50

The video formats look very good in terms of cost. Other tempting considerations are: the cassette format is compact and fits on the shelf like a book; it takes little care and upkeep; and video tape should be good for at least 100 passes over the player heads. Videodisc takes up even less space, and the optical disc is projected to have a very long life. Its playing surface is not affected by fingerprints or scratches. However, there are other considerations that the school library media specialist will want to keep in mind before making a definite decision to buy video over film.

WHICH FORMAT IS BEST?

Film and video are different mediums, and you do not get the same product when film is transferred to video tape. The advantages of film, whether it be 16mm motion picture or a series of stills tied into a sound track by the use of an electronic pulse are better color, better picture clarity, and larger picture size. These technical factors have a major impact on the viewer. There are other points to consider as well. When film is transferred to video, some of the outer parameters of the frame are lost. In the case of artistic or scientific films, this loss must be considered significant. Editing that is done in the process of turning 16mm motion picture film into video tape frequently means that the video copy will not be faithful to the film original. Whether this matters or not depends on to what degree the integrity of the original is of vital concern.

When deciding about video for purchase, the school library media specialist should consider what is unique to the video format—rather than seeing video as a less troublesome, and sometimes less expensive format. Video is intimate and provides a sense of immediacy. The individual or small group watching a video presentation can maintain control over it. The tape or disc can be stopped, reversed, and played over as many times as needed. Video is also a moving medium, and although the disc is being used for storing stills, the emphasis in this situation is on retrieval not program impact. What video does very well is provide one-to-one delivery of factual information—whether to an individual, a small group or a larger audience. When larger monitors or video projectors are used, a video program can bring an important educational stimulus to the classroom. Notes can be easily taken since it is not necessary to darken the room. Video disc has strong possibilities for individualizing instruction. Where video is weak is in providing a shared emotional or aesthetically pleasing experience as compared to film. We recognize that the motion picture "Star Wars" is not going to come off very well on home TV compared to sharing this experience with others in a large screen theater with Dolby sound. By the same token, neither do we really want to see the evening news, our favorite talk show, or "Good Morning America" at the movie theater. It is not just cost or convenience alone—such an experience would mean sensory overkill for what are intimate encounters. For these reasons, video should never be selected as an across the board substitute for film.

A video tape made from slides on writing better paragraphs makes a great deal of sense—and even more so if the student can check it out for home study and use. The slight loss in picture quality will not make that much difference as long as important information is not lost in the transfer process. Convenience and lower cost in this instance help tip the balance in favor of the purchase. On the other hand, the story of Eric Lund from the "Death and Dying" filmstrip series will mean a change in the strength of the emotional impact when viewed on video. There is also the problem of having all the separate filmstrip programs contained in one package which cannot be broken up or quickly located. For some buyers, not having all those separate parts to control may seem a definite advantage, but learner needs should be weighed in the balance.

RESOURCES

Many of the traditional selection tools for school library media centers include video programs among their audiovisual reviews. There are three other comprehensive sources which are useful in selecting or acquiring video tapes and/or discs. All of these resources may not be available in the individual school, but they should be provided at the district level. If they are not at the district level, they may be found in the local college or university library. The most important of these tools in locating reviews of video programs is *Media Review Digest*. This reference work is published annually with semi-annual supplements. It provides title of the work, editor, producer, whether in color or in black and white, date, running time, rental and purchase prices. A brief description of the content is indicated along with a list of reviews. A review rating is indicated by the mediagrapher using plus and minus symbols. The grade level of the work is given, along with Dewey classification number and Library of Congress subject headings. *Media Review Digest* is organized by format and then by title with an alphabetical subject index. A major portion of the book is devoted to reviews of films and videotapes.

The fifth edition of the NICEM *Index to Educational Video Tapes* was published in 1980. It is organized by title with a subject index. It lists over 15,000 titles from 400 producers. This resource is useful in locating what is available and also whether there are mutliple video formats for a given title. NICEM does not provide evaluations of the materials listed.

The Video Source Book is also now in its 5th edition. It lists more than 35,000 programs from 700 sources, including videodiscs and one-quarter inch cassettes. This comprehensive work is organized by title with a main category index. Categories include: movies/entertainment, sports/recreation, fine arts, general interest, education, health science, business/industry, children/juvenile, and how to/instruction. A brief description of the program content is noted along with running time, color, and format options. Potential use is suggested, such as cable TV or school room. Awards are noted, along with audience rating, grade level, and whether available for rent or purchase or other acquisition plans. No prices are given but cast and star notes are, when relevant.

Selecting video materials for the secondary school library media center is a challenge. Knowing what the format options are and where to locate them are important to the successful outcome of the AV selection process. Previewing video programs whenever possible is a must. However, wary producers are concerned with illegal duplication of their materials, so it is increasingly difficult to gain access to review titles. Some charge a rental fee, and others send out a film rather than the video tape. Whatever decision is made must be based on a knowledge of a users' needs on one side of the scale, balanced on the other by cost, convenience, availability, ease of use, quality, and impact. Whoever said that school librarians do not need to be media specialists has never tried to select video materials.

BIBLIOGRAPHY

Colldeweih, Jack H. "Controversial Cuts: Is What You Saw What You'll Get?" *Film Library Quarterly* (Vol. 7, no. 1, 1974) pp. 23, 26–31.

Gross, Lynne Schaffer. *The New Television Technologies* (Dubuque, Iowa: Brown, 1983).

Heath, Ted. "Alternative Videodisc Systems," *Videodisc/Videotex* (Fall 1981) pp. 228–238.

Hickey, Neil. "Ready, Set . . . Glow!" *TV Guide* (July 24, 1982) pp. 13–16.

Kearsley, Greg. "Videodiscs in Education and Training: The Idea Becomes Reality," *Videodisc/Videotex* (Fall 1981) pp. 208–220.

Lipoff, Stuart J. "Is it Success or Failure for the Videodisc?" *Optical Spectre* (March 1981) pp. 60–63.

Wood, R. Kent, Robert D. Woolley, and Stephen W. Zsiray. "Videodisc/Microcomputer Research Opens New Horizons for Libraries," *American Libraries* (April 1981) pp. 208–209.

Pasachoff, Jay M. "A Space Astronomy on Videodisk," *Sky & Telescope* (January 1983) p. 32.

VIDEO RESOURCES

Media Review Digest. (Ann Arbor, Michigan: Pierian Press, 1970–   ).

NICEM Index to Educational Videotapes. (Los Angeles, CA: University of Southern California, National Information Center, 5th ed., 1980).

The Video Source Book. (Syosset, N.Y.: National Video Clearinghouse, 5th ed. 1983).

Selecting Films for Children:
A Bibliographic Essay

Mary Alice Hunt

Short annotated bibliographics are provided in the five sections of this essay: guides, location/availability tools, selection aids, ideas, and reviews. Suggestions of other sources of criteria for selection are given. "Children" in this essay includes the ages of preschoolers through age fourteen.

INTRODUCTION

In beginning an essay on "Selecting Films for Children" the opening words should be "Preview! Preview! Preview!" Preview films with groups of teachers if possible, for reactions as to how it would contribute to various curriculum areas. Use an evaluation form which you keep on file after you preview. Lastly, check reviews of children's films, copy, and attach them to your written evaluations. Talk with teachers about renting or buying films; get some idea of how often a film will be used. In very brief form, these are the essential steps in "Selection."

This essay will not list selection criteria, as such, for these are covered extensively in the literature. For example, Phyllis Van Orden's book, *The Collection Program in Elementary and Middle Schools* has three excellent chapters on selection (Chapter 8–"Selection Procedures," Chapter 9–"General Selection Criteria," and Chapter 10–"Criteria by Format: Visual Materials").[1] Another, older manual, that has extensive coverage on selecting films is Emily S. Jones' *Manual on Film*

---

[1]Phyllis Van Orden. *The Collection Program in Elementary and Middle Schools.* Libraries Unlimited, Inc. 1982.

Dr. Hunt is Professor, School of Library and Information Science, The Florida State University, Tallahassee, Florida.

Evaluation, Revised edition. Educational Film Library Association, 1974.

Instead, this article includes five *bibliographic* sections that could aid school media specialists and library programmers in the selection (and utilization) of films for children. The term "children" covers the age ranges from pre-school through age fourteen.

The arrangement of the bibliographies are as follows:

— *Guides*–Those books that identify or list catalogs, bibliographic tools, selection sources and/or producers and distributors and their addresses.

— *Location/Availability Tools*–Includes indexes, union lists, locator lists of films. These tools usually are not selective or annotated, but indicate only if the film is still available at the time of the book's publication and give complete bibliographic information.

— *Selection Tools*–Books, pamphlets, and lists that include films for children that usually are "selected" and annotated. Each entry usually contains complete bibliographic information. Some selection tools are limited to specific areas, i.e., films based on children's books, films for three to five year old children, or films for children limited to a particular topic.

— *Ideas/Trends*–Articles and books dealing with selection and/or utilization of film for children and articles relating to trends and developments in children's films since 1976.

— *Reviews*–This is a listing of periodicals. One, *Media Review Digest,* is and *index* and *digest* of reviews and evaluations. The others review films for children.

GUIDES

Aids to Media Selection for Students and Teachers/compiled by Beatrice T. Simmons, Yvonne B. Carter. Rev. ed. Indianola, Iowa: National Association of State Educational Media Professionals, 1982.

Children's Media Market Place/edited by Carol A. Emmens. 2nd ed. New York: Neal-Schuman Publishers, 1982.
ISBN 0918212332 (pbk.)

A directory of names, addresses, key personnel and product lines of publishers, producers, and distributors of children's audiovisual materials. Includes section on review media, awards for children's media, and children's television and radio.

Film Programmer's Guide to 16mm Rentals/edited by Kathleen Weaver, associate editor, Richard Prelinger, consulting editor, Linda J. Artel. 3rd ed. Albany, Calif.: Reel Research, 1980.
ISBN 093445602X (pbk.)

Film/Television: A Research Guide/National Education Services, The American Film Institute, edited by Diana Elsas. Washington, D.C.: The John F. Kennedy Center for the Performing Arts, 1977.

Guides to Educational Media: Films, Filmstrips, Multimedia Kits, Programmed Instruction Materials, Recordings on Discs and Tapes, Slides, Transparencies, Videotapes/Margaret I. Rufsvold. 4th ed. Chicago: American Library Association, 1977.
ISBN 0838902324
A guide to catalogs and lists, services of professional organizations and special periodicals which systematically give information on availability of films and filmstrips.

Movies for Kids: A Guide for Parents and Teachers on the Entertainment Film for Children/Ruth M. Goldstein and Edith Zornow, introd. by Joan Ganz Cooney. Rev. ed. New York: Ungar, c1980.
ISBN 0804461945 (pbk.)

Multi-media Indexes, Lists, and Review Sources : A Bibliographic Guide/Thomas L. Hart, Mary Alice Hunt, Blanche Woolls. New York: M. Dekker, c1975.
ISBN 0824763408
Identifies and describes over 400 bibliographic tools and selection sources of both print and non-print media.

LOCATION/AVAILABILITY TOOLS

Bilingual Education Audio-visual Materials/Michigan Education Resources Information Center. Lansing: Michigan Department of Education, State Library Services, Michigan Education Resources Information Center, 1981.

Educational Film Locator/of the Consortium of University Film Centers and R. R. Bowker Company. 2nd ed. New York: R. R. Bowker, c1980.
ISBN 0835212955

Educators Guide to Free Films/compiled and edited by John C. Diffor and Elaine N. Diffor. 43rd ed. Randolph, Wis.: Educators' Progress Service, Inc., 1983

Index to 16mm Films/The National Information Center for Educational Media. Los Angeles: University of Southern California.
An alphabetical listing of films by title and distributor.

National Union Catalog, 1973–77: Films and Other Materials for Projection/compiled and edited by the Catalog Publication Division, Library of Congress. Totowa, N.J.: Rowman and Littlefield, 1978.

SELECTION TOOLS

The Elementary School Library Collection : A Guide to Books and Other Media, Phases 1-2-3/Lois Winkel, editor, assisted by Margaret Edsall . . . et al. 13th ed. Newark, N.J. : Bro-Dart Foundation, 1982.
ISBN 0912654139

"Film: For Children's Eyes"/Tony Gittens. *Essence.* Vol. 10, No. 6, (Oct. 1979), pp. 21–23.
A listing of ten recommended short 16mm films for black children.

"Films for Children"/Patricia Peyton. *Reel Change: A Guide to Social Issue Films.* San Francisco: The Film Fund, Inc., 1979, pp. 92–99.

Films for Children: A Selected List/New York Library Association. Youth Service Section. New York: The Association, 1977.
Highly selective, annotated list of short noninstructional films for use in library programs.

"Films for Kids in the Minority"/Martha Arnoldsen et al. *Film Library Quarterly.* Vol. 9, No. 3, (1976), pp. 46–52.
In an issue devoted to children's films, this article lists se-

lected films for children. Topic headings include Native Americans, Girls, and Black Films.

Films for Three to Five's/Marilyn Collier. Berkeley, Calif.: Instructional Laboratories, Department of Education, University of California, 1976.

Extensive annotation of fifty-seven films for preschool children.

"Films for Very Young Viewers"/Linda Artel. *Sightlines.* Vol. 11, No. 3, (Spring, 1978), pp. 3–10.

Annotated listing of films especially for young viewers.

More Films Kids Like: A Catalog of Short Films for Children/compiled and edited by Maureen Gaffney, assisted in research by Gerry Bond Laybourne and Kay Weidemann Scott. Chicago: American Library Association, 1977.

ISBN 0838902502

A catalog of short films for children with selections based on observed feelings and responses of children themselves. Included are comment on film length and program format and a section on activities relating to films.

A Multimedia Approach to Children's Literature: A Selective List of Films (and videocassettes), Filmstrips, and Recordings Based on Children's Books/edited by Mary Alice Hunt, with a foreword by Ellin Greene. 3rd ed. Chicago : American Library Association, 1983.

ISBN 0838932894

Includes a listing of films based on children's books giving their sources and a brief description of content.

"Notable Children's Films, Filmstrips, Recordings"/compiled by members of Film, Filmstrip, and Recording Evaluation committees of the Association for Library Service to Children. *Top Of The News.* Vol. 40, No. 3, (Spring 1984), pp. 337–342. Also available under the title *ALSC's '84 Notable Films/Filmstrips/Recordings* from American Library Association (pamphlet:cost $0.25 and a SSAE).

Positive Images: A Guide to 400 Nonsexist Films for Young People/Linda Artel, Susan Wengraf. San Francisco: Booklegger Press, 1976.

ISBN 0912932031

Catalog of non-stereotypical 16mm films.

IDEAS/TRENDS

Expanding Media/edited by Deirdre Boyle. Phoenix, AZ : Oryx Press, c1977.
ISBN 0912700033
A collection of articles on the subject of media, including such topics as selection, programming, and evaluation.

Films in the Classroom: A Practical Guide/Hannah Elsas Miller. Metuchen, N.J.: Scarecrow Press, 1979.
ISBN 0810811847
Outstanding resource for the use of children's films. Highlights include "Choosing Films: Previewing" and "Sources of Lists of Films in Special Subject Areas—Appendix D."

"How to Find and Use a Good Film"/Gary A. Wilt. *Instructional Innovator*. Vol. 25, (1980), pp. 43–45.

In Focus: A Guide to Using Films/Linda Blackaby, Dan Georsakas and Barbara Margolis, concept by Affonso Beato, ill. by Tracy Garner. 1st ed. New York: New York Zoetrope, c1980.
ISBN 0918432235
A valuable guidebook for groups organizing a film program, including a useful checklist for film programmers.

Media & Kids: A Real-World Learning in the Schools/James Morrow and Murray Suid. Rochelle Park, N.J.: Hayden Book Co., c1977.
ISBN 0810457989
Classroom techniques for the use of various media.

"Recent Trends in Children's Films"/Robert Grover. *Top Of The News*. Vol. 40, No. 3, (Spring 1984), pp. 285–289.

"Six Years Later: A Re-examination of Trends and Developments in Childrens's Films since 1976"/Martha Barnes. *Film Library Quarterly*. Vol. 15., no. 1, (1982), p. 10.

"The 16mm Treatment: A Prescription for Passive Viewers"/Jeanne Betancourt.
Film Library Quarterly. Vol. 10, No. 3–4, (1977), pp. 4–11, 66.
Article gives helpful techniques for incorporating films into the curriculum.

"Ten Trends in Children's Films"/Mary Alice Hunt. *Florida Media Quarterly*. Vol. 4, No. 3, (Spring 1979), pp. 12–14.

Top Of The News/published by the American Library Association. Vol 40, No. 3, Spring 1984. Special issue titled "Films, Young People, and Libraries."

What to Do When The Lights Go On: A Comprehensive Guide to 16mm Films and Related Activities for Children/Maureen Gaffney and Gerry Bond Laybourne. Phoenix, Ariz.: Oryx Press, c1981.

ISBN 0912700696

Many suggestions are given for activities to follow film programs, including crafts, creative dramatics, and games. Recommended films are annotated with a suggested age level.

REVIEWS

Booklist/published by the American Library Association. Chicago. Published twice monthly September through June and monthly in July and August.
Reviews of 16mm films and filmstrips in each issue.

EFLA Bulletin/published by Educational Film Library Association. New York. Published quarterly.

FLQ, Film Library Quarterly/published by Film Library Information Council. New York. Published quarterly.
ISSN 0160-7316

The Horn Book Magazine/published by Horn Book, Inc. Boston. Published six times a year.
ISSN 0018-5078
Reviews of 16mm films and filmstrips in each issue.

Landers Film Review/published by Landers Associates. Los Angeles. Published bimonthly (5 times a year, Sept. thru June).
ISSN 0023-785X
Film reviews and evaluations covering all age levels and subjects. Reports on award-winning films and yearly source directory of producers and distributors.

Media and Methods/published by American Society of Educators. Philadelphia. Published nine times a year, monthly, except June, July, and August.
ISSN 0025-6897
Contains articles on the use of audiovisual materials in the classroom with regular reviews of 16mm films and filmstrips.

Media Review Digest/published by Pierian Press. Ann Arbor. Annual volume with supplements issued quarterly.
ISSN 0363-7778
An annual index to and digest of reviews, evaluations and descriptions of all forms of film.

Sightlines/published by Educational Film Library Association. New York. Published quarterly.
ISSN 0037-4830

SLJ, School Library Journal/published by Bowker. New York. Published monthly September thru May.
ISSN 0362-8930
Filmstrips and 16mm films are reviewed in the "Audiovisual Review" section which has replaced *Previews* magazine.

Young Viewer/published by Media Center for Children. New York. Published quarterly.
Each issue focuses on a different theme. Issue of special interest include: Winter/Spring 1982, "Using Folktale Films."

Religion Collections and School Libraries

Elizabeth Howard

This bibliographic essay treats the historic problem of religion in public schools, the current imperative that we develop an understanding of the multireligioned (and nonreligioned) society around us, and the need for well-balanced school media collections to include materials on this topic.

Any discussion of collecting materials in religion for school libraries must take into consideration the past and present controversy over the role of religion in public education. Libraries have an important position to play in this area of growing significance for schools and communities across the United States. What makes this a particularly complex issue is that for two decades the public and the schools have generally understood–wrongly–that the Supreme Court declared the schools off limits for religion.

Today the religious/non-religious line is less clear and there are new demands. Whether or not elective courses in religion are offered; whether or not silent prayer is again permitted in the classroom; whether or not students have the right to gather voluntarily for religious purposes, the school library media center has a responsibility to make available appropriate materials for its users. Librarians need to understand the issues, be aware of how they evolved and recognize that collection policies may need to be revised to take into account new interpretations of the First Amendment constraints. There will be more demand for books on religion in school collections, but yet there will also be continuing resistance to the "establishment" of religion.

Dr. Howard is a member of the faculty of West Virginia University.

The first section of this essay reviews briefly the legal history, and discusses the imperatives for and problems in collecting materials in religion. The second section is a history and discusses the imperatives for and problems in collecting materials in religion. The second section is a bibliographical essay on materials recommended for junior or middle and senior high school library collections.

BRIEF HISTORY

Religion has been in American public schools since colonial times. It is not necessary to delve in any depth into the early history. During the formative years of our country and well into the first half of this century, the public schools were expected to provide a good dose of moral education and socialization. Despite the First Amendment restriction against the establishment of religion, there was a distinct Protestant flavor to education. This was Horace Mann's conception of the "common school," for the purpose of weaving one people from the many strands. However, as the United States became more pluralistic and the function of the "common school" began to erode, the Supreme Court handed down several important decisions interpreting the First Amendment. These decisions changed the relationship of religion and public education.

These decisions were designed to set up a "wall of separation" to prevent the state from favoring any one religion. Yet until the *Schempp Case* (374 U.S. 203 (1963)), generalized "American" religiosity (i.e., Protestantism) continued in the background and the public schools carried on the time-honored tradition of some religious exercises, such as prayers and Bible reading, at the opening of each school day. The *Schempp* decision, however, ruled that these types of religious exercises in public schools represented an "advancement" of religion and therefore were unconstitutional.

The immediate reaction in the press was general dismay and anger. The Supreme Court was denounced for "driving God out of the schools." This view the Court's action has not abated and is at the heart of the present movement to restore school prayer. However, this commonly held conviction, that the Court was "against religion," is actually a misinterpretation of the decision.

Justice Clark, writing the opinion in *Schempp,* stated,

> "It might well be said that one's religion is not complete without a study of comparative religion or the history of religion and its relationship to the advancement of civilization. It certainly may be said that the Bible is worthy of study for its literary and historic qualities. Nothing we have said here indicates that such study of the Bible or religion, when presented objectively as part of a secular program of education, may not be effected consistent with the First Amendment."

Justice Goldberg noted in a concurring opinion that the decision ruled out only government sponsored exercises, not teaching about religion. Writing some years later, Justice Clark stated that the perfunctory performance of morning Bible exercises did not help religion, but rather demeaned it. Religion, said Justice Clark, should have a central place in education. But this reading of the decision has not been generally understood.

Not all reaction to the Court's decision was negative, however. In fact, the American Association of School Administrators declared, "Whatever else the Supreme Court decisions may or may not have done, they have stimulated the public schools to search for appropriate means to deal effectively with religion as one of the great influences in man's history." While casual prayer and nominal Bible reading had been the norm, the study of religion had been all but ignored in the public school curriculum. (This lack had been noted in 1953, ten years before *Schempp,* when the American Council on Education called for state departments of education, local school divisions and colleges of education to address themselves to the function of the public school indealing with religion.) Now, in 1963, prayer had been eliminated, but the schools had a clearly stated opportunity to make a place for the study of religion. How did they respond?

There were efforts in some secondary school systems to rise to the possibility, but there were two problems to be overcome: assembling or creating suitable curriculum materials and preparing teachers to handle religion studies objectively and competently. Help was provided by some state departments of education via workshops in curriculum design and teacher preparation. The Public Education Religion Studies Center (PERSC) was established at Wright State University in Dayton, Ohio to provide a national resource center. By 1978, Robert Healey writing in the *Journal of Church and State* (Vol. 20 (1978): pp. 469–489), saw considerable progress in fitting religion studies into the public school curriculum. A national survey in 1979 found 24 percent of secondary schools offering some kind of religion course. But although the challenge was there, most schools either ignored or found too difficult to implement, or did not really comprehend the implications of the *Schempp* decision.

PRESENT SITUATION

The situation in the mid-1980's is complex. Niels Nielsen states that the Supreme Court's distinction between "advancement" of religion and "teaching about" religion is not as widely accepted as previously. The issues are less clear than they were in 1963. This is due, it would appear, to the present religious climate. Indeed, there has been a great deal of ferment and upheaval in the religious atmosphere of America in the 21 years since the Schempp decision.

A growing conservatism in religious as well as political outlook, probably as a pendulum swing from the alleged or actual excesses of the '60's and '70's, has led to such pressures as the movement to legislate prayer back into the schools, and the recent Supreme Court decision to allow voluntary, student led religious gatherings on school property. Fundamentalist religious groups are asking for alternative ways of teaching evolution, leading to the controversy over scientific creationism. The charismatic movement and religious revivalism on the '70's are very much alive, while the mainline churches are losing membership. Religious programming is a lively part of radio and television. Religious publishing is enjoying a boom, including religious publishing for children. Added to all of this and related to it has been the development of textbook watchdog committees, which exert pressure on publishers and on school systems. New religious groups have proliferated, many in the form of cults, where troubled youth turn for answers. And yet, at the same time, in the midst of these conservative trends, the American people are becoming more diversified. Our involvement with other parts of the world, non-Western and non-Christian nations intensifies.

As Thomas Hunt has written (*Religious Education,* v. 74 (1979), schools need an approach to religion that will help students to "understand something of the nature and history of religion without forcing them to abandon, change or adopt a faith stance." Increased understanding of religious issues is fundamental. It is becoming necessary for students to explore the essentially religious issues of war and peace, nuclear developments and environmental dangers, plenty and scarcity, freedom and restraint. Indeed, it appears ever more evident that the public schools cannot avoid religion.

THE ROLE OF THE SCHOOL LIBRARIAN

It is not suggested here that the school library media specialist take any stand or lead any crusade for religion in the schools. What is suggested is that the library media center be equipped with materials on different religions and religious issues for students and teachers. The librarian is the materials expert. There is a vast quantity of materials already available, and more being published. The librarian needs to be knowledgeable about materials in this important area and recognize the necessity of adequate library collections in religion.

DEVELOPING RELIGION COLLECTIONS
FOR SCHOOL LIBRARY MEDIA CENTERS

How does the librarian build an effective collection in religion? The answer must grow out of the selection policy of the school. School library selection policies, if they are based on the School Library Bill of Rights, affirm that controversial issues need to be presented in a balanced way. Some policies specifically state that there must be no purchase of materials designed to promote a particular religion. Since current selection journals used by schools tend not to review books published by the religious presses, materials recommended in the retrospective sources are likely to meet this requirement.

Beyond the general guidelines of the selection policy, the development of an effective collection will depend on its purposes. Is the library media center supporting a specific course in religion studies, e.g., The Bible as Literature, or Comparative World Religions, or The History of Religion? Is the collection aiming to provide supplementary materials for occasional units within regular courses, such as a social studies unit on the Puritans or the Quakers or the Islamic concept of a holy war? Is the collection to supply background or discussion materials on religious issues such as the development of cults, or for topics in ethics such as euthanasia or conscientious objection to military service? At the middle school level, is there primarily a need to have materials on the customs and holidays of different religions?

RECOMMENDED BOOKS ON RELIGION FOR SCHOOL LIBRARY MEDIA CENTERS

This section of the paper is a selected bibliography of nonfiction print materials, i.e., reference and trade books, for junior and senior high school library media collections. Unless otherwise stated, all of the works suggested were listed in at least one recommended catalog or list. The following tools were examined: Petersons's *Reference Books for School Libraries*, Wynar's *Guide to Reference Books for School Media Centers*, the three Wilson catalogs: *Children's Catalog, Junior High School Catalog, Senior High School Catalog*, and the National Council of Teachers of English current booklists for junior high and middle school, and for senior high schools.

Materials are suggested in the following categories: reference works, including general encyclopedias; several versions of the Bible; specialized sources for studying the Bible, i.e., Bible encyclopedias and dictionaries; atlases; concordances and quotation books; biographical dictionaries and Bible stories retold for young readers. Also included are works on history, beliefs, practices and literatures of the major religions of the world (Hinduism, Buddhism, Judaism, Christianity, and Islam; the history of religion in America; biographies of religious figures; and books covering such contemporary topics as cults and current ethical issues. Although not included in the scope of this article, the librarian should attempt to be aware of the fiction in which religion is discussed in any meaningful way.

GENERAL ENCYCLOPEDIAS

A survey of 10 major general encyclopedias likely to be found in school libraries indicated that encyclopedias are major curriculum resources for the study of religion. Objective, authoritative, readable, and well illustrated articles on the five major religions of the world might form the beginning of a study of comparative religion. A careful review of the encyclopedias would uncover briefer articles on specific topics, such as monasticism, Passover, Nirvana, or key personalities, such as George Fox and Pope John XXIII. School librarians can alert teachers considering units or courses in religion studies that usable curriculum materials are already at hand.

The Bible

Several versions of the Bible are recommended in the *Junior* and *Senior High Catalogs*. The King James version, essential for historical and literary study, is available in many editions. One published by Nelson in 1982, "the new King James version" is in more contemporary English. Other suggested Bibles include *The Jerusalem Bible* (available in various editions), the Roman Catholic *New American Bible* (Kenedy, 1970), translated by an ecumenical group of scholars; and the *New English Bible* (Oxford, 1970). Peterson notes also *The Holy Scriptures According to the Masoretic Text* (Jewish Publication Society of America, 1917). *Good News for Modern Man: The New Testament in Today's English* is suggested for easier reading.

Several acclaimed collections of Bible stories are available. For upper elementary and junior high the *Taize Picture Bible* (Fortress, 1969), adapted from the Jerusalem Bible, has 143 stories from the Old and New Testament is highly recommended for its simplified language and appealing illustrations. *Bible Stories You Can't Forget No Matter How Hard You Try* by Marshall Efron and Alpha-Betty Olsen (Dutton, 1976) retells eight of the best known stories (e.g., Noah, Joseph, Tower of Babel, etc.) in contemporary English. Bernard Evslin's *Signs and Wonders: Tales from the Old Testament* (Four Winds, 1981) adds conversation to some well known stories. *City of Gold and Other Stories from the Old Testament* by Peter Dickinson (Pantheon, 1980, 188p.) vividly recalls well known stories (such as Samuel hearing the Lord's voice) from the point of view of people who witnessed or were immediately affected by the events. For younger readers, but also of interest to older children are Meindert Dejong's *The Mighty Ones: Great Men and Women of Early Bible Days* (Harper, 1959, 282 p.) and Walter De La Mare's poetically rendered retellings of the first nine books of the Old Testament, *Stories From the Bible* (Knopf, 1961, 420 p.)

Numerous sources are available to support the academic study of the Bible, including Bible dictionaries or encyclopedias atlases, and books focusing on the history, personalities or life in Biblical times.

Bible Encyclopedias

Cecil Northcott, *Bible Encyclopedia for Children* (Westminster, 1964, 176 p.) has 850 brief entries on people, places and events, and is easy to read. *Eerdman's Family Encyclopedia of the Bible* (Eerdmans, 1978, 328 p.) has chapters on subjects such as archaeology, family life, and an alphabetically arranged section on people and places. *The New Westminster Dictionary of the Bible* (Westminster, 1970, 1027 p.) is a standard reference work on events, places, persons, flora and fauna. It contains about 450 illustrations and excellent full color maps. This is comparable to *Harper's Bible Dictionary*, now in its eighth revision. The Harper volume includes lists under some selected headings such as all the flowers of the Bible wth Latin names and quotations from scripture.

The Times and the People

Handbooks on what it is was like to live in Biblical times are another type of useful source. A.C. Bouqet's *Everyday Life in New Testament Times* (Scribner, 1953, 235 p.) and E. W. Heaton's *Everyday Life in Old Testament Times* (Scribner, 1956, 240 p.) are companion volumes with articles on topics such as family life, food and drink, amusements, agriculture, education, medicine, etc. A highly recommended work dealing with the times of Abraham, Moses, David, Solomon, Jesus and Paul is *Everyday Life in Bible Times* published by the National Geographic Society (1977, c1967, 448 p.) This contains authoritative essays and hundreds of illustrations, 412 in color.

Two biographical dictionaries, companion volumes, are published by Holt: Ronald Bronrigg, *Who's Who in the New Testament* (1971) and Joan Comay, *Who's Who in the Old Testament Together with the Apocrypha* (1977). Each includes approximately 450 black and white illustrations and maps. Elie Wiesel's *Messengers of God: Biblical Portraits and Legends* (Random House, 1976, 237 p.) is a collection of glowing word paintings of major Old Testament figures.

Atlases and Archaeology

Hammond's *Atlas of the Bible Lands* (1948) has full color maps, photographs, city plans, and a time chart. It is recommended for upper elementary and older students. *The Golden Bible Atlas* (1957) by Samuel Terrien is arranged chronologically. F. F. Bruce's *Bible History Atlas* (Garrard, 1982) is recommended in the *Junior High Catalog*. Oxford (Random House, 1974), Macmillan (1977), and the Reader's Digest (1982, c1981) have contributed reliable atlases.

Archaeology of the Bible by Magnus Magnusson, a lively account of research for a television documentary, aims to show how recent excavations relate to Biblical accounts. *Digging Up the Bible: Stories Behind the Great Archaeological Discoveries in the Holy Land* (Morrow, 1980, 240 p.) introduces the most important biblical archaeologists and describes their search for the past. The excitement of archaeological discovery is recalled in Iris Noble's *Treasures of the Caves: The Story of the Dead Sea Scrolls* (Macmillan, 1971, 214 p.)

The Bible as History, 2nd rev. ed. (Morrow, 1981, 413 p.), relates archaeological evidence to Biblical history, partly confirming and partly questioning tradition. Two works by Isaac Asimov add valuable commentary. In a "neither irreverent nor pious" approach Asimov's *Guide to the Bible* (Avon,

1971, 2 v.) is an informal discussion which relates places, persons and events to historical, geographical and scientific research. *In the Beginning . . .* (Crown, 1981, 234 p.) seeks a balance between biblical literalism and science in the story of Creation.

Concordances and Quotation Books

Harper's *Topical Concordance* (1962, 628 p.) and Nelson's *Complete Concordance* are among the several available. Stevenson's *Home Book of Bible Quotations* (Harper and Row, 1949, 645 p.) is an old stand-by.

The Bible As Literature

Teaching the Old Testament in English Classes (James S. Ackerman, Alan W. Jenks and Edward B. Jenkinson, Indiana University Press, 197f, 3, 512 p.) is a handbook for junior and senior high school English teachers, and supplements Ackerman's *On Teaching the Bible as Literature* (1967) T. R. Henn's *The Bible As Literature* analyzes the literary elements and qualities of the King James Version. A helpful handbook is Walter B. Fulghum Jr.'s *A Dictionary of Biblical Allusions in English Literature,* an alphabetical arrangement from both the King James and the Roman Catholic versions.

COMPARATIVE RELIGION

Religion studies courses in secondary school are likely to come under the heading of Comparative Religion. Listed here are selected works which treat the major contemporary religions in the world. Books on mythology, i.e., the religions of the ancient world, are not included, although it is assumed that a media center collection would include important works such as Bulfinch's *Mythology,* Sir James Frazer's *The Golden Bough,* and Edith Hamilton's *Mythology.*

Despite its rather dated black and white photographs, *Their Search For God: Ways of Worship in the Orient,* by Florence Mary Fitch (Lothrop, 1947, 160 p.) continues to be a popular introduction to different religions and their practices, suitable for younger readers and for high school students. For junior high Lavinia Dobler's *Customs and Holidays around the World* (Fleet Press, 1962, 234 p.) includes Christian, Jewish, Buddhist and Islamic religious holidays. Two books by Marietta D. Moskin, published by Atheneum, are thoughtful and highly readable. *In Search of God: The Story of Religion* (1979, 142 p.) ponders why human beings seek God. *In the Name of God: Religion in Everyday Life* is an historical look at comparative religion, with short commentaries on Islam, Hinduism, Buddhism, Mormonism, Protestantism, Roman Catholicism, Eastern Orthodoxy, and Judaism. For upper elementary and older readers A. M. Zehavi has edited *The Handbook of the World's Religions* (Watts, 1973, 203 p.) which considers Christianity, Judaism and the religions of the East. Taken from the *Encyclopedia International,* the material is well organized with numerous photographs. As a reference source for more advanced readers there is Geoffrey Parrinder, *Dictionary of Non-Christian Religions* (Westminster, 1973, 320 p.). This includes definitions, drawings and photographs, and information on all non-Christian religions. Another highly recommended source is *Dictionary of Comparative Religion,* edited by S. G. F. Brandon (Scribner's, 1970, 704 p.). *Great Religions of the World* (National Geographic, 1978, 420 p.) edited by Huston Smith is a gloriously illustrated volume presenting the history, customs, beliefs of Hinduism, Buddhism, Judaism, Islam and Christianity. It is recommended as a reference source.

Three highly recommended volumes consider the religions of east and west. Joseph Gaer, *What the Great Religions Believe* (New American Library, c1963, 192 p.) presents extracts from the literature of eleven major religions (Hinduism, Buddhism, Jainism, Confucianism, Taoism, Shintoism, Judaism, Christianity, Islam, Zoroastrianism, Zen-Buddhism). Larry Kettlekamp, *Religions, East and West* (Morrow, 1972, 128 p.) surveys major religions and includes sections on science and religion, psychic science and archaeology. Edward Rice, *The Five Great Religions* (Four Winds, 1973, 180 p.) is an historical approach which compares Christianity with the other religions, noting how it has been criticized.

Several works dealing specifically with religions of the East complement one another. As a reference work Edward Rice's

Eastern Definitions: A Short Encyclopedia of Religions of the Orient (Doubleday, 1978, 433 p.) covers religions of Asia and Africa. Elizabeth Seeger, *Eastern Religions* (Crowell, 1973, 213 p.) discusses Hinduism, Buddhism, Confucianism, Taoism, and Shinto. *Three Ways of Asian Wisdom: Hinduism, Buddhism, Zen and other Significance for the West* (Simon & Schuster, 1978, c1966, 222 p.) by Nancy Wilson Ross describes each religion showing how it contrasts with western art and culture. An important geographical and historical reference work notably useful for finding information on Asian and African religions is the *Historical Atlas of the Religions of the World,* by Isma'il R. al Faruqi and David E. Sopher (Macmillan, 1974, 346 p.), recommended for junior and senior high school students.

Hinduism and Buddhism

A handful of books on individual eastern religions are available. For younger readers *Hinduism* by I. G. Edmonds (Watts, 1979, 64 p.) considers various aspects of the religion and its relation to Indian culture. *The Hindu Sound* by William Corlett and John Moore (Bradbury, 1980, c1978, 151 p.) considers how Hindu sacred literature deals with basic questions such as "Who am I?"

Buddhism has also received an introductory treatment by I. G. Edmonds (Watts, 1978, 65 p.). A more in depth coverage is presented by Nancy Wilson Ross in *Buddhism: A Way of Life and Thought* (Knopf, 1980, 208 p.). This is a clear explication of the various forms of Buddhism. Recommended also for senior high is Alan Watts, *The Way of Zen* (Pantheon, 1957, 236 p.).

Islam

Islam, by I. G. Edmonds (Watts, 1977, 65 p.) is an introduction, retelling the events of Mohammed's life and the influence of Judeo-Christian teachings on his thinking. It includes the obligations of the Muslim faith and some description of the different forms of Islam. For more advanced readers Caesar Farah's *Islam: Beliefs and Observances* (Barron's Educational Series, 1970, 306 p.) is a description of the religion and of Islam as a political entity. In *Arabs and the Islamic World* (S. G. Phillips, 1979), Frank Ross, Jr. presents information on Mohammed's teachings and on the people of the Arab world. Another work is Fazlur Rahman's *Islam* (2d ed. University of Chicago Press, 1979, 285 p.)

The edition of the Koran recommended for senior high school libraries is the translation by George Sale (Warner; paper back by Dent or by Penguin Books).

Judaism

There is a wealth of recommended material on Judaism. For younger readers an introduction to Judaism is provided by Seymour Rossel's *Judaism* (Watts, 1976, 61 p.) At a more advanced level there is *What is a Jew?* by Morris N. Kertzer (Bloch, 1973, 217 p.). According to the foreword this is "a survey of all those beliefs and customs those ancient values and practices those persisting traditions and inner commitments which taken together constitutes what it is that lies at the heart of Judaism." *Basic Judaism* by Milton Steinberg (Harcourt, 1965, c1947, 172 p) is a brief explanation of Jewish beliefs, history and practices. Rabbi Roland B. Gittelsohn's *The Modern Meaning of Judaism* (William Collins Publishers, 1978) contrasts Jewish and Christian beliefs to allow Christian readers a method of understanding Judaism. *The Junior Jewish Encyclopedia* (Shengold, 1979. 1 vol.) covers topics such as history, customs, communal life, biography, literature and legal structure, and includes hundreds of illustrations. Also recommended for schools is the one volume *New Standard Jewish Encyclopedia* 5th ed. (Doubleday, 1977) with 8,000 short articles. The most comprehensive source on Judaism and undoubtedly beyond the requirements of most school library media collections is the *Encyclopaedia Judaica* (Jerusalem: Encyclopedia Judaica; New York: Macmillan, 16 v., 1972).

Selections from Jewish literature are found in *A Treasury of Jewish Literature: From Biblical Times to Today* (Holt, Rinehart & Winston, 1982, 243 p.), edited by Gloria Goldreich. The excitement of archaeological discovery is recalled in Iris Noble's *Treasure of the Caves: The Story of the Dead Sea Scrolls* (Macmillan, 1971, 214 p.).

Jewish holidays are described in several works. *All About Jewish Holidays and Customs* by Morris Epstein (Ktav, 1970, 142 p.) is a handbook describing holidays and explaining symbols. Individual holidays and customs are portrayed in several books by Howard Greenfeld, and published by Holt, Rinehart and Winston. *Chanukah* (1976, 39 p.), *Passover* (1978, 32 p.), *Rosh Hashanah and Yom Kippur* (1979, 31 pp.) and *Bar Mitzvah* (1981, 32 pp). *Hanukkah: Eight Nights, Eight Lights* by Malka Drucker (Holiday House, 1980) tells the history of the holiday, explains the menorah, and gives recipes and instructions for games and crafts.

Christianity

Introductory materials on Christianity without doctrinal point of view are hard to find. One possibility, not located in the selection tools but suggested by the Children's Department at Carnegie Library in Pittsburgh, is *Christianity*, by Irene Cumming Kleeberg (Franklin Watts, 1976, 87 p.) This concise precis of the origins and history of Christianity, its Jewish roots, major differences between Protestants and Roman Catholics, and short descriptions of Protestant denominations, grew out of a course the author taught in a New York City high school. A useful reference work for senior high schools is Paul Johnson's *A History of Christianity* (Atheneum, 1977, 556 p.). One dictionary of Christianity would be important, such as *The New International Dictionary of the Christian Church* (Revised ed., edited by J. D. Douglas. Zondervan, 1978, 1074 p.) or *The Concise Oxford Dictionary of the Christian Church*, ed. by Elizabeth A. Livingstone. 2d ed. abridged (Oxford, 1977, 570 p.). Middle school children might use Michael Daves, *Young Readers Book of Christian Symbolism* (Abingdon, 1977, 128 p.)

Books on the Life of Jesus

In Search of the Historic Jesus by Lee Roddy and Charles E. Sellier Jr. (Bantam Books, 1979) seeks to corroborate Biblical events with non-Biblical historical accounts. Jim Bishop's *The Day Christ Died* is an hour by hour report of the Last Supper and the events of Good Friday (Harper, 1957, 336 p.). A biographical work of long time acclaim is Fulton Oursler's *The Greatest Story Ever Told* (Doubleday, 1949, 299 p.). *Jesus, His Life and Times* (Morrow, 1979, 224 p.) by the Genesis Project, Inc., is a unique presentation including a modern English rendering of the Gospel of Luke, yellow inserts of background information, and prints from "The New Media Bible." William Barclay's *Jesus of Nazareth* is based on the film by Anthony Burgess, and is copiously illustrated (William Collins Publishers, 1977). A thoughtful volume is Humphrey Carpenter's *Jesus* (Hill and Wang, 1980, 102 p.) which attempts to study the teachings of Jesus in comparison with others of his times. *Christ and the Fine Arts* by Cynthia Pearl Maus (Harper, 1959, 813 p.) is "an antholgy of pictures, poetry, music and stories centering in the life of Christ."

Two books on Christmas customs would be good additions. *Celebrating Christmas Around the World,* edited by Herbert H. Wernecke (Westminster, 1962, 246 p.) includes Africa, Asia and South America; D. Foley's *Christmas the World Over* (Chilton, 1963) describes festival traditions in 34 countries.

The Roman Catholic Church

Two encyclopedias are noted dealing with Roman Catholicism. One is the 17 volume *New Catholic Encyclopedia* (Catholic University of America and McGraw-Hill, 1967), "an international work of reference on the teachings, history, organization and activities of the philosophies and scientific and cultural developments affecting the Catholic Church from its beginning to the present." The other, and more accessible for school libraries, is the one volume work by Robert C. Broderick, *The Catholic Encyclopedia* (Nelson, 1976, 612 p.) with 4000 entries on subjects related to Catholic beliefs and practices.

HISTORY OF RELIGION IN AMERICA

American religious history is fertile territory providing several volumes recommended for junior and senior high collections. Sydney Ahlstrom's *A Religious History of the American*

People (Yale, 1972, 1158 p.) discusses religious thought in the context of social, political and intellectual history. Edwin S. Gaustad in *A Religious History of America* (Harper, 1974, c1966, 421 p.) discusses the three major faiths in the United States and their place in American religious history. Gaustad has also authored *Historical Atlas of Religion in America* (Harper and Row, 1976, 189 p.). Two works give a view of the contemporary religious scene. Leo Rosten's *Religions of America: Ferment and Faith in an Age of Crisis* (Simon and Schuster, 1975, 672 p.) summarizes the beliefs of 16 denominations, includes a statement on agnosticism by Bertrand Russell, and one on the religion of a scientist by Warren Weaver and on the "Unchurched" by Edward Ericson. *Handbook of Denominations in the United States* by Frank S. Mead (7th ed. Abingdon Press, 1980, 320 p.) provides brief facts on the history, organization, beliefs of 250 denominations in the United States. The role of women in the history of American religion from the 17th to the 20th century is surveyed in a collection of essays, *Women in American Religion,* edited by Janet Wilson James (University of Pennsylvania Press, 1980, 274 p.). Daniel Cohen discusses revivalism as an exciting leaven in American history in *The Spirit of the Lord: Revivalism in America* (Four Winds, 1975, 220 p.). This begins with the Great Awakening in Puritan times, and includes Billy Graham and the Jesus movement of the 1970's.

OTHER DENOMINATIONS

Although there were no books about main line Protestant denominations listed in the sources used (the librarian would need to turn to the denominational presses directly) some lesser known religious groupings were treated. *Amish People: Plain Living in a Complex World* by Carolyn Meyer (Atheneum, 1976, 138 p.) combines photographs and fact-filled text to describe sympathetically the life style and beliefs of a typical Amish family. Two books portray the Shakers for junior high and older readers. Doris Faber's *The Perfect Life: The Shakers in America* (Farrar Straus, 1974, 215 p.) and Jane Yolen's *Simple Gifts: The Story of the Shakers* (Viking, 1976, 115 p.) explore history, customs, way of life and art. Another misunderstood religious denomination is sympathetically presented in Leonard Arrington's comprehensive and objective *The Mormon Experience: A History of the Latter Day Saints* (Knopf, 1979, 404 p.).

Cults

The presence of persuasive "cult" groups on the religious scene today is of concern to many who are involved with young adults. Three recent works treat this topic. In *Crazy for God* (Prentice Hall, 1979, 233 p.) author Christopher Edwards describes his sudden conversion to the Unification Church, and his later abduction by his father and deprogramming by the well-known deprogrammer Ted Patrick. Patrick, with Tom Dulack, has told of his experiences in *Let Our Children Go!* (Ballantine Books, 1979). *All God's Children: The Cult Experience–Salvation or Slavery?* by Carroll Stoner and Jo Anne Parke (Chilton Book Co., 1977, 324 p.) is a critical and sensitive investigation of the effect of the cult experience on converts and their parents.

PHILOSOPHY AND ETHICS

Serious high school students might dip into the classic treatise on the psychology of religious experience, William James' time-honored work *The Varieties of Religious Experience* (New American Library, 1936,c1902, 526 p.). Another suggestion for thoughtful readers is *The Christ Story* by William Corlett and John Moore (Bradbury Press (1980, c1978, 153 p.). Ideas in the Gospels are related to adolescence. Karl Menninger's *Whatever Became of Sin?* (Hawthorn Books, 1973, 242 p.) posits that sin, by whatever name, is still very present in the world.

Ethical issues are dealt with in several works. Ann E. Weiss, *God and Government: The Separation of Church and State* (Houghton Mifflin, 1982, 132 p.) asks readers to think about what religious freedom means in the case of conflicting beliefs. John Langone's *Thorny Issues: How Ethics and Morality Affect the Way We Live* (Little, 1981, 220 p.) discusses ethics in medicine, business, science, the press and human rights, presenting alternatives. *Matters of Life and Death* by Edward F. Dolan, Jr. (Watts, 1982, 119 p.) considers issues of abortion and euthanasia in a carefully balanced manner. *The Emerging Order: God in the Age of Scarcity,* by Jeremy Rifkin with Ted Howard (G. P. Putnam's Sons, 19, 272 p.) urges Americans to take seriously the possibility of self-destruction caused by our own selfish disregard of the earth and the environment.

School library media religion collections undoubtedly will be the object of attention as interest in this area continues to develop. It will become increasingly important for school library media specialists to consider these issues in relation to local needs.

Relating Software to Instruction: Problems and Resources in Software Selection and Evaluation

Keith Swigger

This paper discusses problems associated with the collection of software for computer assisted instruction. Sources for reviews and procedures for dealing with problems in evaluating CAI programs.

INTRODUCTION

The ubiquitous microcomputer poses a set of questions and challenges to school librarians and learning resource specialists who must add to their collections the software on which the usefulness of the computer depends. Some of these challenges are new, arising from the unique nature of the technology itself. Others are persistent issues raised in a new guise. The purpose of this paper is to discuss problems associated with collection of software for computer assisted instruction (CAI), to sort out new and older problems, and to identify resources and procedures for dealing with them.

CAI SOFTWARE FOR MICROCOMPUTERS

Publication

The development of relatively inexpensive microcomputers in the late 1970s gave a dramatic boost to the production of CAI materials. Although there were some extensive CAI im-

Dr. Swigger is a faculty member at the School of Library Science, Texas Woman's University, Denton, TX.

plementations on minicomputers and mainframe computers using distributed processing, mostly in universities, CAI had not had a major impact on education mainly because hardware was not widely available to support it. In those institutions where hardware was available, diffusion of CAI through the curriculum was slow because faculty using traditional teaching methods proved reluctant to accept the new technology, just as they have been slow to adopt other nonprint educational technologies. Microcomputers made the use of CAI on a wide scale economically feasible. Advocates of the new technology allied with advocates of educational reform in demanding innovation. The problem shifted suddenly from a shortage of hardware to a shortage of software to run on the new machines. There was a product in search of applications. Many authors and publishers saw the opportunity and CAI software has been appearing in the last few years at a rate dizzying to those who must select among the many programs now available.

What had been the research province of educators and computer scientists suddenly became a cottage industry. Anyone with a microcomputer and a modest knowledge of programming, or of use of a microcomputer-based authoring language such as PILOT, could write CAI programs. Many of these authors established their own software publishing firms or sold their products to publishers eager to enter the new market. Major publishers of educational materials began acquisitions programs and distributors of educational materials also entered the market. Currently it appears the smaller, entrepreneurial firms are being rapidly absorbed by the larger publishing houses. The general "shakeout" in the microcomputer software publishing business also seems to be taking place in the CAI sector of the industry.

These transition stages in the software publishing industry have occurred since about 1980. CAI software publishing for microcomputers has been a commercial enterprise. Even where the enterprise has been one of non-profit institutions, such as the Minnesota Educational Computer Consortium (MECC) the programs available are largely the work of individuals working in isolation from other CAI authors and from producers of other kinds of instructional materials. Consequently the CAI products challenge the purchaser or user—

the librarian or teacher—to find ways to integrate the programs into more broadly conceived curricula and programs of instruction. Because they are usually written as separate pieces rather than as parts of a program of instruction, it is left for the educator to decide which CAI software is appropriate, and where, in the context of the complete instructional program.

CAI As a Tactic

Deciding whether to employ CAI, and if so which CAI programs to use, is ideally a last step in instructional design. It is a tactical decision, as described in Romiszowski's (1981) model: philosophies and theories of instruction determine instructional strategies; instructional strategies determine instructional plans; instructional plans determine tactics; and instructional tactics are applied to determine specific instructional exercises in some medium.

It would seem reasonably simple to select CAI programs in accordance with the above model. The fragmentary nature of CAI publication seems appropriate. Following the textbook models we all learned in school, selection would be simply a process of matching the specifications of a candidate CAI program to the complete specifications of the curriculum (Freeman, 1984); find a match and select it. In practice, things are not so neat. Assuming the philosophy, goals and strategies of the curriculum were cast and specified in detail, it is not the case that programs are so clearly documented. In fact, few curricula are. As most teachers know, curricula are dynamic. What is taught depends in part on what is available with which to teach. New technologies and new products create new teaching opportunities, and real course design is a continuing interplay between curricular strategies and available tactical tools.

CAI has traditionally been seen as a supplement to other modes of instruction. In its current commercially available form, it can only be used as a supplement. What are now available are building blocks, pieces which each instructor must combine with other CAI programs and other instructional materials to make a cohesive whole. Since its inception, CAI has been viewed as a technique for individualizing instruction. Most CAI now produced for microcomputers, however, is centered on presentation of a particular skill or concept and not on the cognitive styles or learning rates of particular types of students. However, since the same subject matter may be taught at various skill levels or in any of a variety of CAI modes (drill and practice, tutorial, simulation, or game) it is possible to build CAI into the curriculum piecemeal. What must happen is akin to the familiar process of selecting any materials to supplement or complement a textbook, or to suit the needs of a particular group of learners. A teacher surveys resources available (starting with what is immediately available locally) to find a tool that works; if no ideal tool is found, and one seldom is, the curriculum subtly changes so that what is found does fit.

The nature of most CAI programs as they are currently published creates a dilemma for those librarians and resource specialists who must select from the universe of materials available. One consideration is the desire to make available as wide a variety of resources as possible in order to support differing teachers' demands and students' needs; one aims to support variety and flexibility and allow for innovation in a rapidly changing field. Yet what is selected must support the existing curricular program. The dilemma is an old one not unique to computer materials. As the editor of this volume expressed it, "Existing collections influence the kind of service which can be provided. On the other hand, demand for services influences the collection" (White, 1984). Few existing CAI software collections are large, but the atmosphere surrounding introduction of microcomputers into the curriculum is so charged with conflicting expectations that the initial acquisitions are likely to "define" the collection in users' minds prematurely, as they rush to judge the value of CAI. In general, it seems that teachers want CAI programs that are compatible with the existing curriculum (Gallagher, 1984), while parents, legislators, and assorted reformers look to CAI as part of an electronic package that will revolutionize education and help take us into what is perceived as a new era.

It is not my purpose here to discuss the merits of CAI as a tactic for instruction. Such discussions are numerous (cf. Coburn, 1982; Salisbury, 1984; Walker and Hess, 1984). It is reasonable to assume that demands for CAI programs will increase and that librarians and resource personnel will be required to participate in the selection of such materials. Survey data (Hawk, 1983) and the current spate of conference programs, library school courses and workshops, and new textbooks (Costa and Costa, 1984; Troutner, 1984) all indicate the expanding role of librarians in CAI selection. In fulfilling that role, it is appropriate to examine these new materials and the stock of familiar selection tools and procedures to see what is new and to see where familiar practices still apply.

Librarians, Media Specialists and CAI—What's New?

CAI obviously requires use of new hardware, but learning to operate microcomputers is fairly trivial and quickly learned. (Learning to program computers or to write CAI is another matter; neither is as simple as sometimes portrayed, but resource personnel need not be involved in the *creation* of programs.) Much of the mystique of CAI derives from the unfamiliarity of the hardware itself. A brief survey of some of the components of CAI programs as they appear to the user shows that many of the characteristics of CAI are characteristics of materials school resource personnel have long been familiar with. CAI employs graphics, and these must be evaluated for aesthetic value, appropriateness, and technical quality. Many CAI programs use sound, in the form of beeps or other noises, music, or in some instances voice synthesis, and these characteristics must be assessed. Media attributes of CAI are reviewed by Leiblum (1982). CAI presents textual material, which must be examined for accuracy, readability, and motivational quality. Most CAI has accompanying instructions (called "documentation") which teachers must read and relay to students. Educators who have experience in selecting books, films, video tapes, film strips and other media are schooled in the criteria to use in assessing such characteristics, and these carry over directly to the evaluation and selection of CAI. For example, the application of evaluative techniques for film to evaluation of CAI has been explored by Della-Piana (1982), who argues that such techniques can help demystify CAI.

What is new about CAI? (1) The degree to which it can combine the features of other media into a single package (2) which *interacts* (apparently intelligently) with students to teach a skill or concept. CAI programs interactively teach in a way that no previous medium has done. CAI programs provide feedback and reinforcement, they repeat instructional sections or frames as required, they branch through material in accord with the interest or achievement level of students, and, in simulation mode, they give students some degree of control over the world being modeled. In the process these programs employ graphics, sound and text. This is not to claim that CAI is better than other media, simply that it is different. Media are combined in a system. The components of the system may not be new to materials selectors, but systematic thinking about the interaction and synergy of the components may be. Selectors must take care in applying their established skills in media evaluation so that the successful interplay of media effects is evaluated.

The evaluation of content of a CAI program is a more difficult matter. There are two problems here. First, what is the content and second, is the content consistent with the philosophy of the full curriculum?

Determining the content of a CAI curriculum is as difficult as determining the content of any record of human thought, and it poses some challenging twists on the problem. Research in the field of discourse analysis has been divided between studies of conversation, focusing on the exchange of information and propositions between speakers/listeners, and studies of text, in which the object is to develop techniques for articulating the content of texts in terms of logical propositions and the ways in which readers derive them (c.f. Kintsch, 1974; van Dijk, 1980; Kintsch and van Dijk, 1983). Techniques for formalizing the content of texts for research purposes have been developed (c.f. Turner and Greene, 1978), but these will not serve for CAI and in any event they are too cumbersome to apply in daily work situations. CAI presents the intriguing case of a combination of conversation and text. A CAI program can only present text, but the text it presents may, due to the branching ability of the program, vary according to the conversation of the student. Researchers have been careful to point out distinctions between conversations and text, yet here we have a case where the two are combined. Development of ways to predict the content, or propositions, that a student will take away from a CAI lesson is an open area of research. The development of "intelligent CAI" in which programs are capable of actually constructing the machine's side of a conversation is another open research field which has yet to produce findings useful to selectors of materials.

There is more to "content" of a work, of course, than the logical propositions one can find in it. There are many kinds of content; there is the content the author intended to convey, the content a panel of objective expert readers might discover, the subjective content an individual derives from experiencing the work, as well as a range of types of "hidden" content that convey and reinforce cultural themes. Works in content analysis (Cary, 1976), semiotics (MacCannell and MacCannell, 1982), information retrieval (Maron, 1975), and discourse analysis (Turner and Greene, 1974; Tannen, 1979), just to name a few of the relevant disciplines, have identified some of the difficulties in specifying the content of a document.

The important content of a CAI program must be the knowledge a student acquires as a result of experiencing it. An indication of our current inability to specify what happens when a student experiences a CAI program is that we have no name for the experience—one *reads* a book, *watches* a film, *listens* to a recording—but what is the appropriate active verb for experiencing a CAI lesson? Verbs commonly used, based on impressions from reading the literature, are "work," "use," and "do." None of these reflect the range of intellectual, emotional, and sensory experiences involved in ****'ing a CAI program. But surely the content of a CAI program lies in the knowledge or information it develops through all the competencies called upon.

Difficulties in determining the content of a CAI lesson can be illustrated with a simple example. "Speed/Bingo Math" (Commodore Electronics, 1983) combines drill and practice in arithmetic with a game. The game may be played by one or two persons. Players select a type of arithmetic to practice (addition, subtraction, multiplication, or division). A matrix similar to a Bingo card appears on the screen for each player. As each problem appears on the screen (—— + 1 = 6), the player must compute the answer, find it on the Bingo card, then move the cursor to the appropriate cell with a joystick within 10 seconds. Incorrect answers produce a buzz, correct answers a pleasant beep. A player wins when a row or column of correct answers is completed.

What is the content of "Bingo/Math"? There is very little text other than the simple instructions for operating the game. Students practice arithmetic, and if a sample of one (my daughter) is valid, the game helps students memorize sums and remainders. Hand/eye coordination is necessary, so that skill is improved also; students learn to operate the joystick. Before she mastered the joystick and the arithmetic, however, and became a consistent winner, Jessica experienced frustration, anger, and resentment at what she felt was unfair competition by the machine, all of which were replaced by confidence and pride, followed shortly by boredom and a desire to move on to something more challenging. This was Jessica's first computer game. Using(?) it, she improved her skill in arithmetic. She improved her hand/eye coordination, and quickly became a formidable PAC-MAN opponent, when that game was acquired. She also learned, in ways I cannot measure, something about patience, about determination (she played about twenty minutes daily for two weeks before she won), about competition and accepting losing, and about winning. Whether she learned more about arithmetic, about the importance of manipulating tools, or about competition, all of which are important in American culture, I cannot say. The content of this very simple game is in fact extremely complex.

Until research on determination of content provides more reliable techniques, selectors will have to rely on descriptions of programs provided by other users, by reviewers, and by publishers, and on their own direct examination of materials. These procedures are described below in the section on selection tools. Determination of content of CAI is in roughly the same situation as determination of content of other instructional materials. Selectors must be aware that there is much more to CAI content than is described in product summaries.

Once content is determined, or approximated, the remaining problem is whether the content and the system of presentation are consistent with the philosophy and goals of the overall instructional design. As Wade (1980), says, "A segment of instruction may teach very well, but unless it is in harmony with the philosophy supporting the instructional system and helps achieve the general goals of the course of study of which it is a part, it would not be considered of value." This problem is one that characterizes all instructional tools and is not unique to CAI. It is one librarians live with daily, and for which they have developed procedures, beginning with the written collection development policy.

SELECTION OF CAI SOFTWARE

Selection of CAI materials is like selection of any other instructional material in that it assumes one begins with a clear statement of educational objectives—an articulated instructional design—and a library collection development policy. The evaluation of a CAI program ought to be based on its content and appropriateness to the curriculum and on its effectiveness as a teacher, which depends largely on its success in appropriately integrating media characteristics. Many of the skills required are those that librarians and media specialists have developed for older materials.

Discovery and Evaluation of Available CAI Programs

CAI software is becoming a very well indexed medium. Given a subject area or content matter as a starting point, there are a number of tools available for locating software. Most useful of these are publishers' and distributors' catalogs and printed and online indexes. Some of the latter include evaluative information.

Several online data bases are useful for locating educational software on the BRS search system. Techniques for searching these databases in tandem are described in "Database Teamwork" (BRS, 1984). The Texas Education Computer Cooperative database (TECC) is produced by the Statewide Microcomputer Courseware Evaluation Network. Among the searchable fields are fields for curriculum area, grade level, instructional technique, and instructional objectives. Each record also includes ratings of the quality of the software as well as student comments. The Resources in Computer Education (RICE) database, produced by the Northwest Regional Educational Laboratory, includes fields for content descriptors, grade level, mode of instruction, instructional objectives, a descriptive abstract, and evaluative paragraphs. CAI software is among other kinds of software indexed in the databases Online Micro Software Guide and Directory (SOFT) and DISC, which comprises tables of contents of major microcomputer journals and may be used to locate product announcements and reviews.

The Educational Products Information Change Institute (EPIE) and Consumers Union jointly publish a printed guide to educational software and hardware *PRO/FILES,* which is also available online through CompuServe. The software profiles include fields on designer's intent, content topics, curriculum role, and a summary analysis and evaluation.

Another print tool for locating software titles and evaluations is *The Digest of Software Reviews: Education.* The digest is intended primarily as an evaluation tool, since it includes only software that has been reviewed in the journals covered, but it may also be used as a finding tool. Each entry includes the publisher's specifications of the product and selected paragraphs from reviews in the library and education literature.

Other print tools useful for identifying (but not evaluating) available software include general software directories and publishers' catalogs. New titles continue to appear; the most useful current lists at the time of this writing are those prepared by Dewey (1984), who describes 27 print directories, and the annotated list prepared by the AASL Committee for Standardization of Access to Library Media Resources (AASL, 1984). There is no standard set of finding aids for CAI software. Just as microcomputer hardware generated a volatile software industry, the software industry is generating a volatile indexing industry.

Freeman (1984) has suggested a scheme for matching learning objectives to available software. "If the CAI field is to progress," he writes, "it will be necessary to develop a set of universal or standard learning objectives. Also, there is a need for an independent agency which will supply ratings for each piece of software. Such an agency might well be supported grants from the major publishers, the government, and private foundations. These ratings could be looked upon much like an Underwriter's Laboratory seal of approval." Freeman also suggests a measure for ranking software items according to their matches to a set of selected objectives. No such system exists and the outlook for specification of a universal set of objectives is dim. For those institutions that have specified objectives, however, selection tools are available which may be searched by content objectives.

Once a CAI program has been identified as a candidate for acquisition, it must be evaluated. The tools described above include evaluations, but before accepting those evaluations at face value, one must be aware of the criteria used by the evaluators. Publication of evaluative guides has been as prolific in recent years as publication of software directories.

Thirteen guides to software evaluation are brought together by Vaughn and Jones (1983) in *A Guide to Guides*. Most of these guides, as well as other works in this genre (cf. Grady, 1983; Costa and Costa, 1983; Fetter, 1984; Truett and Gillespie, 1984) are checklists of the characteristics of CAI in general whereon the evaluator rates a particular program's features on a numeric scale. These guides are designed for use by evaluators in institutional settings such as EPIE as well as by individual librarians and teachers who wish to do evaluation in-house. They are useful because they give the reader of an evaluation an understanding of the evaluators' procedures and because they provide guidance to those unused to evaluating CAI in-house. However, these guides are characterized by two problems.

The first problem in using these guides is that they assume the important characteristics of CAI in terms of learning consequences are known. Yet as Olds (1983) and Caldwell (1983) have argued, and as the *Speed/Math Bingo* discussion above illustrates, neither what CAI teaches nor what features of CAI are most important for achieving the intended objectives are well established. As Olds says, some serious dilemmas "are posed by trying to evaluate a new technology before that technology is well understood." Caldwell points out that many of the evaluative guides give undue importance to unique features of CAI as a medium, such as branching, sound, and graphics, without considering whether these truly contribute to teaching the particular lesson at hand. In evaluating evaluation guides, one must keep these cautions in mind, and ask whether the evaluation guide is intended to select works that are "good CAI" with all the bells and whistles attached, or whether it helps to select works that are good teachers of specific content in a specific curricular context.

The second problem of evaluative guides in general, then, is that they do not provide guidance in determining content. While almost all guides include some provision for describing content, or at least for checking whether the content is "appropriate," the guides themselves do not provide the kind of specific advice for assessing content that they do for assessing such features as presentation style. The "Software Evaluation Checklist" prepared by the National Council of Teachers of Mathematics is an example. In the section on Content, the checklist asks the evaluator to rate a program on a scale of "low" to "high" on the following criteria: instructional focus, instructional significance, soundness or validity, and compatibility with other materials used. The instructions for using the Checklist say, "The program's topic should be clearly defined. The instructional objectives of the program must be viewed as important by the instructor. . . . The content, terminology, teaching style, and educational philosophy should be consistent with those generally encountered by the student" (Vaughan and Jones, 1983, p. 58).

Guidelines and checklists can help in assessing the quality of a program. Ultimately, the best evaluation is to examine materials locally. In the early days of software publishing (two or three years ago) publishers were reluctant to send materials on approval or to allow return of opened CAI, for fear librarians would pirate their products. Whether that fear proved groundless or whether publishers realized they simply could not sell unexamined products, major publishers and distributors now advertise 30-day approval plans. In-house evaluation is particularly important because most software publishers do not conduct extensive field tests of their educational software before releasing it (Truett, 1984).

Determination of content and appropriateness is left to the librarian. In the absence of a complete matching system for content and objectives as proposed by Freeman, the final judgment is left to the selectors. Review sources and evaluating agencies may provide initial guidance, but ultimately evaluation decisions must be made by individual librarians. The reason is simply that we do not understand enough about "aboutness" to specify ways to make those judgments for one another. Panels of experts and professional reviewers may rate the quality of CAI software as CAI per se, but the evaluation of software as teaching tool must be made locally. Determination of content and appropriateness is an expert decision where only those familiar with local circumstances qualify as experts.

Such a conclusion casts the role of the librarian in evaluating and selecting CAI in a somewhat different light than it has been previously understood. Perhaps overwhelmed by the newness of the technology, librarians have tended to make selection of CAI into a problem quite different than it really is. Reviews and institutional evaluations provide technical assessment of CAI for those who feel incompetent to rate those aspects of software. But traditional skills in evaluating multimedia materials do carry over into this class of materials. The real problem in selection of CAI is the familiar problem—does this CAI lesson (story, film strip, recording, picture book, etc.) fit our objectives and our educational philosophy?

REFERENCES

AASL Committee for Standardization of Access to Library Media Resources, "Microcomputer Software and Hardware—An Annotated Source List." *School Library Media Quarterly* 12:2 (Winter 1984): 107–119.

BRS, "Database Teamwork: The Great Software Search." *BRS Bulletin* 8:4 (April 1984): 9–13.

Caldwell, Robert M., "Evaluation of Microcomputer Software: How Valid are the Criteria and Procedures." Paper presented at the Annual Meeting of the Southwest Educational Research Association, Houston, Jan. 1983. (ED 230 171).

Cary, Charles, "Natural Themes in Soviet School History Textbooks." *Computers in the Humanities* 10 (1976): 313–323.

Coburn, Peter et. al. *Practical Guide to Computers in Education.* Reading, MA: Addison Wesley Publishing Co., 1982.

Costa, Betty and Marie Costa. *A Micro Handbook for Small Libraries and Media Centers.* Littleton, CO: Libraries Unlimited, 1983.

Della-Piana, Gabriel M., "Film Criticism and Micro-Computer Courseware Evaluation," in N. Smith, ed., *New Directions for Program Evaluation: Field Assessments of Innovative Evaluation Methods,* No. 13. San Francisco: Jossey-Bass, 1982, 11–28.

Dewey, Patrick R., "Searching for Software: A Checklist of Microcomputer Software Directories." *Library Journal* 109:5 (March 15, 1984): 544–546.

van Dijk, Teun A. *Macrostructures.* Hillsdale, NJ: Lawrence Erlbaum Associates, 1980.

Fetter, Wayne R., "Guidelines for Evaluation of Computer Software (With an Evaluation Form)." *Educational Technology* 24:3 (March 1984): 19–21.

Freeman, Raoul J., "Definition and Evaluation of Computer Support Systems for Instruction." *AEDS Journal* 17:4 (Summer 1984): 46–55.

Gallagher, Francine L., "What Educators Want in Microcomputer Software." *Catholic Library World* 55:7 (February 1984): 290–293.

Grady, M. Tim and Jane D. Gawronski, eds. *Computers in Curriculum and Instruction.* Alexandria, VA: Association for Supervision and Curriculum Development, 1983.

Hawk, Richard L., "Survey Shows Library Media Specialist Involvement in Microcomputer Movement." *Medium* 8:1 (Fall 1983): 8–10.

Kintsch, Walter. *The Representation of Meaning in Memory.* Hillsdale, NJ: Lawrence Erlbaum Associates, 1974.

Kintsch, Walter and Teun A. van Dijk. *Strategies of Discourse Comprehension.* New York: Academic Press, 1983.

Lieblum, M.D., "Factors Sometimes Overlooked and Underestimated in the Selection and Success of CAL as an Instructional Medium." *AEDS Journal* 15:2 (Winter 1982): 67–77.

Maron, M.E., "On Indexing, Retrieval, and the Meaning of About." *Journal of the American Society for Information Science* 28:1 (Jan. 1977): 38–43.

MacCannell, Dean and Juliet Flower MacCannell. *The Time of the Sign: A Semiotic Interpretation of Modern Culture.* Bloomington: Indiana University Press, 1982.

Olds, Henry F. Jr., "Evaluating the Evaluation Schemes." in Larry Vaughan and Nancy Jones, eds., *Evaluation of Educational Software: A Guide to Guides* Chelmsford, MA: Northeast Regional Exchange, Inc., and Austin, TX: Southwest Educational Development Laboratory, 1983.

Romiszowski, A.J. *Designing Instructional Systems.* New York: Nichols Publishing, 1981.

Salisbury, David F.,"How to Decide When and Where to Use Microcomputers for Instruction." *Educational Technology* 24:3 (March 1984): 22–24.

Swigger, Kathleen M. and Boyd Keith Swigger, "Social Patterns and Computer Use Among Preschool Children." *AEDS Journal* 17:3 (Spring 1984): 35–41.

Tannen, Deborah, "What's in a Frame? Surface Evidence for Underlying Expectations," in Roy O. Freedle, ed., *New Directions in Discourse Processing.* Norwood, NJ: Ablex Publishing, 1979, 137–182.

Truett, Carol, "Field Testing Educational Software: Are Publishers Making the Effort?" *Educational Technology* 24:5 (May 1984): 7–12.

Troutner, Joanne. *The Media Specialist, the Microcomputer, and the Curriculum.* Littleton, CO: Libraries Unlimited, 1983.

Truett, Carol and Lorie Gillespie. *Choosing Educational Software: A Buyer's Guide.* Littleton, CO: Libraries Unlimited, 1984.

Turner, Althea and Edith Greene. Construction and Use of a Propositional Text Base. University of Colorado Institute for the Study of Intellectual Behavior, April 1977; *jsas Catalog of Selected Documents in Psychology,* 8:58 (1978), MS 1713.

Vaughan, Larry and Nancy Baker Jones, eds. *Evaluation of Educational Software: A Guide to Guides.* Chelmsford, MA: Northeast Regional Exchange, Inc. and Austin, TX: Southwest Educational Development Laboratory, 1983.

Wade, T.E., Jr. Evaluating Computer Instructional Programs and Other Teaching Units. *Educational Technology* 20:11 (November 1980): 32–35.

Walker, Decker F. and Robert D. Hess, eds. *Instructional Software: Principles and Perspectives for Design and USe.* Belmont, CA: Wadsworth Publishing Co., 1984.

White, Brenda. Letter to the author, Jan. 30, 1984.

Government Documents
and Their Use
in Schools

Hilda L. Jay

Government documents are an important information source
for the student. Despite peculiarities in the purchase, in-library
housing and access to these documents, their value as an information source requires the school library media specialist to
include them in the collection. As an aid to this process, Jay
identifies reviewing sources, discusses indexing systems and
methods of purchasing, and includes lists of recommended
documents.

Library media personnel responsible for providing Reference Services have varying interests and backgrounds in the
use of government documents. One is aware of the separate
departments boldly labeled Government Documents in university and larger municipal libraries. These may be designated as "depository" collections and operate under either
"full" (receiving all) or "selective" (those chosen by the librarian) plans whereby additions to the collection are received directly from the government as soon as they are published. To be designated a depository library the facility must
meet the standards called for in Title 44 of the *U.S. Code,*
Chapter 19, Section 1909, which reads as follows:

> Only a library able to provide custody and service for
> depository materials . . . may be designated a depository
> library.

Dr. Jay, a retired high school librarian, is an adjunct faculty member of the
University of Rhode Island Graduate Library School and the University of Connecticut School of Education.

The *Guidelines for the Depository Library System* states that

> One person should be designated by the library to coordinate activities and to act as liaison with the Superintendent of Documents in all matters relating to depository libraries.
>
> The liaison person should be a professionally qualified librarian.

The determination of whether government documents are to be integrated with the rest of the library holdings or maintained as a separate collection is made by the library director. Variables such as space available within the library, the size of the library collection, the nature of the library community, the size of the staff all influence this decision. When a new library is being planned, or an old one renovated, the library director may be in a position to make decisions different from those usually made when designation as a depository library is made "after the fact" and based upon the size and effectiveness of an existing library operation.

However, when government documents are placed in a separate section, a cursory look around by the user quickly indicates that something is different here. When government documents are housed and classified separately, they are not listed in the card catalog. The SuDocs Classification system is in force, and special indexes must be used to locate needed materials.

Sometimes the user is further confused because frequently referred to references such as the *United States Government Manual* or *Historical Statistics from Colonial Times to 1970* appear on the standard reference shelves. They are government publications but appear not to be placed in the established separate Government Documents section. How does one explain these in-house deviations? Perhaps that library's policy is to duplicate much used references and these titles would be available both places. The provision for instruction of college students or the general public using that special section of the collection is usually a departmental responsibility. The user can be certain that a Government Documents Librarian will be available to assist with the use of government documents in any depository library.

But what about our public schools? Do they purchase government documents? If so, how do they handle these publications? Do the students recognize government documents as a unique and significant type of reference? If not, why not? Or should they?

To try to find out answers to these questions, and to identify common thought among trained school library media specialists, a questionnaire was distributed. Individual copies were sent to representative Division of School Media Services building level and/or system-wide supervisors including elementary, middle, junior high, and senior high schools across the country. In addition, the questionnaire was placed in the Connecticut Educational Media Association newsletter and also in the Ohio Educational Library Media Association quarterly, *Ohio Media Spectrum.* Open-ended questions provided numerous responses that shed light on the use, or non-use, of this type of reference.

But before going into the questionnaire responses and their implications, a look at the possible use and potential of government documents as a genre is of value.

The largest number and range of statistics available to searchers are compiled by the federal government. The government conducts some of the most avant garde experimentation done in the United States, and the results are normally reported in publications of the agency doing this work. The government is involved in a very wide range of disciplines. There is almost no area in which they have no interest. These publications range from pamphlets of just a few pages to ponderous volumes. There are numerous periodical publications.

Subject matter is presented in readibility level ranging from that suitable for the average layman to that suitable for the most technically trained scientist. Collectively, this body of publishing constitutes an impressive library in and of itself. How, then, does one find out about what is available and, even more to the point, where to get hold of it when wanted?

Most library science and information services curricula include a course in the use of Government Documents. If one does not favor enrolling in a course, then some private study sessions using a good government document text will help a great deal. One newer example of texts available is *Congressional Publications: A Research Guide to Legislation, Budgets, and Treaties* by Jerrold Zwirn, Libraries Unlimited, 1983.

Myriad changes have taken place over the years among agencies that have been transferred from department to department, gone out of existence, or been newly created. The indexing that has been provided has undergone as many changes, at least regarding inclusiveness. Not all public documents published are made available for sale. Some, listed in indexes, are also considered suitable "for official use only." Various classified documents have, since the passage of the Freedom of Information Act of 1973, become de-classified. These are located through the use of the *Declassified Documents Quarterly*. Some documents are only mimeographed in small numbers. Like other publications, government documents do go out of print after a period of time. It is a valued art to become adept at retrieving these so-called "fugitive" documents. It must not be forgotten that for many citizens access to these sources of information are urgently necessary in the course of their business or professional pursuits. Although public schools do not have to be concerned with the ultra esoteric or elusive materials, they can make excellent use of government documents in general.

Some problems pertaining to the acquisition of government documents apply to everyone. First, the government is divided into three branches, and each branch with its attendant departments, committees, agencies, etc. individually has publishing capabilities. The Government Printing Office is the primary source for these publications and stocks some 25,000 titles. Finding out what is in print, its cost, and ordering information can be something of a challenge.

Prices may be obtained from the *GPO Sales Publications Reference File*. *PRF* is a 48x microfiche catalog of publications currently for sale by the Superintendent of Documents. It lists forthcoming and recently out-of-stock items as well as current items. The cumulative file of approximately 300 microfiche is issued to subscribers and to depository libraries every two months. The supplement (consisting usually of one or two microfiche) is issued monthly. The supplement lists new and reprinted publications added to the active sales inventory in the past month.

PRF is invaluable to anyone who wants to verify a title, to determine the availability of a title, and to ascertain the price and stock number of a government publication. It is also extremely useful for finding out what the Government is publishing on a particular subject. The microfiche in the *PRF* are arranged in three sequences: stock number, catalog number, and alphabetical sequence. The alphabetical listing is a dictionary arrangement of all titles, series, key words, key phrases, subjects, and personal authors.

Prices are available in current price lists that may be requested from the various government publishing agencies. Prices are also listed in *Monthly Catalog,* but it should be realized that unless one is using the latest *Monthly Catalog* it would be unwise to rely completely on this source for prices. The *Monthly Catalog* indexes materials that have been published, but it is of no value in determining the current availability of a document. This is the role of *PRF* as discussed above. Much help can be obtained from the nearest depository library and its government documents librarian.

There is no extensive reviewing done of government publications. A small number of selected reviews appear in *Booklist, Choice, Library Journal, Publisher's Weekly, RQ, School Library Media Quarterly,* and *Wilson Bulletin.* Two periodicals are directly concerned with government documents and are a splendid source of articles on their use as well as reviews of new releases. These are *Government Publications Review,* a quarterly, and *Dup, Documents to the People,* a bimonthly newsletter from the ALA Government Documents Round Table (GODORT). However, many of the traditional reviewing services ignore government publications. Bookstores do not, as a rule, stock them. One's best source for leads of what might be available are *The Monthly Catalog of the United States Government Publications* which is the basic bibliography of government documents, and the *U.S. Government Books,* a quarterly in existence since 1982 that annotates some 1,000 popular government publications. (This is the successor to the monthly *Selected U.S. Government Publications* and is a means by which the Superintendent of Documents advertises government publications.) Indexes provide some useful suggestions for purchase. *Public Affairs Information Service* (PAIS) includes some government documents. In addition, there is the *Index to Publications of the United States Congress,* known as the *CIS/Index* and begun in 1970, and the *Index to U.S. Government Periodicals,* quarterly, with coverage from 1970 to the present. Up to two hundred periodicals are listed by subject in this index. Statistical references published by the government are indexed in *American Statistics Index*, covering 1970 to date. This tool, begun in 1973, appears annually and has monthly supplements. The problem of popular name vs. official name sometimes impedes acquisition. Prime examples of this are the "Warren Report" and the "Shafer Report," both well known and sought after. *Popular Names of U.S. Government Reports: A Catalog* (since 1966) provides facsimile catalog cards in alphabetical order for a large (but not all) number of documents under their popular names. Here one would be led to title terminology *Report of President's Commission on the Assassination of John F. Kennedy* or to *Marihuana, Signal of Misunderstanding*. The real problem is the incompleteness of indexing and the effect of "indexer's choice." Not all documents are listed under suitable subject headings in subject indexing. Persons who are inclined to look in one place and expect 100% coverage will have problems with government document searches of any sort.

As effective as the *Monthly Catalog* and the *CIS/Index* are, the user will have to learn to read and apply the Superintendent of Documents' arrangement scheme. This so-called SuDocs Classification is not formidable and should not scare anyone out of using government documents. Explanations of sample entries are readily available, and it is just one more application of letters and numbers that are used in traditional sequences. (However, a small number of questionnaire responses termed this system "unwieldy" and claimed it was a deterrent to their use of government documents.)

Law is often an important segment of school curricula, but few schools could justify owning the *United States Code*. They may own their own state statutes, and they will usually own their own state handbook. Whether a copy finds its way to the school library media center or not is another question. There is the *Index to Legal Periodicals,* a monthly index of some 400 + periodicals, begun in 1908 that is helpful. A less esoteric index that includes legal references of common interest is the familiar *Reader's Guide to Periodical Literature.* (It might be worth mentioning that the book *Effective Legal Research* by Miles Price and published by Little, Brown, 4th ed. 1979, although not a government publication or limited to legal documents, is a handy guide to working one's way through legal treatises and decisions.)

Although it is the responsibility of the individual states to publish their own laws, the federal government has published compilations of state laws based on specific topics or themes. These publications might be on topics such as aging, air pollution, health, labor, public welfare, etc. The pulling together of this sort of information into a single location is something the individual would have trouble doing.

County, city, township, and town also produce documents. These are government documents just as much as are state and federal publications. Budgets, building codes, and the regulations of such things as waste disposal, use of firearms, fire making, running tag sales, and much more are addressed "locally." When these are published, they, too, become government documents. Using answers and comments from the questionnaires, a number of current thought patterns and practices or trends can be identified. Government documents have special value in the school library media center collection. Their authority is paramount. Government prepared statistics tend to have a common base which makes comparisons more valid. Their element of timeliness is important.

Selection procedures reported included use of periodicals that contain limited numbers of reviews (those listed above), and the *Monthly Catalog*. No one reported having the *Monthly Catalog* within the school (current annual subscription price is $125). They used them when they were available at public or university libraries. Some have started using *U.S. Government Books*. Sometimes a request will be made by a teacher or student. Responses to the questionnaire included favorable comment regarding the formerly available *Selected U.S. Government Publications*. It's annotated format was appreciated. No evaluative comment was received regarding *U.S. Government Books*. Additional comments regarding selection procedures suggested that school library media specialists tend to think of government documents in a restricted manner. Statistics and career publications used in social studies appeared in collections that had any government documents at all. A few respondents mentioned "science," but this was more often general than specific. "Space" and "weather maps" were individually cited. No one seemed to be aware of the extensive services of the National Cartographic Information Center (507 National Center, Reston, VA 22092) or of the User Services Section of EROS Data Center (Sioux Falls, SD 57198) from whom remarkable assistance is given in acquiring maps and aerial photographs.

Government documents begin to be used in the elementary schools, although use increases with the age of the student. Government documents are not generally put aside into a special collection in the schools. The usual system of handling them is to catalog them according to Dewey or LC classification schemes and interfile them with the rest of the collection. At least, this is true of those publications that are hardbound or thick enough paperbound not to get lost on the open shelves. Thin pamphlets are more often kept in a Vertical File or Princeton File type of storage. Maps always require specialized storage.

There were some complaints among the questionnaire answers. Prominent was the statement that government documents are expensive. Certainly, they have gone up in price. The effect of inflation on publishing costs is one reason. A second is the reduction in government funding for the purpose. Many items that once were free must now be purchased. Respondents did indicate that the state manuals, by and large, are provided to schools free of charge. Often this is a service of the local legislator.

A greater problem seemed to be the matter of actual purchase. The use of vouchers has been discontinued; however, orders may be charged to MasterCard or to Visa. Respondents reported that many business managers of school systems have a reluctance to provide a check to accompany an order before actual receipt of the item ordered. Some stated that to do so was illegal in terms of their own state laws. Inasmuch as the federal government requires pre-payment, the school library media specialist is caught between the two directives. This situation effectively prevents many school libraries from stocking as many government documents as would be desirable from the point of view of curriculum. One response explained that the school library media specialist, if she wanted to purchase government documents, had to spend her own money and hope for reimbursement on an annual basis.

Could it be that too many of us take the easy way out in not mounting an organized campaign against short-sighted directives? It should be easy to understand the federal government's need to insist upon pre-payment, and methods cited above are accepted by the federal government to accomplish this. The numerous comments on the questionnaires indicate that in many instances these plans are not acceptable to local authorities. Laws may need to be modified, or the school business managers may need to be educated as to the need for a workable system permitting school library media centers to obtain these excellent publications. It is probable that these directives cannot stand up to the glare of publicity, if that is what it will take to accomplish proper authorization. Perhaps this is a concern that American Library Association Government Documents Round Table (GODORT) could help with.

Another complaint was that regional offices selling government documents are not stocked suitably for school needs. This comment was not wide-spread enough on the questionnaires to indicate whether this is true in all regions or only for this one region. It may be, also, that supplies in these offices ebb now and then. Could the timing of a shopping trip mismatch adequate stocking by the center?

The need for Cataloging in Publication Data (CIP) or printed card sets to accompany purchases was noted several times. Wherever school library media specialists are not in the habit of doing original cataloging, or are normally supplied cataloging with their purchases, the absence of at least card sets places one more deterrent to use before them. Surely CIP should not add excessively to the production costs of government documents even though many items would be filed using SuDocs Classification and be accessed through government published indexes instead of card catalogs. This CIP information is available in the *Monthly Catalog* entries, but this usually requires a trip for the school library media specialist to a distant library to examine the cataloging in either print or on-line version. For some time yet schools will use card catalogs. Goodly numbers of them will not have membership in regional networks that could provide printed cards through online sources.

Respondents indicated that about one percent of their collections were government documents. There could be some speculation about this figure because direct conversation with a number of school library media specialists, especially those serving younger students, did not seem to have thought much about their use of government documents. When their thinking was directed toward specific titles or types of materials in common use, they realized that these were indeed government documents. They did have them in the collection, and they did use them with the students. There was a combination of not realizing that a given title was published by a governmental agency, and of not realizing that a publication by anything but the *federal* government could be a "government document."

Questions such as "But surely your students use your state handbook when they study state government?" brought forth answers such as, "Oh, yes, of course. That unit is in fifth grade. I forgot about it." State road maps, state park brochures, historic house literature were in common use. And further questioning indicated that weather maps, even if an on-going subscription was not needed, were used. *Background Notes,* published by the Department of State, were useful with younger students. Here again, a full subscription was not needed. Only those countries that were emphasized in the curriculum were represented. In some cases multiple copies or classroom size collections were acquired.

Familiar titles that were actually Department of Agriculture Yearbooks were also overlooked as government documents. The 1949 issue, *Trees;* 1952, *Insects;* 1961, *Seeds;* 1966, *Protecting Our Food;* 1968, *Food For Us All;* plus more recent issues in the series seemed to be rather standard fare.

This suggests that whether the students are aware of government documents as a specific type of reference source or not depends to some extent upon the awareness of and value placed on them by the school library media specialist. One comment was made that it was difficult enough to get the students to become fully aware of the library, never mind trying to make them aware of a specific type of reference. On the other hand, where responses indicated that the students did have some awareness of the role of government documents in information gathering, the reasons expressed were that there were "courses," that "certain teachers require their use," that "government documents are referred to as possible sources by the school library media specialist," "that we often refer students from a secondary statistics source to the government source," and that "we include these publications in our teacher in-service sessions." One response described taking high school seniors to the depository library at the local college where their staff introduced students to the range of government documents and instructed them in the use of the three major *indexes—Monthly Catalog, CIS,* and *Statistics Index.* This awareness was considered important both for the college bound and for those who would, as citizens, use local facilities.

And, speaking of awareness, students should realize that the publications of Congress receive special treatment. The common conception that the *Congressional Record* is an exact documentation of what goes on and is said in Congress is false. The editorial privilege that has been given Congressional members to verify copy before it is printed has been abused. Outright changes—both deletions and additions—are so extensive that the document is not a "record" at all. Some government documents texts discuss this problem, and the article "Congressional Record: Congress's License to Lie," found in the February 1983 issue of *Reader's Digest* addresses the problem in detail. This does not mean that the *Congressional Record* is of no value, but anyone using this source needs to be aware of its limitations.

When asked to identify the curricular areas for which use of government documents was made, a wide range of answers was given. Social studies, government, science, home economics, health, industrial arts, foreign language, and consumer education were mentioned specifically. Several responses indicated that "all areas" made use of them. It appeared that the extent of use was related to the degree of push given their use by the school library media specialist. Those responses indicating more extensive use being made of these materials were, as might be expected, the ones that provided the longer lists of titles considered basic to a standard school library media collection.

Four government document title lists follow. The first is a compilation of titles cited on the questionnaires as being basic to school library media center collections. The second is the basic reference collection list that all depository libraries are expected to have readily available. The third and fourth are lists of additional titles found by analyzing a number of standard selection, reference, and government document texts. The third is a list for general search interests, and the fourth is for potential professional use.

TITLES RECOMMENDED ON QUESTIONNAIRES

Almanac of American Politics
American Revolution 1775–1783: An Atlas of 18th Century Maps and Charts
Background Notes (Department of State)
Biographical Directory of the American Congress, 1774–1971
Book of the States
Climatic Atlas of the U.S.
Common Environmental Terms: A Glossary
Constitution of the United States of America, Analysis and Interpretation
County and City Data Book (Supplement to Statistical Abstracts)
Daily Weather Map
Department of State Bulletin
Federal Reserve Bank free publications
Guide to the Study of the United States of America and Its Supplement 1956–65
Handbook of Air Pollution
Historical Statistics of the US Colonial Times to 1970
House Manual
If Elected . . . Unsuccessful Candidates for the Presidency
Inaugural Addresses of Presidents of the U.S. from George Washington to Nixon
Monthly Labor Review
National Atlas of the United States
National Aeronautics and Space Administration publications
National Parks and Landmarks
National Zip Code Directory
Occupational Outlook Handbook
Official Congressional Directory

Pocket Data Book USA
Postage Stamps of the United States
State Government Manual
State Maps
State Statistical Abstracts (Michigan)
State Statutes
Statistical Abstracts of U.S.
Statistical Yearbook (Annual)
Topographic Maps of the US Geological Survey
U.S. Reports: Cases Adjudged in the Supreme Court
U.S. Army Area Handbook Series
U.S. Department of State Fact Book on Countries of the World
U.S. Government Manual
Yearbook of Agriculture

TITLES FOUND ON DEPOSITORY LIBRARY BASIC REFERENCE LIST

Budget of the United States Government
Catalog of Federal Domestic Assistance
Census Bureau Catalog
Census of Housing
Census of Population
Code of Federal Regulations
Congressional Directory
Congressional District Data Book
Congressional Record
County-City Data Book
Federal Register
Historical Statistics of the United States
Monthly Catalog
Numerical Lists and Schedules of Volumes
Slip Laws
Statistical Abstract
Statutes at Large
Subject Bibliographies
Supreme Court Reports
United States Code
United States Government Manual
Weekly Compilation of Presidential Documents

TITLES FOUND IN GOVERNMENT DOCUMENT SECTIONS OF SELECTION, REFERENCE, AND GOVERNMENT DOCUMENTS TEXTS

100 Native Forage Grasses in Eleven Southern States
200th Anniversary of the First Continental Congress 1774–1974
Agricultural Statistics
Air Almanac
American Ephemeris and Nautical Almanac
Annual Report to Congress of the Atomic Energy Commission
Assassination of Rep. Leo J. Ryan & the Jonestown, Guyana Tragedy
Atlas of Issues in the Middle East
Basic Construction Techniques for Houses & Small Businesses
Biographic Register (Dept. of State)
Biographical Sketches & Anecdotes of . . . Indian Chiefs
Birds In Our Lives
Blueprint Reading and Sketching
Bureau of the Census, Fact Finder of the Nation
Checklist of Native and Naturalized Trees of the U.S.
Code of Federal Regulations
Commercial Fisheries Review
Commercial Fisheries Abstracts
Common Weeds of the US
Congressional District Atlas
Congressional Record
Conservation in Action Pamphlets
Conservation Yearbooks
Country Periodical
Dictionary of Economic and Statistical Terms
Digest of Educational Statistics (Annual)
Earthquake History of the United States
Eastern Forest Insects
Employment & Earnings: United States 1909–1971
ERA of FDR: Bibliography of Annotated Periodical and Dissertation Literature

Explorers and Settlers: Historic Places Commemorating
Early . . . Settlement
Fact Book of U.S. Agriculture
Federal Register
Field and Seed Crops: Usual Planting and Harvesting
Dates by States
Fishery Bulletin
Geographic Areas Serviced by Bell and Independent Tele-
phone Companies . . .
Glossary of Oceanographic Terms
Guides to Outdoor Recreation Areas and Facilities
Handbook of South American Indians: North of Mexico
Handbook of Labor Statistics (Annual)
Handbook of Mathematical Functions: With Formulas,
Graphs, & Tables
Highway Statistics (Annual)
How Our Laws Are Made
International Control of World Resources: Handbook for
Debaters
Manual of Grasses of the U.S.
Mineral Facts and Problems
Monthly Catalog (U.S. Government Publications)
Municipal Yearbook
National Wildlife Refuges
Navigation Dictionary
Overseas Business Reports
Presidential Inaugurations (Bibliography)
Presidential Portraits
Presidents of the U.S., 1789–1962 (Bibliography)
Public Laws (Slip Laws)
Rare and Endangered Fish and Wildlife of the U.S.
Records, Computers, and the Rights of Citizens
Senate Manual
Shopper's Guide
Signers of the Declaration
Sixty American Poets, 1896–1944
Social Security Programs Throughout the World
State Conducted Lotteries
State Law Digest

Style Manual and Word Division (Supplement)
Survey of Current Business (Monthly)
Tools and Their Uses
Treaties and Other International Agreements of the USA (Annual)
Treaties in Force
United States Code
UFO's and Related Subjects: An Annotated Bibliography
Uniform Crime Reports for the U.S.
United States Statutes at Large
U.S. Budget in Brief, Fiscal Year . . .
U.S. President's Commission on Campus Unrest Special Reports

TITLES OF PROFESSIONAL INTEREST

Aids to Media Selection for Students and Teachers
Alcohol and Alcohol Safety: A Curriculum Manual for Elementary Level
Alcohol and Alcohol Safety: A Curriculum Manual for Junior High Level
Alcohol Safety: A Curriculum Manual for Senior High Level
American Education
American Revolution: Selected Reading List (Covers events through the 1780's)
Basic Guide to Microfilms
Care of Books, Documents, Prints and Films
Civil War in Motion Pictures: A Bibliography of Films Produced Since '79
Creating Independence, 1763–1789 Bicentennial List of Books for Chidren
Current Index to Journals in Education
Environmental-Ecological Education: Bibliography for Elementary & Secondary Schools
Fact Book: Office of Education Programs
Index to U.S. Government Periodicals
Library of Congress Subject Headings
Monthly Checklist of State Publications

Periodical Literature of the American Revolution . . .
 1895–1970
Research in Education
Source Materials for Secondary School Teachers of Foreign
 Languages
Subject Bibliographies
Thesaurus of Eric Descriptors
U.S. Government Films: A Catalog of AV Materials for
 Rent and Sale by the National AV Center

In spite of the problems encountered when identifying, purchasing, or merely locating materials for examination through
an index, government documents do provide valuable information found no where else. Students who are not made
aware of the purpose, scope, and availability of these materials are being cheated of an awareness of information that
surely handicaps them as searchers. The fact that some
schools do so very well in this area suggests that in the spirit
of equity school library media specialists will want to review
the use of government documents in their schools.

Note: The author wishes to acknowledge gratefully the assistance given by Martha Croft, Government Documents Librarian, Central Connecticut State University, New Britain,
CT checking for inaccuracies and suggesting additions to the
author's initial draft. Here is absolute proof of the gracious
readiness to help that an informed and dedicated government
documents librarian offers the inquirer.

Management of Periodicals in a Small School LMC

Judith M. Bury

The aim of management of periodicals is to provide an efficient delivery of services to patrons through a streamlined operation. This article provides suggestions for implementing a plan for controlling periodicals with all the factors which make this difficult. Topics addressed are selection, indexing—both commercial and in-house, sources, curricular and recreational uses, storage, alternate formats, record keeping and more.

INTRODUCTION

This article is directed to the managers of small public school library media centers (LMCs) whose collections range from a casual dozen titles to several hundred. Management means deliberate control according to a consistent plan based on well defined goals. Ultimately it need not be complex, but, in drawing up a management plan for periodicals, many factors must be considered before decisions are made. These factors will be discussed but final details of execution will vary from school to school and must be custom tailored by the LMC specialist. The target is a streamlined operation which will provide efficient and effective patron service, expanding and enhancing educational opportunities for all students.

The first thing to remember about periodicals management is that they resist management. They come in a variety of shapes and sizes, usually with flimsy bindings and slippery covers. Dark cover backgrounds defy a legible LMC stamp. Publishers play hide and seek with the cover dates and issue numbers. Periodicity varies widely from the reliable weekly to

Judith Bury is the instructional aide at the Ridgefield High School Library, Ridgefield, Connecticut, and a graduate student at the University of Connecticut.

313

whenever the editors get around to it. Many are not indexed. Some have questionable accuracy. They are torn or lost in the mails. Maintaining an uninterrupted subscription in the computer age can be a challenge. An unbroken file is difficult to preserve. Magazines can take up an incredible amount of space and are heavy as the back files grow and grow and grow. Nearly everything about periodicals is untidy and offends the neurotic sensibilities of the LMC conservator, so why bother!

Because periodical articles are an unparalleled source of timely information and opinion. They contain material that may never appear in book form. They reflect social history through ads and commentary. They appeal to the reluctant reader in their brevity and layout. They are entertaining. Many have a heterogeneity of material that seductively leads a reader far beyond the information originally sought. Those that are specialized provide breadth and depth to a subject inexpensively. Besides, they are the bread and butter of writers who otherwise might not produce the more impressive tomes we cherish.

GOALS AND POLICIES

The first managerial decisions are ones of goals and policies. Are periodicals to be a here and now LMC peripheral that disappear after a few months of use or are they to be a research tool with a core of indexed back files? Are periodical search skills and the unique strengths of magazine content to be incorporated into curriculum and class assignments? Does the administration concur?

Most LMC goals and supporting policies focus broadly on advancing literacy and expanding horizons, providing informational support of curriculum, teaching and reinforcing search skills, promoting critical thinking and pleasure reading. Seldom are periodicals or their role mentioned specifically. If periodicals, current subscriptions and indexed backfiles are to be an integral part of the LMC collection and program, then specific, formally approved, written statements of long and short range goals and supporting policies are needed to provide the necessary base on which to function. It can not be stressed enough that a good periodicals collection and program must have administrative commitment.

Elementary schools that have good LMC skills instruction integrated into their comprehensive programs still may give low priority to periodical search skills because there is so much other basic material to cover and the relative cost of a periodicals based program is disproportionate to the curricular applicability.

They may maintain a short list of magazine titles appropriate to the lower grade reading levels primarily to lure the reluctant reader and casually expand the interest horizons of all students. Some of these periodicals such as nature, history and National Geographic publications have content related to curriculum but their use is not structured. The wise LMC specialist knows that teaching skills that are not immediately relevant to class projects and not continually reinforced is usually a waste of time.

Periodicals management in these circumstances is usually restricted to the simplest selection, ordering, processing, display, circulation and disposal procedures. This is as it should be but it also can include some of the basic management techniques described later on.

Middle schools, junior and senior high schools are apt to use periodicals more extensively. Even the smallest collection should have a management plan for use today and expansion tomorrow based on curriculum, budget and space available.

Active and even aggressive promotion of periodical search skills, content and critical thinking in class projects is appropriate at these levels concomitant with the reinforcement of what has been taught earlier. Periodicals can be intentionally integrated into nearly every LMC assignment, progressively increasing the content variety and degree of difficulty.

An extensive range of titles or back files is not essential initially. The greater the use of what is available, the greater the demand for an expanded collection and more use. This curricular use management and the degree to which demand is created is for the most part the direct responsibility of the LMC specialist consistent with stated goals. Physical management of the collection and its possible expansion is directly related, but somewhat less important, although the two go hand in hand. There is little point in developing an efficient, well controlled physical management system if it is infrequently used. Thus, the first decisions must be based on how and for what purposes periodicals are to be used in the school setting.

SELECTION

Selection of titles, the form in which they will be acquired and where they will be filed are key decisions to be made by the LMC specialist. According to *The IMS '84 Ayer Directory of Publications* (page Aviii) there are 10,809 periodicals published in the United States alone. The average school LMC specialist can hope to personally evaluate only a fraction of them. Without consulting annotations for the entire list, how can appropriate selections be made for an individual school's collection?

Accessibility to articles, suitability of material, cost and space factors immediately narrow the field. What titles are indexed? How many comprehensive indexes can be consistently carried in the budget year after year? How many magazine titles? What is the patron reading level? What are the curricular demands and how can and should they be expanded? What are the goals in teaching information retrieval skills? What is the magazine's reputation for accuracy? Can students detect any editorial bias through their own critical analysis or must it be pointed out? Is the physical layout and literacy level attractive to students? What space can be devoted to shelving or microform machines? Is the LMC staff willing to manage the negative aspects of periodicals because they believe in the benefits and will promote them accordingly, or will periodicals be neglected?

Titles in any category that come to your attention as possible purchases should be personally scrutinized even though they seem to meet the necessary criteria, especially if you are pinching pennies. Advertising, word of mouth and even reviews in reputable sources can be misleading. A visit to another LMC wth a subscription or a request to a publisher for a sample copy can save the aggravation of correcting a costly mistake and be well worth the effort. Canceling a subscription and attempting to obtain a refund is an unrewarding exercise.

COMMERCIAL INDEXES

The availability of indexing can not be stressed enough. The most relevant material is useless unless the staff and patrons can find it. Lack of LMC time during the school day, student short interest span and laziness usually preclude the issue by issue search for material. Such tedium should not be a student's introduction to research. Introduction to a periodical index when relevant to the project at hand prevents much frustration and forms a base for good attitude and search skills development.

There are dozens of comprehensive, cumulative indexes published, most fairly specialized. Only a few are relevant to K–12. *Children's Magazine Guide* (formerly *Subject Index to Children's Magazines*) is geared to the lower grades in vocabulary, type size, spacing, and magazines covered, yet has generally the same features and format as adult indexes. It is relatively inexpensive and can be useful to the LMC staff and teachers even if cumulative index search skills are not part of the elementary school curriculum. *Reader's Guide to Periodical Literature* and/or *The Magazine Index* and a newspaper index such as *The New York Times* are some of the most basic for grades 6–12 purposes. They cover a wide range of topics that relate well to most curricula and are written on an appropriate level.

Access, General Science Index, Biography Index, Book Review Digest, Index to Free Periodicals, Personal Names Index (New York Times), Theater Review Index (New York Times), and *Biology Digest* are among other titles that can be appropriate supplements for use with these older students. Some of these supplementary titles are actually indexes to indexes or abstracts, research formats that college bound students should be introduced to if possible.

Obviously, the bulk of magazine subscriptions should be chosen from the list of those supported by the LMC's indexes. Conversely, there is diminished value and high frustration in having an index series with few of the magazines available. A balance is essential.

Some LMCs who find their budgets inadequate to support both an index serial and enough magazine subscriptions to make it seem worth while may use the *Abridged Reader's Guide.* Although comparably priced with the full version when the Wilson service price structure is used, it does list fewer titles, lessens the frustration factor among users and takes up less shelf space. On the other hand, since cost is not a factor, using the complete index permits students to see the full range of information generally available and perhaps find sources at their public LMC.

Another answer lies in the self indexed magazines such as *National Geographic, American Heritage, Horizon,* etc. A single title index is an excellent introduction for young students and useful to all. Unfortunately, the cumulative indexing often lags badly, and search in multiple annual indexes can become tedious. Nevertheless, single title indexes deserve their niche on the shelf. Some come as individual units and others can be photocopied from the terminal issue of a volume and bound in a loose-leaf notebook. In the latter instance, as many copies as are needed for class use can be made as a teaching aid.

OUTSIDE SOURCES

If used with discretion, outside sources can also help to extend coverage of titles infrequently requested but found in the LMCs indexes. Periodical holdings lists should be exchanged among schools in the district. Although there may be a great deal of overlap, unique titles can be high lighted. Procedures should be developed to interchange articles from these sources when possible, perhaps by interschool mail.

Similar cooperation and coordination should be encouraged with the local public LMC. Access through networks, universities and Union Serials Lists should also be explored for the highly specialized information that high school students sometimes need. Approached properly and in moderation, the use of school based indexes to obtain information from other LMCs expands a students research base rather than underscores local deficiencies.

In-House Indexes

In practical terms of needing the most basic access here and now, some small LMCs will be continually frustrated until budget adjustments can be made and a general index serial purchased. They can eke out subscriptions to only a few curriculum oriented titles, not all of which are self indexed, and cite this as an excuse to use only the most recent issues for their timeliness or recreational value. Research value is neglected due to the inefficiency of searching through every issue for some dimly remembered article.

The time spent in such a search would be better put to use in systematically maintaining a simple, informal in-house index of the ready reference type for topics predictable in the curriculum. Staff time spent on such indexing is not necessarily wasted because once the essential curricular need illustrated by use is established, professional time can be translated into the dollars that justify purchase commitment to a commercial index, and back files have already been established.

In-house indexing of this sort is also applicable to a well indexed LMC on a more limited scale. There is always a time lag, several weeks to a year, for nearly all commercial indexes. Locating a pertinent article of a month ago that might have been in one of the dozens of magazines can be impossible when an entire class is clamoring for service.

Before a newly arrived magazine is shelved, the person who deals most with magazine use in curriculum should scan the table of contents and fix in memory or mark for in-house ready reference indexing those items most apt to be useful in that dead period before the commercial index arrives.

Familiarity with special features standard to a title is important for often they are not included in commercial indexes nor is the topic indicated in the table of contents. *Congressional Digest,* for example, routinely prints a chronology of legislative events that is accessed only by first-hand knowledge. In-house indexing helps here.

This familiarity with periodicals content and predictable patron demands can not be stressed enough. Know what student projects are and will be, as individuals and as classes. When teachers see how this can benefit student research, they will be more apt to keep in constant contact about assignments and so will students. Not every article should be indexed, however. Only those of unique value to a predictable curricular need, and within the unindexed time span, should be considered.

This also holds true for the few totally unindexed magazines of proven curricular value which may find their way into the collection. *Biblical Archeological Review* is an example of one title that simple, selective in-house indexing makes invaluable to Ancient History courses.

Simple in-house indexing is by subject, listing article and magazine title, date of publication and page number. It may be annotated in unusual instances. Cross referencing is minimal and not every article is included. It is filed on 3x5 cards completely separately from the main card catalog and weeded as is desirable. The articles to be indexed can be checked in the table of contents and subject headings assigned by the LMC specialist. The actual preparation of the index cards can be done by a clerk or volunteer following a set format.

In-house indexing can also be done on a microcomputer, using one of the better commercial file programs. If the computer can be dedicated to this use, it can also serve as a student introduction to the simplest type of data base searching, either by subject or key word.

The least desirable option to article retrieval is clipping for the Vertical File. Except in unusual circumstances, Vertical File space is better devoted to other source material than commonly accessible magazine articles.

CURRICULUM AND PERIODICALS CONTENT

Periodicals, like other LMC materials, are multipurpose in relation to the curriculum. Primarily, their use advances literacy, develops search skills and provides information although additional uses can be cited.

In evaluating indexed titles for the collection classroom applicability is a prime consideration. What topic coverage is desirable at what reading level and at what depth? Curriculum guides should be consulted for every course and major study units noted. Key teachers, those readily identified by their LMC orientation and peer leadership, should be specifically interviewed.

Not every course or study unit needs or should have its own specialized periodicals, but the possibility should be considered in the selection process. Periodicals could be the prime source for a course in ecology, but play no part in the assignments for Algebra I. Often, broad coverage titles such as *U.S. News and World Report* or *Time* will meet the needs of a number of possible assigments. Opinion magazines, representing a variety of outlooks on social, political or literary topics, help to sharpen critical skills and provide the base for position papers or debate. Technical magazines may be necessary for science or specific career exploration courses.

Periodicals and curriculum are both organic, constantly changing in form, content, and emphasis. Editorial policies are altered. Magazines come and go. Indexes add and drop titles. Teaching styles and projects vary from year to year. It is essential to stay in close touch with what teachers are contemplating, help them to plan in relation to resources available and then stay three jumps ahead of them and any district or state curricular revisions.

New and creative uses of the periodical material available should be constantly sought to reinforce skills already learned and widen research horizons. Good teachers appreciate suggestions that will add variety and vitality to their lesson plans and have a multiple purpose. Even stodgy teachers can be enlivened if they feel the LMC will share the work load.

Periodicals are versatile tools and should not be confined to being one of the sources for The Research Paper. They can be the perfect vehicle for very short reports, such as practice in expository writing or public speaking. Watch trends and fads. What works one year, may not the next, and sometimes the periodicals collection must be adjusted.

Larger comprehensive periodical collections are usually adaptable to curricular fluctuations and seldom require more than an occasional title addition or deletion. The minuscule budget, small collection manager, however, must often decide between books and magazines when changes occur. The Crusades may be better served in hard cover, but current scientific developments and politics are not. If the small basic collection is chosen carefully, usually serials can be preserved that are appropriate to a number of topics in breadth if not depth. It is at this time that policy application is particularly important and goals must be kept clearly in view.

A knee jerk response to project change and teacher short term demand for highly specialized magazines results in title additions and cancellations that interrupt back file integrity and are a time consuming nightmare. Nevertheless, the collection should be systematically reviewed annually in relation to every course and predictable assignment to ascertain holes and redundancies.

That way deliberate choices have been made for intelligent reasons. The LMC specialist is on firm professional ground, the collection content is kept in balanced perspective to the curriculum and managed instead of just happening by default.

Pleasure Reading

Most magazine and newspaper choices, by budgetary limitation, must be curriculum related, but pleasure reading should not be neglected. Luckily, many multitopic periodicals can serve both purposes, but a few titles featuring sports, short stories, puzzles, grooming, etc., can capture the reluctant as well as the avid reader as nothing else can. Educational? Of course. Curricular? Not necessarily. Important? Very. But to be used, they must be invitingly visible and available without hassle.

Newspapers

Newspapers are a nuisance. They are also a vital part of a collection, indexed or not. Curricular applications are numerous and varied. As a primary source they are invaluable.

Local, state and national news coverage is desirable. When these are all in one newspaper, so much the better. Otherwise, subscriptions to several should be carried. Money can be saved if subscriptions are only for the same 180 days as the school year. Extensive hardcopy back files need not be kept; a few months are usually more than adequate. Sometimes the format is such that only one or two sections of an edition need be saved.

More and more major newspapers with cumulative indexing are available on microform so a back file of regional as well as national news can be collected. If coordinate hard copy is ordered be sure to specify the edition used for cumulative indexing to avoid bibliographic confusion. Content and paging can vary in the several daily editions.

Professional Magazines

One group of periodicals that is often overlooked because of budget or presumed lack of interest is the professional collection. Some teachers prefer their own subscriptions, some don't care, and some would welcome and use a few titles. The collection need not be extensive. *Reader's Guide* and *Education Index* can provide a basic list from which to choose although other titles are also available.

Poll the staff for focus preferences–general education theory, classroom management, organizational news, how-to projects, new approaches to specific disciplines, etc. Where is the most interest and, just as important, will those who express interest honestly use them? Request staff members to discard any personal subscriptions into your hands for possible inclusion on the shelf.

Routing slips can be attached to new copies which are passed to interested and cooperative staff members but sometimes the route has fatal detours. Having time limits with the principal the last person on the route sometimes helps. A better solution is to have a quantity of mimeographed notices prepared in advance saying only that the new issue of a specified title is available. These are then placed in staff mailboxes and the initiative is theirs.

Before any professional magazines are circulated, they should be scanned by the LMC staff for new ideas and trends in any discipline that could have creative LMC application or should be brought to a specific teacher's attention. This sort of internal public relations increases the professional creditability of the LMC immeasurably.

Storage

You have carefully chosen a list of appropriate, indexed periodicals that you can afford to maintain in the forseeable future. Now you can go ahead and subscribe, right? Wrong! Where are you going to put them, for how long and in what form?

Even the newest, most carefully designed school LMCs have space limitations. Older facilities have reached the saturation point and periodicals are in a vulnerable position.

There are combination display and limited storage units

available commercially but they are expensive and take up a lot of space. Small LMCs, particularly older ones, may not find them feasible. Many school LMCs use common shelf space, in a main periodical area and/or in storage closets, with perhaps a simple display rack for the most recent issues.

Periodicals may be stacked horizontally on the shelf or vertically in Princeton or similar box files. Filing and retrieving slippery magazines that are stacked is an exercise in frustration to be avoided if at all possible. The small expense and slightly greater space that labeled, cardboard, Princeton files require more than compensates for staff time spent keeping piles of periodicals in order.

Periodicals, by their very nature, are predictably cumulative. If the number of issues of one title in one year occupies eight inches of horizontal shelf space, the same number of issues the next year probably will also. Multiplying all of your titles by their predicted shelf space inches for ten years adds up to a big problem. And ten years is an arbitrary figure.

If the indexed collection is to fill a research role, back files should be available indefinitely, give or take a bit of title weeding. From time to time, new titles may be added, or old ones dropped, but a discontinued subscription does not necessarily mean clearing the title from the shelves. *The Reporter* magazine, for instance, has not been published since 1968, yet its articles can be a valuable resource, accessible through the indexes of that period.

The easiest solution is to hold magazines for a limited time and then get rid of them. The rationale is often that they are in such tattered condition that they have become useless. The irony is that the most ragged issues become that way through use, indicating that the material within has patron value. Only unused magazines remain in pristine condition.

Another solution is to severely limit the number of subscriptions so that there is plenty of room for future issues. By doing so, today's patrons will be shortchanged unnecessarily in information availability while waiting for the shelves to fill with back files.

Bound Volumes

Some LMCs go to the trouble of binding back issues according to volume. This has a preservative advantage but the cost is high if missing or damaged issues must first be re-placed, patron use is denied while they are at the bindery and they still use shelf space, although, perhaps, in a different location. They can also be cumbersome to use, particularly for younger students. Nevertheless, this is often the best way to handle selective, heavily used titles such as journals with lengthy articles or publications where microform reproduction is inadequate or unavailable.

Bound volumes may be assigned classification numbers and be shelved with the book collection. This practice can be confusing to students who expect to find all periodicals in the same location, and also can distort collection of periodical use statistics.

Microforms

Microforms have been the salvation of many collections. Their weight and volume is a fraction of that of hard copy so space requirements are vastly reduced. Microforms are easy for staff and patrons to handle. They are conveniently filed and accessed, reproducible, more durable and less vulnerable to loss and vandalism than hard copy. Back files predating a LMC's hard copy collection may be available. The cost of replacing a hard copy backfile with microform is at least comparable to and often less than having it bound in most instances.

Microforms are not ordinarily a substitute for current hard copy, however. Most microform publishers wait until an entire volume of hard copy has been publicly distributed before they start filming, and then reproduce copies according to orders received. This is eminently sensible from a business point of view but it means that a LMC relying entirely on microform subscriptions always would be at least 6 months to a year behind.

However, at least one microform publisher is now offering a limited number of titles on microfiche issued within a month of hard copy publication at a comparable price. If this becomes the standard within the industry and an extensive list of titles becomes available LMC collections heretofore limited by space availability will benefit considerably.

For some titles that do not deal with dated material complete reliance on microform subscription might be acceptable.

The value of a *Newsweek* or *Science News,* however, would be vastly diminished if it were not available immediately upon hard copy publication. Some titles cannot be sold in microform unless current hard copy subscriptions are also held.

Microform Machines

If microforms are part of the management plan then supervisable space must be allocated to microfiche/film readers and reader-printers. This is a different type and amount of space compared to shelving, however, and is limited only by the availability of electric outlets.

Although the list price is fairly high for some budgets, these machines are often given as bonuses for large fiche/film purchases such as when back files are originally converted. Microform readers are quite durable and three or four are usually enough for the impact of a class of 25 students with a multiple reference form assignment. Reader-printers, although initially even more expensive, speed user turnover and fewer machines overall are needed. It is advisable to charge a modest fee, say $.10 a printout page, to avoid copying abuse and help defray costs. Printers can be self supporting. Parent or class groups sometimes find fund raising for microform machine purchase a worthwhile project. A realistic supply of light bulbs, printer paper and toner should be on hand at all times. Some printer paper is dated, however, and a large quantity should not be ordered at one time since deterioration of quality can occur.

Microfilm vs. Microfiche

Microfiche is preferable to microfilm in a school setting. The machines are less vulnerable to breakdown since there are fewer moving parts and introductory instruction is simpler. Class resource management is better when the single issue of a title can be distributed on a fiche card instead of a number of issues on a microfilm reel. This becomes most apparent when an entire class is researching a limited time period such as their birthdays and two or three years worth of certain titles must be divided twenty-five or more ways. (This is another problem with bound hardcopy back files, incidentally.) It must be noted that many magazine titles, pre 1970, are available only on microfilm, as are many newspaper titles.

Mixed Form Planning

Practically speaking, a combination of hard copy, microforms, perhaps bound volumes, and judicious weeding best serve the research function of an established periodical collection with space limitations. A long range plan must be adopted and followed consistantly. This requires administrative as well as LMC commitment because of the fiscal implications. The index serials and core periodical subscriptions, hard copy and microform, must be considered a consistently supported budget item, as important as almanacs, electricity or pension plans.

The pattern adopted by Ridgefield (CT) High School might serve as an illustration of mixed form planning. It is based on observation of student use, pragmatism and technological developments. They found that the bulk of student research requiring overnight circulation of magazines encompassed the most recent two year span, thus hard copy is desirable for this time period. Microforms, with occasional student purchased printouts of previewed material, cover all other needs. Student resistance to microforms is minimal.

The basic plan is that current subscriptions are for hard copy, run from January to December and are kept for 2-1/2 years. At the end of a school year, the oldest hard copy year, showing many signs of wear, is discarded and replaced by duplicate microfiche (a standing order, renewed annually.) In other words, in June, 1983, all 1981 hard copy issues of a title were replaced by its fiche counterpart, leaving hard copy issues for 1982 and half of 1983 on the shelf.

The emptied Princeton files which had housed the 1981 hard copy were moved to the other end of the title span on the shelf to await the arrival of the rest of 1983 and the first half of 1984, when the procedure would be repeated. Using this sort of shelf rotation of Princeton file boxes for each title dedicates a predictable and consistent amount of shelf space to that title and avoids the massive shifts of back files often necessary when all years of all periodicals holdings are filed together.

Backfiles not replaced by or predating microforms are stored alphabetically in Princeton files in an adjacent area since use is less frequent.

Even if microform replacement is not part of a LMC's plan, the idea of keeping only the most recent several years of the collection in a separate, more accessible area deserves consideration. If separating forms and definite time periods of a title file would seem to generate staff confusion, cardboard dummies indicating the pattern for each title can be filed with that title in the primary filing area.

Speed and efficiency in retrieving and filing issues are desirable and the less distance that has to be covered per transaction, the better. Ridgefield High School LMC also found that the most frequently requested titles were toward the end of the alphabet so current hard copy is filed alphabetically with XYZ nearest the magazine circulation desk.

Since space is the problem, the ongoing cost of replacing hard copy with microfiche, in essence two subscriptions to the same title, different forms, different years, is minuscule compared to the alternatives of building a LMC addition, massive remodeling or drastic collection reduction resulting in curricular limitations. Not all educational costs are measured in dollars.

Originally, a large number of back issue titles were replaced at one time and bonus microform readers and reader/printers acquired. At that time 1970 was the earliest date fiche was available for most titles and was chosen as the uniform fiche/film dividing date. Pre-1970 holdings are on microfilm or retained in hard copy for eventual replacement as more space is demanded and budget permits. Some title files have been extended back to the first date of publication.

The pattern makes it easy to fill a request. Pre-1970, film or hard copy; current 2 years, hard copy; anything else, fiche. A few periodicals whose content is not too dated and in low demand or those subject to vandalism, such as *Rolling Stone,* are direct fiche subscriptions, within the fiche time pattern. Color is an important component of some publications such as art magazines and until good color microform is available they will remain in hard copy.

The practice of binding *National Geographic* and *Life* volumes predated the availability of microform. Established curricular use patterns made it advisable to continue this format for these titles although space limitations may force a reevaluation. They are filed with periodicals.

NEW TECHNOLOGIES

Experience with a variety of resource forms as well as content evaluation should be part of every students education. The introduction of microform technology has vastly widened the possibilities for periodical research in small LMCs. Previously it would have been unthinkable to hold a complete file of the *New York Times,* indexed, from its inception in 1851. Now it can be a practical goal if funding can be found.

Advances in microcomputer technology have widened horizons even further although, at the moment, on-line access to full text articles and their local reproduction is limited and expensive. When this becomes financially feasible for smaller LMCs and the available title range of current publications broad enough, supporting some hard copy titles on site for research may no longer be as necessary. Any holdings on fiche and film will continue to be useful, however.

New teletext, optical and video lasar disk technologies also hold promise and their development as a source of periodicals would be interesting if technical problems are overcome and they become cost effective for small LMCs. Accurate color reproduction with good resolution in all the various formats is another technological step to be anticipated.

Although the development of new technologies relevant to periodicals is exciting to contemplate, the school LMC must view them in terms of the number of necessary patron or staffed access stations, basically a cost and space problem. Considered in the context of classroom groups needing supervised access to indexing and individual magazine issues in a 40 minute period, this is not a minor matter.

Patron Access to Periodicals

The degree of access students have to the files is a question of policy and the physical arrangement of the LMC. One of the secrets of efficient periodicals management is close supervisory control of the file area. A separate room or enclosure with controlled access is more important to effective physical management than any other factor yet patrons should feel comfortable about requesting material. Recent copies of popular titles can be on display for browsing and a small area within the controlled space can be set aside for a "reading room," or periodicals can be checked out for use in the main reading area. This is a space related circulation policy issue to be decided and consistently followed.

Periodical files, circulation control, microform machines and indexes should be in physically distinct but related supervisable areas so that all may be used in an orderly way when a number of students are working on similar projects. A dedicated counter top or tables should be used for indexes so they remain in one area.

Closed Stacks

Although freer access to displayed recent issues is desirable, the "closed stacks" concept should be applied to most periodical files, hard copy and microform, as far as patrons are concerned.

Misfiled fiche or a date scrambled Princeton file box results in wasted time and poor service to patrons. The staff time spent in "closed stack" retrieval is nothing compared to time spent sorting out the chaos that one class can create when let loose among the files.

More importantly, the disciplined order of well maintained files that results in efficient and responsive service subtly conveys to students a respect for their endeavors and a proper attitude toward the LMC as a whole.

This does not mean that the atmosphere should be harsh, dictatorial and forbidding. On the contrary. Every effort should be made to indicate that because the files are in order the staff will be more efficient, friendlier and more responsive to a student's particular needs.

Staff members who service the periodicals circulation desk do more than fetch and carry, however. They are in a prime position to spot students with research difficulties, suggest other sources, help with bibliographic formats and give a great deal of other informal instruction.

TECHNICAL MANAGEMENT OF PERIODICALS

Basic decisions have been made: overall goals and policies, title selection, space allocations, format pattern and parameters. Now is the time to consider in detail the day to day management of the periodical program. Additional policies in this area must be established, tailored to the individual LMC and consistant with its other operations. Procedures for acquisitions, record keeping, processing, circulation and overdues, deaccession and other functions must be developed.

Purchasing

Purchasing can be approached several ways. The least efficient and most frustrating is for the LMC to deal individually with each title publisher. Some school systems require that subscription lists be submitted to the central purchasing office which in turn deals with the publishers directly, ordering and, sometimes, trouble shooting.

Many LMCs use subscription agencies. The price may be a bit more than the total of individual orders or there may be quantity or institutional discounts, depending on the agency chosen and the services it offers. The justification lies in saving the school clerical (or LMC specialist) cost of processing and following through on individual purchase orders, maintaining detailed subscription and correspondence files, time consuming SNAFU tracing, headaches and postage.

Shop around. Different agencies offer different prices and services. Needed above all are reliability of accurate renewals and speedy effective troubleshooting. Magazine publishers have circulation idiosyncrasies. The good agencies know them and act accordingly and their size gives them clout that the individual subscriber doesn't always have. To be fair, most publishers seem to be sensitive to subscription problems but foul-ups do occur.

One big exception to using an agency can be made if there is a really good introductory cut rate offer, often multiyear, for a title addition necessary to the collection. The savings may be well worth the extra record keeping. The new title should be added to the agency list at renewal time.

Sometimes there will be an attractive multiyear cut rate

offer for a title already on your agency list. Resist it unless it is very, very good. Too many titles out of phase with the agency annual renewal pattern will result in missed renewals, broken serials or too much record checking. The administrative use of a microcomputer periodical management program lessens the risk but the human element of remembering to enter and check properly one more minor file type is still vulnerable.

The persistant problem of some publishers charging higher rates for institutional subscriptions is with us still. Some LMCs obtain these titles as "gifts" from individuals, others pay the higher price and seethe. A case can be made for all points of view.

Subscription Patterns

It is desirable to establish a subscription pattern so that all renewals occur in the same month and coordinate well with the availability of funds, adequate agency lead time and LMC staff time for evaluation and order preparation. For instance, if the school fiscal year runs from July 1 to June 30, the tentative subscription order might be prepared in mid May and the purchase order, dated in July, be ready to cover the definite order to the agency as soon as the exact LMC budget is known and funds are released. Be sure to place orders at the beginning of the fiscal year before monies are frozen for unforeseen reasons.

Starting in October, the subscription agency will appropriately pace ordering renewals and new titles for subscriptions that will run from January to December. A catalogue and the list of titles up for renewal the next year is then sent to you in the spring along with prices and other data which makes evaluation, title adjustment and reordering of the bulk of the collection quite efficient. Annual renewals with microform publishers generally follow the same pattern.

Exceptions break the subscription pattern. For whatever the reason, a magazine may fall behind and not be published for one or more issues, then extend the subscription by the number of omitted issues to make up for the lapse. Or, it may be necessary to individually enter a subscription to an additional title off-pattern because of unforseen curricular demands or a new desirable title might start publication out of phase with the subscription year.

In bringing these vagrants within the fold of the established subscription time pattern, try to maintain unbroken serials. The vagrant title should be added to the next year's January–December subscription list. Duplicate issues may be received for a few months or there may be a lapse of a few issues. If the latter, then an effort should be made to anticipate and purchase the few predictable missing issues on the newsstand as they appear. An alternative is to wait a year or so until the missing issues can be ordered from a back issue supplier or the complete volume can be purchased on microform. This is less desirable since the relevance of timely material may be lost.

Why bother to have consistent expiration dates since agencies can renew appropriately any variations they are handed? The problem is not agency management of renewals, but it is LMC management of a collection. Local record and budget management is vastly simplified if as many renewal dates as possible are the same. Professional time is too valuable to spend verifying new expiration dates on address labels for a different group of periodicals every month and checking them against the agency order or tracing missing issues to a subscription lapse. Routine perusal of all address labels following the uniform renewal date should be enough to spot any problems and alert the agency.

Gifts

To extend your collection beyond the limits of the budget, take advantage of free magazines, but with discrimination. They come from a variety of sources. Donations from private citizens or teachers may be duplicates of subscription holdings. If they are high usage titles, accept them with gratitude. Two or three copies of the same issue will increase the circulation of the material and the extras can be weeded out after peak usage is over. If they are low usage duplicates, accept them graciously, fill in any holes in the file and discard the rest immediately and discretely.

If they are titles not in the collection, evaluate them as carefully as any other perspective acquisition would be evaluated and accept or reject accordingly. Do not accept blindly; a bit of paranoia at the time may be good for the LMC's reputation in the long run. Not all periodicals are appropriate for school use.

Public relations is paramount in dealing with these gifts. Donors should be made to feel their thoughtfulness is appreciated even if they are basically interested in unloading their trash to claim a tax deduction. Most donors are not so mean spirited, however, and their donations should have a warm written acknowledgement that also can be used for tax purposes if they wish. Rejections can be made on the basis of curriculum irrelevance, non-indexing and/or space availability while still praising the generous gesture.

Free Publications

There are some very fine freebies available directly from the publishers. *Free Magazines for Libraries* (Smith, Adeline Mercer. *Free Magazines for Libraries*. Jefferson, N.C.: McFarland and Company, Inc., 1980) has a long annotated list of titles that will be sent free on a continuing basis for those who have a specific use for them. Most are not covered in standard commercial indexes but some have self-indexing or are in *Index to Free Periodicals*.

Many promote a particular point of view and should be evaluated according to the patron level of critical analysis and what other balancing material is available.

Some sources and examples are Foreign Information Offices (*Japan Report, South African Panorama*), industry or labor unions (*ARAMCO World, Ecolibrium, AFL-CIO News*), civic groups (*Rotarian*), religious organizations (*The Plain Truth*), lobby groups (*Right to Life News*), or military services (*Leatherneck*).

This is by no means an exhaustive list, nor are those listed appropriate for all schools. Nevertheless, this type of material should be explored and might prove a useful adjunct to the core subscription list.

Discards from other LMCs that are weeding or converting to microform can help to start or fill in back files in selected titles. One LMC has an arrangement with a local advertising analysis company to cull their discards and has thus built up an unusual collection of microcomputer titles. It came about through a chance conversation on a bus! Be alert for opportunities to extend the collection appropriately and with discretion beyond budgetary limitations.

Log Cards and Record Keeping

When magazines arrive in the LMC each should be logged in. Log cards are a good and simple way of maintaining and updating a variety of data for each title efficiently. These 3x5 printed cards are available from LMC supply houses and are formatted with spaces for days or months. Each title is assigned its own card and when the magazine arrives the arrival date is recorded in the appropriate space for the magazine cover date. This forms the basis for inventory control similar to a book shelflist.

Frequency varies from title to title, but each log card will show the individual pattern, weekly, 22 times a year, quarterly, etc. By recording the date of arrival as well as the cover date, confusion can be avoided, for with some titles the two dates are separated by several months. The "December" issue may not be published until March! With a predictable pattern of recorded publishing frequency, undelivered issues can be quickly identified at a glance for further action.

Those LMCs fortunate enough to take annual inventory cross out missing issues or otherwise indicate temporary unavailability if replacement is planned. Arrival of replacements or duplicate issues are also recorded. Other managerial data on the log card can include extent, form and location of all holdings in that title, the renewal month and agency, index source and arrival of special issues or indexes.

One LMC with multiform holdings of back files logs in current hard copy issues in ink. When hard copy is replaced with fiche a colored transparent highlighter is drawn through the relevant dates to indicate the new form. A different color is used for microfilm and another for bound issues. Form usually indicates location. Any variations can be noted.

The monthly style log cards can contain 12 years of data for a title and are adaptable for quarterly publications also. The daily style of card, commonly used for weekly, biweekly and irregularly spaced publications, only accommodates one year's data, but several years can be stapled together along with a monthly style card showing the condensed record.

Log cards are filed alphabetically by title, but may be removed from their file box and temporarily sorted by other categories such as frequency, major subject matter, aberrant renewal date, etc. Color coded clips can be affixed for easy recognition of these categories if desired when they are interfiled.

Missing Issues

Cards for undelivered issues, detected by a break in logging pattern, or titles with subscription problems can be placed on end in the file box and thus demand attention. When the source of the problem is located and corrective action initiated, a succinct explanatory note can be paper clipped to the log card and it can resume its normal position in the box. Additional notations concerning the problem are made until it is resolved so that an up-to-date status summary is readily available and correspondence files and telephone records need not be consulted constantly.

Notations for one problem might read: 10/9/84–Form to agency re: missing issue for 9/84; 11/15/84–Agency reply. Publisher sent issue but will replace anyway. Another notation series might be: 1/23/85–Phoned Postmaster re: erratic delivery of *People*. He disclaims responsibility, suggests in-school mail distribution system faulty; 1/26/85–Conference w. principal and secretary, new mail distribution procedure agreed upon; monitor for a while.

When a problem is resolved, the paper clip is removed and the notations discarded or, in rare instances where the same title is always a problem, the record is stapled to the log card for future referral. Occasional checks of paperclipped log cards should be made to identify futile cases. The card can then be marked appropriately and revert to normal status.

Letters do not usually need to be sent in routine no-show cases. Agencies often supply forms or accept telephoned complaints. It is essential to check the sequence of issue numbers as well as the dates before claiming non delivery. A date gap is not necessarily an issue gap.

For individual subscriptions or when an agency is laggard, a pre-printed request form postcard need only have the title, date, volume and issue number written in before it is sent off to the publisher. Correspondence with a publisher should usually be directed to the subscription or circulation manager whose address may be different from that of the editorial office. There are wide variations and frequent changes, so the very small print on one of the first pages of the most recent available issue should be consulted.

Although other forms of record keeping may be developed, the multiple use of a log card vastly simplifies and consolidates data referral, freeing the staff for other tasks. Management programs on a dedicated microcomputer can do the same thing but are not necessarily faster, more accurate or efficient. A very sharp pencil is a lot less expensive.

But is all this data necessary? Each type of data has a distinct management purpose and the extent to which it is recorded and used determines the degree of control exercised over a collection. The degree of control is directly related to the degree of patron service that can be rendered.

Each LMC must determine the minimum data necessary for its own most effective operation. Some initial log card data entry is merely a convenience to avoid seeking other sources or cross referencing. Some is necessary to make sure files are as complete as possible and provide a record of claims or other correspondence in progress. Some is used for verification when overdue notices are challenged, particularly when there are multiple copies of an issue.

Holdings Lists

Some LMCs only record issue arrival on log cards and place them in plastic flip folders that serve primarily as a list of holdings for patron referral. It is unnecessarily time consuming for managers to remove each log card from its plastic sleeve to record the arrival of an issue and patrons can take them for their own selfish purposes effectively destroying the inventory record of a title. Log cards are better and more versatile used solely as a more comprehensive record and managerial tool.

Another form of holdings list for patron use, however, is a time saver for all. It should list titles, frequency, date span, form and location of all magazines. It can be updated and typed once a year or, better yet, it can be recorded on a microcomputer diskette using one of the many filing or periodicals management programs, updated when convenient and printed automatically in multiple copies. Since this only needs to be done occasionally and takes little time or skill once the original data is entered, the LMC does not even have to own its own computer and the updating can be done off-site.

It is helpful to have holdings lists in notebook binders located at index, reference and periodical circulation stations.

Processing

After a magazine is logged in, the LMC identification should be stamped prominently at least once on the cover near the binding if possible. Today this is a real challenge when the cover art has intense dark colors. Duplicate issues should be marked c.1 or c.2, etc., near the date. Filing and retrieval are made more efficient if a pressure sensitive white label with date and copy number is affixed to the cover, in the upper left hand corner when Princeton files are used, for instance. The LMC stamp can also be put on this label. Logging and most processing can be done by a clerk, aide or faithful volunteer.

Skimming for content and subject assignment for in-house indexing as described earlier is then done by the LMC specialist. This need take only a routine 5 or 10 minutes a day. In-house indexing should not be allowed to pile up. Periodicals should be made available to patrons as soon after arrival as possible.

These are the only preparations needed before the magazine is ready for circulation in some LMCs. Other LMCs insert the most recent issue of a title into a protective plastic folder that may contain a pocket and circulation card and place it on a display rack. The previous issue is then filed on the shelf.

A few LMCs go to the trouble of typing pockets and circulation cards and pasting them in each individual issue permanently. This is more costly in supplies and staff time than warranted when other, simpler, equally effective circulation control methods are available. The same can be said of bar code labels that are part of a computerized circulation system.

LMCs with circulation security systems must decide if magazines should be sensitized. There is usually no question in the case of bound volumes or expensive journals that are attractive to patrons. The garden variety of magazine, however, is too easily vandalized and the sensitized strip removed. The cost of material and labor to bring all periodicals within the security fold is usually greater than the value of individual replacements. There should be no need to sensitize periodicals kept in closed stacks or a well supervised area.

Hard Copy Circulation Policies

Circulation can be handled in several ways and depends to some extent on the physical layout of the LMC. Some LMCs choose to handle it by not allowing magazines to leave the LMC at all and may make coin operated photocoping facilities available instead.

This non-circulation may help to insure unbroken files so that the material is always available for students to use, but it also restricts the time available for individual student use without cost, an important consideration when student access to the collection is limited by school schedule, LMC hours or transportation.

Some LMCs allow circulation of all but the most recent issues, and some have no restrictions Since most articles are fairly short and demand may be heavy, a uniform overnight borrowing period with renewal option is usually adequate. A longer borrowing period seems to generate unnecessary wear and tear and possibility of loss as well as deny timely access to others who may have the same assignment.

It is desirable to limit the number of issues requested by a student at one time. Four or five is a reasonable number for most situations.

The size and extent of the collection, average type of assignment and available staff for retrieval and filing are some factors to consider in formulating these policies.

Hard Copy Circulation Procedure

If the LMC is arranged with closed magazine stacks, a student written request form, one per issue, can also double as the circulation card and be left at the request desk for filing when the magazine is produced. These request forms may be commercially printed on card stock or duplicated in-house in quantity on standard paper and cut to filing size. Simplicity is the key and usually only the title, date, and pages of the magazine and patron name, I.D. number/class numeral/home room and date checked out are necessary. A good supply should be kept by the indexes as well as at the magazine request area.

When the magazine is given to the patron, the copy number is added if necessary and the request form checked for completeness and legibility of all items. The student I.D. or LMC card is also checked if that is part of the system.

School issued I.D. or LMC cards with the student's photograph laminated on are a highly desirable component of circulation control unless the school is small enough so the staff knows each student by name and face. Even ordinarily honest students may resort to unusual subterfuge under academic pressures without this sort of control and needless time can be spent trying to track down the true borrower.

Consistent application of circulation procedures is essential in even the most informal LMCs, but no procedure should be so inflexible that students are denied legitimate use of material. One alternative to lack of an I.D. card might be to have a temporary one issued by the main office or attending teacher. Another is to have use restricted to the periodicals reading room if it is a controlled area. Student paid, in-house photocopying of articles can be done. Another means (officially discouraged but unpreventable) is to have the magazine cheked out properly by a student who assumes full responsibility for it but in turn lends it to a friend. Although such options should be available they should be used seldom and with discretion or circulation control becomes ineffective. Some of these measures are also applicable to individual students whose borrowing privileges have been temporarily rescinded.

Magazine request forms/circulation slips are filed alphabetically by magazine title. Unfulfilled requests can be filed separately for statistical purposes. If the consistent borrowing period is merely overnight, no notation of due date is necessary; it is automatically due the next school day. When the magazine is returned, the request form/circulation slip is removed from the file and saved to be tallied eventually for circulation statistics. If the magazine is overdue, the circulation slip is left in the file until overdue procedures are instituted.

Microform Circulation, Policy and Procedure

Microform circulation to the machines and back is handled the same way. The request form becomes the circulation slip and is retained until the microform is returned. It is usually not necessary to designate on the slip if the request is for hard copy or microform; the date of the publication should be sufficiently indicative.

Instruction on the use of microforms and the readers or reader/printers should be part of the circulation procedure so that each student receives a quiet, individualized demonstration with the requested microform. Usually such an introduction takes less than 3 minutes and is far more effective than holding a group demonstration since the student is effectively launched without fanfare and not intimidated by preconceived ideas.

The use of the printer should be taught at the time it is needed. Fees for the use of a microform printer should be collected when all prints have been made. Policies should be set on the cost per print (students and teachers), whether or not IOUs are acceptable and concerning illegible copies. A possible rule of thumb is that a charge is made if a poor print is the fault of the patron in not following directions. A small charge is important to prevent copying abuses.

Out-of-LMC circulation of microforms is not advised even if portable readers are available. A reader/printer printout should cover all needs and avoids the possibility of loss or damage. Microforms can be replaced by individual reel or fiche issue but patron access is lost in the process. Student care of a portable reader is another concern.

Shelving

Returned magazines and microforms should be shelved as soon as possible. This is obvious, but an accumulation has a way of sneaking up without warning. Nothing is more frustrating and unprofessional than to have to paw through a yard high stack of unfiled titles to fill a request. Trained student or adult volunteers can be a big help here.

Overdues

If all LMC circulation transactions take place at one desk, a procedure to rescind all borrowing privileges of a student until overdue magazines are returned may be coordinated with the procedure used for books. If there is a separate circulation desk for periodicals, coordination with other circulation stations for every transaction is impracticable and no restriction is imposed. Students who are flagrant overdue offenders can be dealt with as individuals.

Fines for overdue magazines are still charged by some schools, but a LMC specialist's time is money, and the record keeping and tracking down of offenders is seldom justified by the amount collected. The writing and distribution of daily overdue notices also falls into this category. An effort to retrieve overdue materials in high demand may be desirable occasionally, however, and direct contact with the offending student's teacher is usually the most profitable route.

This seemingly casual attitude toward overdue magazines does not mean that no control is exercised, however. A distinction must be made between punishing the offender and getting the periodical back. The threat of a scolding or a few pennies fine has little effect on today's student, and heftier penalties are usually disproportionate to the unavailability of a magazine for a few days. The reappearance of the periodical for use by others is the important focus.

Some schools follow the lead of the many colleges which withhold grades until the obligation is met. To do this, the list of offenders and missing materials is compiled quarterly and posted a week or so before report cards are issued. This public notice can bring peer and teacher pressure into play and usually results in many returns. Then revised lists or individual forms are sent to the school office and the report cards are retained there until the obligation is satisfied. Parental pressure now becomes a factor. If the magazine is lost, the student must either pay for replacement or replace it himself.

This latter is the more desirable since the effort involved has an educational value and does not involve the LMC's time in determining the replacement cost, usually more than the cover price, and placing the order. A selection of businesses that specialize in handling out of print periodicals should be listed without preference and the list given to offending students along with standard ordering procedure directions. The rest is up to them.

An exception to student replacement is made when the missing magazine would be soon converted to microform. Then a simple fee, $2.00 in the author's school, is charged and applied to the cost of the microform.

If the obligation is still outstanding at the time of graduation or when a student moves to another school, the diploma or transcript can be withheld. This all requires the cooperation of the administration, but once the procedure is in place, publicized and enforced, the more extreme steps are seldom necessary.

Circulation Policies for Faculty Members

Faculty members have different uses and time demands for LMC materials than students and sometimes a different set of policies are formulated for them. Although standard check-out and check-in procedures remain the same, staff members may be given unlimited time and quantity borrowing privileges (unless student need for the periodicals materializes) during a semester or school year. If this is the case, then individual status reports should be periodically issued so any misunderstandings can be resolved. The administration should develop a policy regarding teacher accountability for unreturned periodicals.

Although sometimes difficult to control, unrestricted teacher browsing among the files should be discouraged and any photocopy costs should be collected for the same reasons pertinent to students.

STATISTICS

Circulation statistics can be a useful managerial tool if not over done and if used with a full understanding of what they represent. They do not represent the usefulness of material or the fact that it was used! There is much in-house use that is not recorded and some material is checked out but not used.

Circulation slips provide the basic data. Statistics can represent the number of formal transactions handled by the staff. They can represent the number of requests for a title, giving a general indication of its probable usefulness. They can indicate unfilled requests. They can indicate peak periods of borrowing if slips are dated and sometimes can be identified with specific assignments. They can show the number of different students using periodicals. They are not infallible and should be used as general indicators, not absolutes, and with perspective of the total program in mind. Be aware of the soft spots and shortcomings. Compilation of statistics should not be disproportionately time consuming compared to their value.

The most important uses are in evaluating the collection, patron use and staff time. What are the monthly circulation figures? Are they reasonably consistent? What titles were frequently requested that are not in the collection? What titles held are never requested? What is the ratio of current issues to back files or microform to hard copy requested? Is concurrent demand for one title so great that duplicates are needed? Is staff time for circulation (direct patron attention, retrieval and filing, check-in, check-out time estimates for one issue multiplied by total daily, monthly or annual circulation figure) so great as to require assignment adjustment, procedural alteration or hiring another person? Conversely, is there so little demand that staff time is inefficiently utilized manning a sporadically used station?

The numbers will not tell the whole story but are a useful starting place. "Why?" is equally important. Inconsistant monthly circulation figures may mean class assignments need to be timed somewhat differently. Great demand for an unheld title may be a temporary aberration. Nonuse of certain titles may occur because the relevant course is offered every other year or a new teacher needs orientation to their use. The microform/hardcopy request ratio may reinforce the observed need for another microform machine, suggest longer holding of hard copy or indicate need for better student orientation to microform. Staff time figures may be used with discretion and explanation to buttress a case with the administration.

Hard Copy Repairs

It is unreasonable to expect that magazines will remain in pristine condition. The most common repairs are mending torn pages with clear tape and reattaching covers. If the cover has become separated from the body of the magazine, clear tape or stapling is too insubstantial a repair. The front and back cover should be cut apart and rejoined on a strip of wide masking tape, leaving enough room between them for the body of the magazine to be affixed to the tape. If additional reinforcement is desired, a long necked stapler can be used. Heavy brown paper from a paper bag is used to replace an irreparable cover or one defaced with graffitti.

Some LMCs prefer to remove pages that have unerasable graffiti, particularly if they are not text crucial, rather than have them circulate and invite further marking. If the culprit can be firmly identified, of course, replacement can be required. Missing pages that are text crucial can be photocopied at another LMC and pasted in. Badly battered issues should not circulate. Not because further damage is feared but because it implies that extreme dilapidation is an accepted standard and invites abuse of other materials. They may be used in a supervised area, however, with appropriate explanation if replacement is impractical.

Students often have a throw-away attitude toward periodicals because this is how they are regarded at home for good and practical reasons. General LMC instruction should include alteration of that attitude but still some students persist in clipping material, usually pictures to illustrate reports.

This problem should be brought to the attention of teachers and their cooperation sought in handling it as follows. Only hand drawn or photocopies of an illustration are acceptable in reports or the entire publication with referral to the proper page and illustration must be submitted. Projects such as art collages should be done in class from a classroom supply of discarded periodicals and an explanation made that they have been acquired solely for that purpose. Oral current event reports should be done from notes, photocopies, or the entire publication, not clippings. If there are justifiable exceptions, the teacher should require proof of the source although there is really no fool-proof way to distinguish between home or LMC sources of clippings.

Repair of Microforms

Microfilm is repaired in much the same way that other film is although this is seldom necessary if the reader machine area is supervised. There are inexpensive splicing kits available with templates to align the film and clear tape packaged like strip bandages that is quick and simple to use on broken or torn film. Too short leaders can be lengthened with excess from an extra long leader. Missing frames of text can not be easily reproduced and the reel must be replaced if the text is of significance. Crumpled film or fiche is uncommon but wrinkles can occasionally be straightened by carefully heating it near a warm light bulb. Splicing or replacement is preferable.

Weeding and Deaccession

A word more about weeding and deaccession. Judicious weeding is essential, but indiscriminate weeding can be disastrous. A case in point. Most science magazines are valued for their most recent information on research developments. Backfiles are usually considered less important. Yet, the most recent work published on a particular topic may have been five years ago, or a recent bibliography may refer to techniques described in detail eight years ago that are still in use. Even the most dated material can have historic value, so weed with a close eye to curricular need in every field, but be realistic. Don't wait until the dust on a file is an inch thick.

Some school districts have specific procedures to cover deaccession of periodicals. Others look the other way. A small quantity of magazines can just fade away. Periodicals in large quantity are not always easy to get rid of. In any case, each issue should be clearly marked "discard" or it will come back to haunt you. Tying each title series into a separate bundle or sealing it in a labeled, strong paper bag makes handling easier.

Some can be offered to students, teachers or the general public. After all, the reasoning goes, they were purchased with public funds. If this route is taken, be prepared to offer a clear explanation, again and again and again, justifying the deaccession. Occasionally, a school district will have a deaccession fair or sale of a variety of materials. Take advantage of the positive publicity. There may be willing takers at prisons, veterans' hospitals, convalescent or retirement homes or state institutions. Sometimes they can be sold to dealers in used periodicals, but make sure the delivery charges don't exceed the price offered. Occasionally a home for them can be found in another school.

Recycling centers love them and, as a last resort, there is the trash collector. If the latter two options are taken, be prepared to answer irate citizenry who do not understand or approve of such disposal of public property. Whatever method is used, try to get rid of them all at the same place. Don't spend time doling them out bit by bit.

BUDGETS

LMC budgets are so individual and sensitive that little can be said of a general nature beyond what has already been mentioned. Administrators must be convinced and often reminded of the importance of unbroken serials and their curricular value. In allocating funds, indexes and subscriptions head the list of items to be considered. Microform machines, reader/printer or computer service contracts, microform printing supplies and light bulbs, computer programs supplies, bindery costs, mending supplies, labels, file boxes, circulation forms, index cards and other small items may be on the list also.

Compare prices. Check to see if some items can be included on school or system wide bid lists or if centralized purchasing will result in quantity discounts. Sometimes special sales of equipment or supplies that usually occur toward the end of a school year can be advantageous if there is still money left.

It is desirable to thoroughly document requests for new equipment, additional staff or other expensive items. The necessary statistical data, justifications and other supporting information may take several years to accumulate to make a strong case, so plan ahead.

STAFFING AND SCHEDULING

One LMC specialist alone can't possibly manage periodicals and the rest of the collection, consult with faculty, conduct instructional programs and special events, supervise volunteers and provide patron assistance on the floor unless the school is very small, the collection minuscule, and patronage thin. That, and budget limitations, are the main reasons that good periodical programs fall by the wayside.

Train and delegate. Professional skill is most important initially in determining goals, policies, procedures and title selections and formats, in other words, at the planning stage. Annually, professional acumen is needed in title and statistical evaluation, budget decisions and ordering. Daily, the professional focus is on skimming publications for content and in-house indexing, instruction and curricular application of materials. Troubleshooting is sporadic. If well thought out policies and procedures are adopted, the rest can be done by a clerk, aide or faithful volunteers, adult or student. Computer programs for periodicals management can be of assistance in exercising firmer control but the data input and physical work is still done by people and is not necessarily faster. An overall streamlined management program saves everyone time and effort in the long run.

Although personnel can be assigned various responsibilities, nothing has been said about how to schedule magazine management. With the best intentions in the world, a busy library media center can not keep to a rigid management schedule. Everything should have been done yesterday. A quiet library media center doesn't need one.

A large master calendar can help everyone, however, and time guidelines should be tailored for each library. These would include target dates for such predictable things as inventory, compilation of statistics, collection evaluation and ordering, moving files, checking mailing labels for new sub-scription expiration dates, preparing obligations and routine machine maintenance. Logging in, processing, and filing, of course, goes on continually. Shelf reading to keep dates in order, repairs, replacement of missing issues and in-house indexing are done as necessary.

CONCLUSION

Comprehensive long range planning, starting with careful attention to all the elements of realistic goal setting, policy formulation, selection and technical procedures, is the basis of successful periodicals management. Smooth, efficient daily operation of a successful periodicals program flows from this.

The information explosion of the last decades and the need to foster good student research skills and guided critical thinking opportunities make it more important than ever for periodicals in school libraries to be managed and not to just happen.

SECTION V
INTELLECTUAL FREEDOM AND
COLLECTION MANAGEMENT

Freedom and censorship are examined in two geographically dissimilar areas.

Intellectual Freedom
as Practiced
by Public and School Librarians
in Texas

Barbara Immroth

Based on surveys completed by school and public librarians at workshops in various regions of Texas, the author explores attitudes and practices of a sample of professionals. Their similarities and differences are detailed and suggestions for improvement of certain practices are made.

INTRODUCTION

Intellectual freedom is considered a basic principle of modern American library practice, an area of professional responsibility reflecting cherished First Amendment rights of freedom of expression. The *Intellectual Freedom Manual* defines the concept as follows:

> In basic terms, intellectual freedom means the right of any person to hold any belief whatever on any subject, and to express such beliefs or ideas in whatever way the person believes appropriate. The freedom to express one's beliefs or ideas through any mode of communication becomes virtually meaningless, however, when accessibility to such expression is denied to other persons. For this reason, the definition of intellectual freedom has a second, integral part: namely, the right of unrestricted access to all information and ideas regardless of the me-

---

Dr. Immroth is an assistant professor in the Graduate School of Library and Information Science at the University of Texas at Austin.

dium of communication used. Intellectual freedom implies a circle, and that circle is broken if either freedom of expression or access to the ideas expressed is stifled.[1]

The American Association of School Librarians (AASL) has taken a position of leadership in advocating intellectual freedom in school libraries. It adopted the "School Library Bill of Rights" in 1955 in response to the climate of fear during the McCarthy era. During the following years, the concept of free access to libraries for minors evolved and was included in the American Library Association's (ALA) *Library Bill of Rights* in 1967. The matter of age was addressed in policy number five: "The rights of an individual to the use of a library should not be denied or abridged because of his age, race, religion, or national origins, or social or political views." AASL revised its own "School Library Bill of Rights for School Media Center Programs" in 1969. However, having two similar professional documents was confusing to the community at large, and unnecessary because both documents agreed on the question of access for youth. In 1976 the AASL Board of Directors took action to clarify their position by voting to endorse the ALA's *Library Bill of Rights* and stating that "This document replaces 'The School Library Bill of Rights for School Library Media Center Programs' adopted in 1969.[2] Further emphasis was given by the statement that "These rights are fundamental to the philosophy of school media programs as stated in *Media Programs: District and School*."[3]

The appearance of new standards written by an experienced, highly regarded group of professionals was an important reference point for practitioners. The national guidelines published jointly by AASL and the Association for Educational Communication and Technology (AECT) in 1975, *Media Programs: District and School* demonstrate a philosophical orientation toward intellectual freedom in the introductory statement of purpose, "A vital concern of the media program is the guarantee of intellectual freedom for learners, teachers, and staff members."[4] This thread is again picked up in the Guiding Principles for access and delivery systems: "Access to a variety of materials gives the user opportunity to grow in ability to make choices, compare ideas, and discover new interests."[5] The chapter devoted to collections has a section "Selection Policies and Procedures" which again states "The selection policy reflects and supports principles of intellectual freedom."[6] The concept of intellectual freedom is well established in the basic documents used by school librarians to guide them in their operation of school library media programs.

The transition between adopting principles in theory and adhering to these principles in the face of real world situations has often been difficult for school librarians. These principles are tested time after time from reports, on the one hand, of individual librarians being confronted by angry parents or authoritarian administrators, and on the other hand, by cases being argued over points of constitutional law in the courts.

TEXAS WORKSHOPS

While serving as chair of the Texas Library Association, Intellectual Freedom and Professional Responsibilities Committee, the author was asked to present workshops on censorship and selection. Attending these workshops were school and public librarians with a common interest in selection and from a wide variety of backgrounds and library settings. At four workshops a brief questionnaire, developed by Dr. Blanche Woolls for a Pennsylvania School Librarians Association workshop, and adapted by the author, was used as a self pre-test of attitude and as a focusing device for participants. These workshops, held during the period of September, 1981 through August, 1982, were at sites in different parts of the state: one in the southeast, one in the south, one in the central area, and one in west Texas. Two workshops were given for librarians from a single district. In one case the group began to formulate a district selection policy as a result of the workshop experience. The questions were reworded according to the participants' work situation in public or school libraries, but retained the same basic concepts in each case. In many cases participants selected more than one answer for a question or left a question blank. Written comments qualifying or explaining an answer were also frequent. A total of 41 public and 34 school librarians returned usable questionnaires. This self-selected group of librarians could be considered a biased sample. Some of the school librarians were required to attend a workshop as a continuing education (in-service) requirement, some of these chose not to return the questionnaire. The responses could be considered a best case group, the cutting edge of those with an interest in selection and censorship in what is considered by the rest of the world to be a conservative state. Answers to these questions provide a glimpse of current practice in Texas. Because of the nature of the use of the questionnaire as a focusing device, respondents were not limited in number of answers per question. Many checked more than one answer and then wrote comments to explain or qualify the answers.

SELECTION POLICIES

When asked "Do you have a selection policy for your library?" (Question 5), public librarians were more likely to have a board-approved policy. Seventy-four and thirty-six hundredth per cent of the public librarians had a Board approved policy while 46 per cent of the school librarians had a board approved policy. In each of two workshops, all of the participants were from one district, six librarians were working in a school district which had a board approved selection policy. In the other district without a board approved policy, seven librarians were in attendance. Seven school librarians answered that they had a policy but it was not board approved. Thirty-five and nine-tenths per cent of the school librarians reported that they have no policy, while only 10.26 per cent of the public librarians had no policy. Since the Texas Association of School Boards has a sample policy available in the *Policy Reference Manual for Texas School Districts*,[7] it is not clear why over half of the districts have no board approved policy.

Two questions were asked about community influence on the selection process and the use of recommended lists in selection. Pressure from the community to select or reject certain titles or subjects might influence the process. The use of recommended lists might offer guidance in selection and the protection of expert authority beyond the community. When asked "Do you consider your community's reaction when you purchase a title?" (Question 3) many librarians stated that they buy needed items which appear on recommended lists: 53.66 per cent of school librarians and 40.82 per cent of public librarians. Some librarians chose to qualify that statement by answering that they buy those titles from recommended lists which would be acceptable to their community: 19.51 per cent of school librarians and 30.61 per cent of public librarians. A sizable minority in each group, 24.39 per cent of school librarians and 16.33 per cent of public librarians, answered that they select titles regardless of recommended lists while a small minority, 4.08 per cent of public and 2.44 per cent of school librarians, buy those titles which will be non-controversial.

There was a significant difference in what each group bought based on patron requests. (Question 4) School librarians were much more likely to buy requested materials without checking review sources first. Fifty six and seventy-six hundredth per cent of the school librarians said they buy everything teachers request while only 7.69 per cent of public librarians do so. Both groups seem to be influenced in their selections by recommended lists. Public librarians buy everything patrons request which appears on a recommended list in 50 per cent of the responses while school librarians do so in 37.84 per cent of the responses. A small minority of public librarians, 7.69 per cent answered that they never buy any materials requested by patrons.

SELECTION OF CONTROVERSIAL MATERIALS

A book which is challenged in one collection may later be challenged in another collection. Special interest groups may circulate lists of titles for exclusion from collections. An individual may be aware of attempts at exclusion and seek to exclude the same titles in his local library. To see if this was happening in these collections a question was asked about a specific controversial title, *Go Ask Alice*. This novel was used as an example of a title on recommended lists which has been challenged in many collections. (Question 2) In this sample public and school librarians were almost equally likely to have *Go Ask Alice* on open shelves in their collection, 60.53 per cent public, 57.14 per cent school. More school than public branches had the title on closed shelves, 17.14 per cent school, 2.63 per cent public, meaning that it would be available though restricted in more school libraries. More public librarians had never read or heard of *Go Ask Alice* than school librarians which might account for its increased availability in schols. Elementary, middle and junior high librarians commented that it was not appropriate for these grade levels. Of the eleven school librarians who identified themselves as high school librarians, only one had the title on a closed shelf.

Two questions about inclusion of controversial material in collections were asked only of school librarians. Although no comparison of answers with public librarians is possible, the questions and answers are included for further background. The film version of Shirley Jackson's short story "The Lottery" is one of the reportedly most often censored films in this country. When school librarians were asked if they would recommend the film to a seventh grade English teacher who wished to present an American short story visually, they answered as follows:

> 7 would
> 8 would if felt the teacher could handle the situation
> 2 would if seventh graders in the class were mature
> 3 would if students brought parental permission
> 8 would NOT

The rest of the group chose not to answer the question. One person who would recommend it to an English teacher commented "the teacher would know her classes well enough to decide upon using it."

The other question concerning inclusion of specific titles asked about purchasing three well-known modern literary novels, *Catcher in the Rye, 1984, Slaughterhouse Five.* These titles have been repeatedly challenged over a number of years, inspite of critical recognition of their place in modern American literature. When asked "Would you purchase *Catcher in the Rye, 1984,* and *Slaughterhouse Five* for the English teacher?" school librarians answered as follows:

19 yes
1 yes, because they are found on
recommended lists
8 yes, but would warn the teacher of potential
problems
5 yes, but would limit circulation to that
particular class
2 no

The rest of the group chose not to respond. Two made specific comments about *Slaughterhouse Five:* "that's literature?" and "no, only because I don't have full responsibility for purchasing." In all of these cases of specific examples of materials known to be controversial, the majority of librarians responding have included them in their collections, sometimes with restrictions, but nevertheless available to users.

Two questions were asked about the selection and purchase of materials on topics which might be controversial. When asked about purchase of books about death, divorce, child abuse, drugs, handicaps (Question 9) 89.19 per cent of all public librarians and 86.11 per cent of school librarians purchased books on all five topics. Purchase was qualified by recommendation, in the case of public librarians, 10.8 per cent and in the case of school librarians, 2.70 per cent, would purchase those titles which were recommended. One school librarian commented that she placed the child abuse books on the professional shelf.

When questioned about selecting a sex education title that showed a nude male and female, the public librarians were significantly more likely to answer with an unqualified yes than the school librarians. (Question 11) Eighty six and eleven hundredth per cent of the public librarians answered yes, while only 30.77 per cent of the school librarians answered yes to this question. The school librarians would more often select a title only when the "pictures" are sketches or labeled diagrams. Forty-eight per cent of the school librarians and 8.3 per cent of the public librarians chose this response to the question. Just under 3 per cent (2.78) of the public librarians and just over 15 per cent (15.38) of the school librarians would never select a sex education title that showed a nude male and female. One commented specifically, "not in junior high."

When asked about replacing books stolen from the topic categories of death, divorce, child abuse, drugs and handicaps (Question 10), the school librarians were more likely to replace those titles which are still relevant (75 per cent) than public librarians (70 per cent). School librarians would replace two books for each one lost on the topic (13.89 per cent) more often than public librarians (2.50 per cent).

CHALLENGES TO MATERIALS AND REEVALUATIONS

Whether a librarian has secured a carefully written, board approved selection policy or has not been able to do so, there is still the possibility that at some point in time, someone will question the choice of material in the collection. A challenge to materials in the collection may come from a variety of sources, a staff member within the institution, a Board member, a parent or any individual or group in the community. An administrative procedure used sometimes in children's services to prevent such challenges to materials is to require that the student obtain parental permission before being permitted to use controversial material. This is a philosophical compromise between free access to minors and parental rights. The ALA's position on parental rights is "that it is the parents—and only parents—who may restrict their children—and only their children—from access to library materials and services."[8] Reevaluation of material usually follows a challenge to its presence in the collection. The three basic options after reevaluation are to retain the item; to retain the item, but restrict access; or to remove the item from the collection. A question was asked to determine how librarians were responding to reevaluation on two subjects considered to be controversial, racism and sexism. Since the final result of defending the professional principle of intellectual freedom for some librarians has been dismissal from their positions, a question was asked about the extent to which a librarian would go to defend this principle.

When asked about challenges to the library collection and the sources from which challenges arise there was a significant difference in the experience of school and public librarians. (Question 1) Public library materials were more often challenged than those in schools. This can be seen in the respondents selecting the negative statement "Materials in the library collection have *NOT* been challenged." School librarians responded that 26.53 per cent have not been challenged while public librarians replied that 18.75 per cent have not. As for the sources of the challenges, staff members in schools (24.49 per cent) were more likely to initiate a challenge than staff members in a public library (12.5 per cent). Parents were likely to challenge materials about equally in each institution, school, 30.61 per cent and public, 29.17 per cent. Other community members were much more likely to challenge materials in a public library (35.42 per cent) than a school library (10.20 per cent).

Several librarians added explanatory comments about challenges. One school librarian who had been challenged said: "Teachers and principal have objected to several books. I pulled the records for the two my principal kept." Another commented that students questioned materials in the collection. A school librarian whose collection had not been challenged commented "All materials should be made available; the student should have a choice." Thirteen of the public librarians wrote comments about challenges and challengers. The occult, religion and sex were subjects being challenged. *Rachel, the Rabbi's Wife, Dr. Knock-Knock's Book of Knock-Knock Jokes, Where Do Babies Come From?* were specific titles mentioned. One parent complained that picture books containing witches, goblins, and demons are more numerous than those with Bible stories and that a book based on "Genesis" was not "according to the *Bible.*" Challengers included a staff member of whom the librarian said "I consider staff member ignorant and make clear my judgment is to prevail. (This is not a flip remark, staff member does not read—knows virtually nothing of books.)" Another commented "community member is old and single and just walks in and grabs any book as long as it's got a new cover and then gets home and hates its contents." Several librarians suggested that patrons complained and then did not return the written complaint form. One librarian commented "more complaints about not buying enough 'sexy' books rather than complaints about books that are too explicit."

In response to the question of securing parental permission

before permitting a student to take a questionable title from the library, (Question 7) the majority of public and school librarians never ask for parental permission, public, 69.23 per cent and school, 56.76 per cent. School librarians are more likely to have another authority approve questionable titles than public librarians, 18.92 per cent of school librarians said that the principal approves questionable titles before the titles are placed in circulation while only 7.69 per cent of the public librarians received Board approval on individual titles before circulating them. A small minority of each group always requires permission only for materials on sex, 3.85 per cent of public and 2.70 per cent of school. Almost 20 per cent of the public librarians (19.23 per cent) always require permission for questionable titles while under 10 per cent of the school librarians (8.11 per cent) always require permission. There was a difference in the groups about not having questionable titles in the library. None of the public librarians chose the response that they have no questionable titles in the library while 13.51 per cent of the school librarians chose that response.

One question explored removing all books from the library which show racism and sexism. (Question 8) Two-thirds of librarians in each group responded in the negative, 73.68 per cent of public, and 67.5 per cent of school librarians. A small number in each group answered yes to this question, 2.63 per cent of public and 5 per cent of school librarians. None of the people in either group has appointed a committee to consider the question. More school librarians, 15 per cent, have removed those titles which are the most racist and/or sexist while only 2.63 per cent of the public librarians have done so. Some librarians in each group responded that they have never considered the problem, 21.05 per cent of the public and 12.5 per cent of the school librarians.

When the difficult choice has to be made between upholding the principle of intellectual freedom and remaining employed (Question 6) the most frequent choice of librarians in each group is that they prefer to defend intellectual freedom, but to keep their job, public, 57.89 per cent and school, 47.5 per cent. Job security is apparently higher in public libraries than school libraries, or the fear of job loss is less for public librarians. School librarians expressed the fear of job loss for insubordination for not obeying a demand from a supervisor that an item be removed from the collection. More public, 31.58 per cent, than school librarians, 15 per cent, would not fear the loss of job. On the other hand, the fear of job loss probably explains why more school librarians, 20 per cent, remove anything that is questioned by a principal or teacher, than public librarians, 5.26 per cent, remove anything that is questioned by their Board. Also the fear of job loss might explain why school librarians are more likely to remove any item that is questioned, 12.5 per cent than public librarians, 2.63 per cent. A small percentage of each group claims that they would go to jail to defend this principle, 2.63 per cent of public and 5 per cent of school librarians.

SUMMARY

A group of 75 Texas librarians, 41 public and 34 school, attended workshops on censorship and selection. Each completed a brief questionnaire used as a focusing device. Comparisons between the group of public librarians and the group of school librarians were made from answers to questions about selection policies, selection of controversial materials, challenges to materials and reevaluation. Although this could be considered a best case sample, because of participants choosing to attend a workshop, differences between the groups were found. In the matter of selection policies public librarians were more likely to have a board approved policy than school librarians. The two groups showed similar patterns about considering their community's reaction when purchasing a title by most often purchasing items on recommended lists. School librarians were more likely to buy requested materials without checking review sources while public librarians were more likely to purchase patron requests which appear on a recommended list. This might be attributed to the smaller size of the school community or its institutional purpose of serving the curriculum.

In the area of selection of controversial materials several questions were asked about specific titles and subjects. *Go Ask Alice* was almost equally likely to appear on open shelves in school and public libraries. Books about death, divorce,

Public (No.)	(%)	School (No.)	(%)	(1) Materials in the library collection:
9	18.75	13	26.53	Have NOT been challenged
6	12.50	12	24.49	Have been challenged by staff member
14	29.17	15	30.61	Have been challenged by parent(s)
2	4.17	4	8.16	Have been challenged by Board member
17	35.42	5	10.20	Have been challenged by other community member

(97 observations; x^2 = 9.9646; P < .0419)*

Public (No.)	(%)	School (No.)	(%)	(2) Do you have Go Ask Alice in your library?
23	60.53	20	57.14	Have it on open shelves
1	2.63	6	17.14	Have it on closed shelves
1	2.63	2	5.71	Are going home and order it
7	18.42	5	14.29	Have never read it
6	15.79	2	5.71	Have never heard of Go Ask Alice

(73 observations; x^2 = 6.3348; P < .1755)

Public (No.)	(%)	School (No.)	(%)	(3) Do you consider your community's reaction when you purchase a title?
8	16.33	10	24.39	Select regardless of recommended lists
20	40.82	22	53.66	Buy needed items which appear on recommended lists
4	8.16	0	0	Buy only from recommended lists
15	30.61	8	19.51	Buy from recommended lists those titles which would be acceptable to your community
2	4.08	1	2.44	Buy those titles which will be non-controversial

(90 observations; x^2 = 6.1185; P < .1905)

Public (No.)	(%)	School (No.)	(%)	(4) Do you ask your patrons to help evaluate new selections before purchase?
2	7.69	21	56.76	Buy everything patrons request
13	50.00	14	37.84	Buy everything they request which appears on a recommended list
8	30.77	2	5.41	Buy those titles which are recommended by TWO patrons
1	3.85	0	0	Buy titles which are suggested by patrons with MLS degrees, only
2	7.69	0	0	Never buy any materials requested by patrons

(63 observations; x^2 = 21.0539; P < .0003)*

	Public (No.)	(%)	School (No.)	(%)

(5) Do you have a selection policy for your library?

	Public (No.)	(%)	School (No.)	(%)
Do and it has been tested by any community case	8	20.51	9	23.08
It is approved by the Board	21	53.85	9	23.08
Have a policy but it has not been approved by the Board	5	12.82	7	17.95
Have no policy	4	10.26	14	35.90
Feel you do not need a selection policy	1	2.56	0	0

(78 observations; $x^2 = 11.7477$; $P < .0193$)*

(6) Would you forfeit your job rather than remove any questionable material from your library?

	Public (No.)	(%)	School (No.)	(%)
Would go to jail	1	2.63	2	5.00
Would not fear loss of job	12	31.58	6	15.00
Prefer to defend intellectual freedom, but keep your job	22	57.89	19	47.50
Remove anything that is questioned by your Board	2	5.26	8	20.00
Remove anything that is questioned by anyone	1	2.63	5	12.50

(78 observations; $x^2 = 8.7740$; $P < .0670$)

(7) Do you secure parental permission before permitting a student to take a questionable title from your library?

	Public (No.)	(%)	School (No.)	(%)
Never ask for parental permission	18	69.23	21	56.76
The Board approves all questionable selections before placing in circulation	2	7.69	7	18.92
Require permission only for materials on sex	1	3.85	1	2.70
Always require permission for questionable titles	5	19.23	3	8.11
Have no questionable titles in the library	0	0	5	13.51

(63 observations; $x^2 = 6.7951$; $P < .1471$)

(8) Have you removed all books from your library which show racism and sexism?

	Public (No.)	(%)	School (No.)	(%)
No	28	73.68	27	67.50
Have appointed a committe to consider the question	0	0	0	0
Have removed those which are the most racist and/or sexist	1	2.63	6	15.00
Yes	1	2.63	2	5.00
Have never considered a problem	8	21.05	5	12.50

(78 observations; $x^2 = 4.5670$; $P < .2064$)

Public (No.)	(%)	School (No.)	(%)

(9) Do you purchase books about death, divorce, child abuse, drugs, handicaps?

33	89.19	___ Purchase all five topics	35	83.79
0	0	___ Purchase in four of the five	5	13.51
4	10.81	___ Purchase only those which are recommended on the five topics	1	2.70
0	0	___ Purchase in one of the five topics	0	0
0	0	___ Purchase in none of the above topics	0	0

(78 observations; $x^2 = 6.6712$; $P < .0356$)*

(10) Do you replace books that are stolen from the above categories?

1	2.50	___ Replace two books for each one lost on the topic	5	13.89
28	70.00	___ Replace those titles which are still relevant	27	75.00
6	15.00	___ Replace only those which were recommended	3	8.33
5	12.50	___ Replace only those which are WORTH IT	5	13.89
0	0	___ Say "No, good riddance"	0	0

(80 observations; $x^2 = 3.6848$; $P < .2976$)

(11) Would you select a title on sex education that showed a nude male and female?

31	86.11	___ Yes	12	30.77
0	0	___ Yes, when pictures are on separate pages	2	5.13
3	8.33	___ Only when the 'pictures' are sketches or labeled diagrams	19	48.72
1	2.78	___ Only for grades 11 and 12	0	0
1	2.78	___ Never	6	15.38

(75 observations; $x^2 = 26.5256$; $P < .0001$)*

child abuse, drugs and handicaps would be purchased by over 80 per cent of school and public librarians and over 70 per cent in each group would replace stolen titles about these topics if still relevant. The selection of a sex education title showing a nude male and female would be made almost three times as often in a public library as in a school library. School librarians would select books with sketches or labeled diagrams as illustrations more frequently.

The sources of challenges to materials and the process of reevaluation were explored in several questions. Materials in public libraries were more likely to be challenged than materials in school collections. Of those materials challenged, school staff members were twice as likely to challenge materials as public library staff members; while parents were equally likely to challenge materials in either institution. Other community members were much more likely to challenge public library materials than school library materials. While the majority of both groups do not ask for parental permission before permitting a student to take a questionable title from the library, school librarians are more likely to have another authority approve a questionable title before placing it in circulation than are public librarians. Over two-thirds of each group had not removed from the collection all books which show racism and sexism. Rather than making the difficult choice between upholding the principle of intellectual freedom and remaining employed, the majority of librarians in each group make a compromise by choosing to both uphold their principles and retain their jobs. The fear of job loss is twice as high among school librarians as it is among public librarians.

CONCLUSION

Texas public and school librarians in this sample practice intellectual freedom by selecting and purchasing materials about controversial topics, by having a selection policy in the majority of cases, and by respecting free access for minors. While there are some significant differences in practice in some areas between the groups of school and public librarians, there are also areas of agreement as shown in practice. As in any human endeavor to uphold ethical principles, there is room for improvement. Those librarians which do not have board approved policies might try to gain such approval. Those librarians who are unfamiliar with highly acclaimed and popular materials might become acquainted with some of those titles, especially if the material is controversial, it might also be informative and thought-provoking. There are both public and school librarians in Texas who are working to implement the principles of intellectual freedom on a day-to-day basis in their collections; in the dawning era of renewed pursuit of excellence in education, one would hope that they flourish and multiply.

REFERENCE NOTES

1. "Introduction," *Intellectual Freedom Manual,* Second Edition (Chicago, American Library Association, 1983), p. viii.

2. "AASL Notes," *School Media Quarterly* 5, no. 1 (Fall 1976): 36.

3. Ibid., p. 37.

4. *Media Programs: District and School* (Chicago: American Library Association and Washington, D.C.: Association for Educational Communications and Technology, 1975), p. 6.

5. Ibid., p. 48.

6. Ibid., p. 64.

7. "Instructional Resources: Instructional Materials Selection and Adoption," *Policy Reference Manual for Texas School Districts* (Austin: Texas Association of School Boards, 1977), unnumbered.

8. *Intellectual Freedom Manual,* p. 23.

The Impact of Censorship
on Collections Development

Harriet Selverstone

Through a survey of school library media specialists in one Connecticut county and a review of the literature, Selverstone has identified sources of pressure on and support for collection development decisions. Potential supporters are identified.

The investigation into the identification and impact of forms of censorship of school library media collections has been conducted as one means of determining the degree of support offered by students, parents, faculty, and school administators for school library media programs.

The support systems for school library media programs include library use, collections, new technologies, administrative budgetary allocations, funding sources other than from school budgets, the degree of faculty and professional acceptance, professional organizations, parent support, communication and/or cooperation with outside agencies. When dealing with the issue of censorship, it is important to identify support by the school administration, student and parent groups as a basis for determining collection development and management.

A study was conducted to assess the impact of factors identified as providing support systems for school library media programs. The research was limited to the school library media programs in Fairfield County, Connecticut.

A basic assumption of this study was that censorship of the collections of school library media programs reflects both an internal and external support system for the collection. With reference to internal support, one can ask the rhetorical ques-

Harriet Selverstone is a school library media specialist at Norwalk High School, Norwalk, Connecticut.

tion of school library media specialists, "Are we our own censors?" For external support, the school library media specialists must turn to several groups—students, parents, faculty, and administration.

It is important to realize that a support system might be represented by an individual, group, or program which helps the school library media specialist cope with the pressures which often place major constraints on school library media programs. The various sources of pressures may also be, in turn, those very factors which provide support.

Support systems are the insurance policies of school library media specialists, available, when needed. Support systems, represented by groups of persons, may be fellow professionals from other school library media centers or from public or academic libraries. These persons should be carefully identified for their varying and unique expertise. Also, existing groups of people within the same building in which the school library media center is located can often function as excellent support systems. Well-informed department chairpersons, on the middle school and secondary level, can be among the greatest of support systems. Student and parent groups, too, welcome some type of constructive school library media role.

In addition to the above named individuals and groups of individuals, the school library media specialist can look beyond his/her immediate school environment and identify a number of groups and organizations which are established that are support systems already in place and eager to help. These would be professional library media organizations— national, such as the American Library Association, the American Association of School Librarians; regional, such as the Southwestern Connecticut Regional Library Council; state, the Connecticut Educational Media Association, and local, the Fairfield County School Librarians' Association. The Connecticut State Board of Education was the first State Board of Education to adopt the "Free to Learn" policy, a policy on academic freedom and public education. Other support groups are the professional organizations of other disciplines, such as the National Council of Teachers of English, the Office of Intellectual Freedom, the Freedom to Read Foundation, the Society of American Archivists, and the Connecticut Association of Independent Schools.

The area of censorship, as one support system in the role of collection development, is a prominent one. Censorship, in its various forms, may be applied to either the existing collection, or, in the process of collection development-acquisitions. Support may be achieved in this area with clearly articulated and written policies. The latter are major allies for the school library media specialist. If a policy for the handling of controversial materials and the appropriate forms for follow-up action are ready to be distributed to the would-be censor, the issue can be handled as a routine matter and not be an instantaneous pressure point. Even though an individual case might become a major issue, the plan of action would be readily available.

The study of the impact of types of censorship as one means of support of school library media programs, was conducted during the Spring semester of 1983. One hundred forty questionnaires were distributed to Fairfield County, Connecticut school library media centers, and 103 were returned. Censorship was the concluding major area covered on the questionnaire. Not all of the library media specialists responded to this particular area on the survey. However, the number of respondents in each of the three areas—elementary, middle, and high school—will be delineated and the responses provided.

Ten of the fifty-eight elementary school library media specialists responding to the questionnaire included comments on the section devoted to censorship issues and ensuing support. The comments were as follows:

> 'Sometimes chapters or words are questioned; however, the principal supports media center decisions'; 'Parent objected to Judy Blume book, however, support from all administration and staff'; 'Case involving born-again Christians and witchcraft in a fiction book-resolved in library's favor by panel of townspersons, school board member and teacher involved'; 'System has form to follow-works well'; 'One or two parent objections, but no one filled out "Citizens' Request for Recommendation of a Book" form-Students' Right to Read Program'; 'Judy Blume's *Deenie,* five years ago, problem, yet still on shelf—was parent's concern'; 'Have a good board

policy, forms to fill out if objection is made'; 'Book challenged by parent, *Scary Stories to Tell in the Dark* by A. Schwartz—used challenge form, support from district-wide committee meetings'; 'Three questions in last ten years, resolved informally'; 'Wrote new policy on book selection and weeding-accepted with commendation by the Board and the Administration.'

Two of the twenty-one middle schools responded to the issue of "Problems With Censorship." Their comments were: "Language in books by one parent, necessary to pull book to keep area quiet"; the second response was "Administrative reluctance to put materials on birth control on shelves. Also, extreme caution on candor of sex education materials."

Five of the twenty-four high school library media specialists addressed the issue of censorship with the following comments:

'Revised book selection policy just in case, supported by Adminstration and Board of Education'; 'Have written policy just in case'; 'Problem in 1960's, not directed to library books, but to textbooks, support from Superintendent and Principal'; 'Parental objections to two titles—removed both: *Go Ask Alice* and *Down These Mean Streets;* the administration, including the Superintendent, requested my selection policy'; 'Administrative objection to subscription to *Mademoiselle* Magazine.'

With few exceptions (three out of seventeen responses from all three academic levels, or 17%), the administration or local Board of Education seemed to lend its support to the school library media program and its book selection policy, regarding censorship issues.

Censorship has been an area both vulnerable to attack from outside sources and a recipient of support.

"The American Library Association reported that in a six month period of 1981–82 more than one hundred titles were either removed, or threatened with removal from school and public libraries in thirty states."[1] The ALA indicated that ultraconservative political and religious organizations were prominent forces in the above endeavors. Materials were condemned for vulgar language or descriptions of sexual behavior or for "undermining the family or for containing radical political ideas."[2] It was pointed out that some liberals:

> believe our society may have become too permissive. Feminists have condemned books said to promote sexism and pornography. Blacks object to materials that they consider racist and demeaning. A number of Jews believe that young people should not be exposed to such characterizations as Shylock in *The Merchant of Venice* and Fagin in *Oliver Twist.*[3]

The United States Supreme Court, in June of 1982, was somewhat supportive in their Island Trees Board of Education vs. Pico 5-4 decision, "the Constitution prohibits the removal of books from school libraries for 'official suppression of ideas.' "[4] Justice Brennan maintained that "School boards possess significant discretion to determine the content of their school libraries . . . but that discretion may not be exercised in a narrowly partisan or political manner."[5] The student plaintiff, Steven Pico, in this case, responded with, "A school board should not have the final decision on book selection. A Board of Education is not necessarily a board of educated people."[6]

A judge in a Massachusetts city told panelists in a Right to Read Committee that his primary criterion for deciding on censorship cases is the "motivation behind the action to remove a book. If the motive is mind control, then that clearly goes against the First Amendment."[7] Dong also reported on the concern of the Editor-in-Chief of young readers' books at the Knopf publishing house who believes that the ultimate censorship is not at the selecting level, but at the publishing level. The latter considers twice before publishing controversial titles.

There was a unique suit involving censorship in a California community. That involved the restricted access to copies of *MS* Magazine in school libraries. An ACLU attorney thought that this was the "first suit to protest the placement of material on a restricted list rather than an outright banning."[8] The restriction was seen as banning, but in this manner the authorities were hoping to avoid a First Amendment challenge by acting in this way. The community was not against the assigned articles from the magazine, but against the fact that *MS* contained articles on birth control and abortion. The Principal requested the removal of *MS* from the library's shelves because of complaints. The school board, after hearing a suit would be filed if *MS* were removed from the shelves, decided to restrict its availability to those students with parental permission. However, the ACLU was most supportive of the librarians' efforts to present all types of materials by forcing a preliminary injunction to place *MS* back on the shelves on an *un*restricted basis until the case were to come to trial. The ACLU was not the only support group for the librarians. The National Organization for Women, parents, and teachers, were also on the librarians' defensive. A similar effort to ban *MS* in a high school library in Nashua, New Hampshire, was rejected by a federal district court on the "ground that mere conclusions that a publication is 'offensive' because it is contrary to the beliefs of individual school board members or because it represents an unpopular political point of view are not sufficient for removal."[9]

An editorial in a local Fairfield County newspaper reflected on the banning by one town of the viewing of Shakespeare's play, *Romeo and Juliet* by 9–11 year olds. The play was shown at the American Shakespeare Theater in Stratford, Connecticut. It was reported that 32,000 school children from seven states were seeing it—all but those students from one particular town in Fairfield County. The managing editor's thesis was that propriety or decency is subjective. The major points he raised were:

> If the kids understand the sexual references in the play, then how does hearing those references hurt the kids? I mean, if they get the joke, it's not telling them anything they don't already know, right? If the kids don't understand the references, some of which are quite obscure, then there's no harm done. Much of Shakespeare's language is simply going to get past them anyway. Nothing in the play is more suggestive than what kids watch on television all the time. There is scarcely a show on commercial T.V. which is not riddled with sexual innuendo, at the least.[10]

The editor was still hoping that the play in book form was available in that particular town's school library.

A recent *New York Times Magazine* article was devoted to censorship and to the major exhibition at the New York Public Library "that deals directly with the issues of freedom, of the silencing of opinion, and of the persistent effort by some to control the minds of others."[11]

Ms. Joan Hoff-Wilson of Indiana University contends that:

> Since the mid-1970's there has been an epidemic of attempts to censor books and films in the schools, a contention supported by others. The Washington-based citizens' group, People for the American Way, which supports First Amendment rights, claims that last year there were attempts to remove, alter, or restrict textbooks, library books or teaching materials and courses in 48 states.[12]

Censorship is an issue of major concern to school library media specialists. They have been confronted by widely varied audiences: from parent groups, community organizations, students, faculty, administration, and Boards of Education. However, with articulately written policies substantiating the philosophy of their collection development and collection maintenance, these policies can act in the capacity of insurance policies, to be used when necessary.

NOTES

1. Ira Peck, "Mr. Jefferson's Offer . . . and the Issue of Book Banning," *Senior Scholastic*, Vol. 115, No. 4, October 15, 1982, p.21.

2. Ibid., p.21.

3. Ibid., p.22.

4. Ibid., p.22.

5. Ibid., p.22.

6. Stella Dong, "The Week," *Publishers' Weekly*, Vol.218, No. 3, July 18, 1980, p.16.

7. Ibid., p.16.

8. Wendy Smith, "California Suit Protests School Library Restrictions," *Publishers' Weekly*, Vol.219, No. 1, January 2, 1981, p. 14.

9. Lisa Cronin Wohl, "Caution—These Pages Maybe Banned In Your School," *MS*, Vol.IX, No. 3, September, 1980, p.82.

10. Timothy Sullivan, "Romeo, Oh Romeo, Wherefore Art Thou Risque?" *Fairpress* Newspaper, May 23, 1984, p. A12.

11. Richard Bernstein, "Opening the Books on Censorship," *New York Times Magazine,* May 13, 1984, p.29.
12. Ibid., p.91.

BIBLIOGRAPHY

Bernstein, Richard. "Opening the Books on Censorship." *New York Times Magazine,* May 13, 1984, pp.28–92.
Dong, Stella. "The Week." *Publishers' Weekly,* Vol. 218, No.3, July 18, 1980, p. 16.
Peck, Ira. "Mr. Jefferson's Offer . . . and the Issue of Book Banning." *Senior Scholastic,* Vol.115, No.4, October 15, 1982, p. 21.
Selverstone, Harriet. "The Identification and Impact of Factors Which Provide Support Systems For School Library Media Programs." Unpublished Masters' Thesis, October, 1983.
Smith, Wendy. "California Suit Protests School Library Restrictions." *Publishers' Weekly,* Vol. 219, No. 1, January 2,1981, p. 14.
Sullivan, Timothy. "Romeo, Oh Romeo, Wherefore Art Thou Risque?" *Fairpress* Newspaper, May 23, 1984, p. A12.
Wohl, Lisa Cronin. "Caution—These Pages Maybe Banned In Your School." *MS,* Vol. IX, No. 3, September, 1980, p.82.

Index